Manchester United
Official Yearbook 2003

Contributors:
Martin Edwards
Sir Alex Ferguson
Barry Moorhouse

Thanks to:
Cliff Butler, Ian McLeish, Niall Hampton, Hazel Brown, Sarah Dyson, Tim Scott,
Wayne Cyrus, Aubrey Smith, Steve Morgan, Scott Morgan, Cormac Bourne, Jane Cullen,
Jon Hotten, Robert Jeffery, David Meek, Wolfgang Harles, Diane Clifford, Ben Gardener,
Brian Finch, Mark Lloyd, Karl Evans

Thanks also to all the clubs who kindly granted permission in allowing their official club
crests to be reproduced in this publication.

Photographs:
John and Matthew Peters/Manchester United FC, Action Images, Empics

Design and Editorial:
Haymarket Customer Publishing

First published in 2003

10 9 8 7 6 5 4 3 2 1

Published, manufactured and distributed by
Carlton Books Limited
20 Mortimer Street
London W1T 3JW

Design and text copyright © Manchester United PLC 2003

A CIP catalogue record for this book is available from the British Library.

ISBN 0 233 00997 3

Printed and bound in the UK by Times Printers

CONTENTS

Manchester United Football Club PLC

Chairman Martin Edwards
Chief Executive Peter Kenyon
Managing Director David Gill
Group Finance Director Nick Humby
Directors J M Edelson,
Sir Bobby Charlton CBE,
E M Watkins LI M, R L Olive
Manager Sir Alex Ferguson
Secretary Kenneth R Merrett

Honours

European Champions Clubs' Cup – winners:
1968, 1999

European Cup Winners' Cup – winners:
1991

FA Premier League – champions:
1993, 1994, 1996, 1997, 1999, 2000, 2001, 2003

Football League Division One – champions:
1908, 1911, 1952, 1956, 1957, 1965, 1967

FA Challenge Cup – winners:
1909, 1948, 1963, 1977, 1983, 1985, 1990, 1994, 1996, 1999

Football League Cup – winners:
1992

Inter-Continental Cup – winners:
1999

UEFA Super Cup – winners:
1991

FA Charity Shield – winners:
1908, 1911, 1952, 1956, 1957, 1983, 1993, 1994, 1996, 1997
Joint holders:
1965, 1967, 1977, 1990

CLUBTELEPHONENUMBERS

Website: www.manutd.com
Ticket and match info line: +44 (0) 870 757 1968
Main switchboard: +44 (0) 161 868 8000
Ticket sales: +44 (0) 870 442 1999
Match hospitality, Museum and Tour centre, Ticketing Services inquiries,
Membership Services: +44 (0) 870 442 1994
Conference & Catering and Events Team: +44 (0) 161 868 8300
Megastore: +44 (0) 161 868 8567
Mail Order: +44 (0) 870 162 0212
Red Café: +44 (0) 161 868 8303
Development Association: +44 (0) 161 868 8600
United in the Community: +44 (0) 161 708 9451
United Radio: +44 (0) 16 868 8888
MUTV: +44 (0) 870 848 6888
United Review Subscriptions: +44 (0) 870 442 9407
MU Finance: +44 (0) 870 442 2001
Textphone for deaf/impaired hearing: +44 (0) 161 868 8668

Our eighth FA Premier League title in 11 years and our 15th championship overall was good cause for celebration at the end of another fantastic season. The triumph came at the end of a marvellous run-in, which saw Arsenal, clear favourites in the opinion of most observers, overhauled in spectacular fashion.

That amazing run of games during the closing few weeks of the season, which included Newcastle United and Arsenal (both away) and Liverpool at Old Trafford, proved to be the turning point. It was a remarkable series of high-profile fixtures and the team came through magnificently to put themselves in pole position for the final sprint to the winning post.

It did appear that the destination of the title wouldn't be decided until the final day of the season, but Leeds United's win at Arsenal the previous weekend meant that the Gunners were unable to match our points total. It was fantastic to reclaim the title and a wonderful testimony to the resolve and belief that Sir Alex, the players and staff have in their own strengths and capabilities.

It was hugely disappointing that we were unable to claim a place in the UEFA Champions League final, staged at Old Trafford this year, but at least we went out

of the competition with all guns blazing against a fabulous Real Madrid side. I don't think anyone could deny that both quarter-final games against Real were memorable occasions with the football played by both sides being of the very highest calibre. It was just a pity that one team had to fall by the wayside.

We also reached the Worthington Cup final for the first time in several years and while the trophy was ultimately won by Liverpool, the visit to Cardiff's Millennium Stadium was another splendid occasion for everyone to enjoy.

All in all, I think it would be fair to describe the 2002/03 season as one of success, excitement and great memories. Many of which can be recalled in the pages of this latest edition of the *Manchester United Official Yearbook*. I've always found this publication an indispensable point of reference – a view shared by many people in football.

Martin Edwards **Chairman**

SIR ALEX FERGUSON

It's been one of the most memorable seasons in recent times, from the charge towards another Premiership title to those epic Champions League clashes with Real Madrid – here, Sir Alex looks back on another glorious year for United

Well, they made us sweat, and none more so than the manager, but they came brilliantly at the end to win our eighth Championship in 11 years. What a remarkable season it proved to be, with so many people writing us off before Christmas and ready to suggest our empire was crumbling. When we were eight points adrift of Arsenal, it was a real test of faith.

I don't like to talk about making people eat their words or think in terms of revenge, because it's the vagaries of the game that make it so compelling. At the same time, I have got to be honest and say that this success was extra sweet and satisfying because it was achieved against all the odds.

In fact, I would put this Championship up alongside many of our other trophies because of what the players had to pull out to make up the lost ground. The situation called for them to dig deep and they were not found wanting. They displayed the character and determination that tipped the balance our way and I am so proud of them.

Their form towards the end was unbelievably good. They defended well and always looked full of goals, especially of course Ruud van Nistelrooy.

This title was a collective achievement, but there can be no doubt that Ruud was a particularly inspiring figure. How appropriate that when we played Charlton in our final home game of the season he should have marked his 100th United appearance with a hat-trick to take his scoring total with us over two years to 79?

It's a superb strike rate, and while reluctant to pick out a player of the year I think Ruud's goals must single him out for some kind of accolade – even if he did miss out on the national awards because the voting came too early in the season, with perhaps a little London bias as well!

United fans know who is the best and Ruud is clearly on his way to becoming one of the all-time great strikers in the club's history. Having said that, the team has had individual successes in every department, and it was

gratifying to note the tremendous progress made by young players like Wes Brown and John O'Shea. Our captain, Roy Keane, came in for some criticism, but few made allowance for the time he was out for major surgery. Roy was back by the end and he played his part in those testing matches when the pressure was mounting. Ryan Giggs was another who answered his critics in a way that brooked no argument.

There were a number of players missing for surgery in the early part of the season and I am positive that the absence of seven for operations had a lot to do with our inconsistency before Christmas. Conversely, they were back strong and fit for when it really counted – at the time when Championships are won and lost! The momentum towards the end of the season was fantastic and importantly, the players did not let the set-backs that came our way destroy their rhythm.

Losing to Liverpool in the final of the Worthington Cup was a major disappointment, for instance, but we kept things in perspective. We didn't get the breaks that day, but that kind of thing happens and what matters is the reaction. The fact that we promptly launched into a winning League run, including a 4-0 success against Liverpool, tells you about the make-up of our team.

It was a similar story after the major blow of losing 3-1 to Real Madrid in the *Bernabéu* in the first leg of our Champions League quarter-finals. Four days later, we went to Newcastle and won 6-2. That was a tremendous and highly significant result, though one I truly didn't expect. I never thought for a moment we would score six at Newcastle and I rated it as our best

continued overleaf

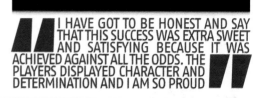

I HAVE GOT TO BE HONEST AND SAY THAT THIS SUCCESS WAS EXTRA SWEET AND SATISFYING BECAUSE IT WAS ACHIEVED AGAINST ALL THE ODDS. THE PLAYERS DISPLAYED CHARACTER AND DETERMINATION AND I AM SO PROUD

Ruud van Nistelrooy scored 44 goals in 2002/03

Real Madrid: Old Trafford visitors in April 2003

performance of the season. Every player in the team was flying and if ever we needed a tonic, this was it. Four days later, we went to Arsenal to come home with a key point from a 2-2 draw and in fact we deserved more.

By then, though, Arsenal had lost at Blackburn. I felt it was the turning point of the season. There was a definite change in Arsenal's performances after that, while we went from strength to strength.

I have always believed that what is important in a team is the reaction to disappointment and after a set-back I always ask the players what do they intend to do about it. Are they going to roll over with a shrug or are they going to redouble their efforts? I think the team last season made their reaction quite clear, and they also answered just as emphatically my perennial question of whether they have lost their hunger for success. Their

fightback demonstrated that despite suggestions they had perhaps left some of their desire in the comfort zone, they are as committed as ever. It didn't surprise me because they are people of character. Manchester United needs players who are strong mentally and the club has been blessed in this department over the years from men like Nobby Stiles, Pat Crerand, Denis Law and Bobby Charlton through to the likes of Bryan Robson, Mark Hughes and Steve Bruce and now the latest generation.

I really enjoyed the season, and not just because we ended up winners. I relished every step of the way – even our defeat against Real Madrid, because it was a tremendous experience to have been involved in two such marvellous games of football.

At the same time, we must address the European question. Three successes in 35 years is not in keeping with a club of the stature of Manchester United and the Champions League remains the big challenge for us. It's important for the club and it's important for me, too. I have restructured the coaching staff and we have won the FA Youth Cup as well as the Championship and I am excited as I look to the future.

I made the right decision when I decided to stay on as manager. I feel younger and fresher, and like you the Members, I am already looking forward to the coming season! Your support helped us over the finishing line this last time and I am sure you will be there with the same splendid encouragement in the coming months.

Alex Ferguson

AUGUST

With memories of the World Cup fading, United fans couldn't wait for the new league campaign – and with it the Reds' quest to bring the Premiership trophy back to Old Trafford

Following a lengthy World Cup, the Premiership programme didn't start until 17th August. United played just three league games in the first month, but the players were kept busy with nine matches in August – the rest coming in friendlies and a two-legged tie against the Hungarian champions Zalaegerszeg, in which United reversed a 1-0 away defeat with a 5-0 romp at Old Trafford.

The haul of five points from the three Premiership games wasn't spectacular, more so when you consider that two of the opponents were relegation favourites West Brom and Sunderland, but both sides were fired with early season optimism. United ended the month in an uncustomary mid-table position, having played one game less than most other sides due to their European commitments.

Elsewhere, a 16-year-old called Wayne Rooney made his debut for Everton, who became the first club to accumulate 100 years in the top-flight. In the league, West Ham got off to a characteristically slow start, as did Sunderland, Southampton and West Brom, who appeared punch drunk after losing their first three games against United, Arsenal and Leeds. Welcome to the Premiership.

More surprisingly, Champions League qualifiers Newcastle United started poorly but as every fan knows, early form and league tables can be misleading. Tottenham fans enjoyed their brief spell at the top in late August, ahead of North London rivals Arsenal, then Leeds and Liverpool.

Barclaycard Premiership fixtures this month

Saturday 17th	West Bromwich Albion	Home
Friday 23rd	Chelsea	Away
Saturday 31st	Sunderland	Home

In the Barclaycard Premiership this month

156,772
watched United play three games

United scored	United travelled
4 goals	**716** miles to and from games

but conceded

3 goals

United fielded a total of

15 players

FOCUS ON JOHN O'SHEA

When John O'Shea reported for pre-season training in July, Sir Alex was forced to do a double-take. "I looked up and said, 'Look at the shoulders you've got now!'" he laughed. "Last year he was a big beanpole, but he has grown and developed his strength. He looks like a centre half." The young Irishman was pitched straight into the new season's opener against West Brom, alongside Laurent Blanc. The Brummies couldn't get past this beguiling mixture of youth and experience and the new central defensive pairing headed for Stamford Bridge and a Friday night battle royal with Chelsea. Unusually for a match containing four goals and a dazzling array of attacking superstars, it was a defender who walked away with the man of the match award that night. John O'Shea had arrived.

Manchester United 1
Solskjaer 78

West Bromwich Albion 0

The matchwinner once again – Ole is engulfed by his team-mates

Giggs keeps his eye on the ball

Off the bench and breaking Brummie hearts

Saturday
17 August 2002
Old Trafford
Attendance: **67,645**
Referee: **Steve Bennett**

REVIEW

Manchester United: Barthez; P Neville (Scholes 71), O'Shea, Blanc, Silvestre (Forlan 77); Beckham, Veron (Solskjaer 59), Butt, Keane; Giggs, van Nistelrooy **Subs Not Used:** B Williams, Tierney **Booked:** Keane

West Bromwich Albion: Hoult; Sigurdsson, Moore, Gilchrist; Balis, McInnes, Gregan (Taylor 83), Johnson, Clement; Dichio (Dobie 60), Roberts (Marshall 70) **Subs Not Used:** Jensen, Wallwork **Sent off:** McInnes

Possession		
75%		25%
Shots on target		
9		3
Shots off target		
7		1
Corners		
9		1
Offsides		
10		2
Fouls		
10		13

Man of the match
ROY KEANE

Back to business. Another inspirational effort as the captain, playing in a more advanced role, got forward to considerable effect. The first United player to trouble Baggies keeper Russell Hoult, and unlucky not to score on two subsequent occasions, Keane also had a hand in the goal.

It had been seven years since United had lost an opening league fixture, defeated 3-1 by Aston Villa, and after a feisty encounter the Reds eventually made sure Villa's Brummie neighbours didn't repeat the trick. The Premiership debutantes finally caved in after being reduced to 10 men and facing an unlikely 2-5-3 formation for the last 20 minutes – attacking even by United's legendary standards. It could be quite a season...

Assured performances from O'Shea and Carroll, deputising for Ferdinand and Barthez, settled the nerves and the first half saw a bagful of chances created. Keane, Butt, van Nistelrooy and Giggs all came close to opening United's account for the season but the best chance of the first 45 came when Beckham released an on-rushing Nicky Butt. He burst through the West Brom defence and rounded the keeper... only to see the ball run agonisingly wide.

It wasn't all one-way traffic though, with Baggies forward Jason Roberts proving a handful for Blanc and O'Shea. But at the start of the second half United had a solid penalty shout when Giggs was nudged by Balis, adding to the frustrations of the players and fans. Was it to be one of those days?

After a tempestuous spell of midfield tussles Keane was booked for a challenge on Gregan, but it was West Brom captain Derek McInnes who was soon in deeper trouble. Booked for timewasting over the initial free-kick, minutes later he was given a straight red for a rattling two-footed lunge on Nicky Butt.

Time, then, for the cavalry charge. An industrious Veron had already been sacrificed for Solskjaer just after the hour mark, and the sending-off was the cue for Sir Alex to throw on Scholes and Forlan in place of Neville and Silvestre. Hoult was performing heroics in the Albion goal, but finally United got the break. Keane fed the ball through to Scholes on the edge of the box. He found Solskjaer, who found the back of the net for the 100th time in a Manchester United shirt.

The last few minutes saw West Brom throw everyone forward but ultimately Ole Gunnar Solskjaer's century strike was enough to secure the three points.

Premiership results
Weekend beginning 17/08/02

Aston Villa	0-1	Liverpool
Arsenal	2-0	Birmingham City
Blackburn Rovers	0-0	Sunderland
Charlton Athletic	2-3	Chelsea
Everton	2-2	Tottenham Hotspur
Fulham	4-1	Bolton Wanderers
Leeds United	3-0	Manchester City
Newcastle United	4-0	West Ham United
Southampton	0-0	Middlesbrough

Premiership table
Top 10 at the end of 17/08/02

	P	PTS
1 Newcastle United	1	3
2 Fulham	1	3
3 Leeds	1	3
4 Arsenal	1	3
5 Chelsea	1	3
6 Liverpool	1	3
7 Manchester United	1	3
8 Tottenham Hotspur	1	1
9 Everton	1	1
10 Blackburn Rovers	1	1

Sir Alex Ferguson

THIS RETURN TO THE BIG TIME WAS A SPECIAL OCCASION FOR A CLUB WITH ALBION'S HISTORY. THEY GAVE THEIR ALL AND MADE IT VERY DIFFICULT FOR US. I WAS PLEASED WITH THE WAY THE TEAM PERSEVERED AND I THINK WE MUST TAKE SOME CREDIT FOR THE RISK WE TOOK TO WIN

Chelsea 2
Gallas 3, Zenden 45

Manchester United 2
Beckham 26, Giggs 66

Desailly fails to stop Beckham's equaliser

Cudicini looks on in despair as Giggs levels again

Ruud shows his authority in the challenge

Friday
23 August 2002
Stamford Bridge
Attendance: **41,541**
Referee: **Graham Poll**

The season had only just opened for business but fans of the Premiership enjoyed their first edge-of-the-seat thriller, as United twice came from behind to earn a point at Stamford Bridge. With Rio Ferdinand recovering from his ankle injury, John O'Shea filled in alongside Laurent Blanc. In search of goals, Sir Alex Ferguson partnered Paul Scholes with Ruud van Nistelrooy up front.

It was Chelsea who took charge of the game early on. After just three minutes, Boudewijn Zenden swung in a low free-kick and William Gallas got a slight touch at close range to knock the ball past Roy Carroll. The London club pushed for a second goal and Jimmy Floyd Hasselbaink missed two chances to put the Blues further ahead, while Zenden threatened the United defence with his swift runs.

Nearing the half-hour mark, David Beckham received a delightful 50-yard cross-field pass from Mikael Silvestre. His left-foot shot took a slight deflection off Marcel Desailly before looping over Chelsea keeper Carlo Cudicini. The game came alive: Ryan Giggs struck the post, while at the other end Gianfranco Zola skimmed the bar and Carroll had to save at the feet of Hasselbaink. As the interval loomed, an attempted counter-attack throw from the United keeper was intercepted and Zenden unleashed a fierce left-foot shot into the top corner of the net.

If Chelsea had the better of the first half, United stepped up a gear in the second. O'Shea's hard work enabled the midfield to get a stranglehold on the game. Beckham struck the crossbar with a delicate chip and Cudicini had to block a goal-bound shot from Scholes. There was controversy near the hour mark when Scholes broke clear and seemed to be brought down by the Chelsea keeper in the area, but referee Graham Poll waved play on.

Minutes later, Silvestre made another run down the left flank, then cut the ball back for Giggs. The Welshman hit a first-time shot past Cudicini to level the score and rack up his 100th goal for United. After that United continued to attack sporadically and by the final whistle, the Reds were entitled to feel unlucky not to leave the capital with maximum gains.

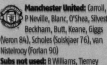

Chelsea: Cudicini, Melchiot, Desailly, Gallas, Babayaro, Zenden, Lampard, Petit (Gronkjaer 75), De Lucas, Hasselbaink (Cole 80), Zola (Gudjohnsen 80)
Subs not used: de Goey, Ferrer
Booked: Desailly, Hasselbaink, De Lucas

Manchester United: Carroll, P Neville, Blanc, O'Shea, Silvestre, Beckham, Butt, Keane, Giggs (Veron 84), Scholes (Solskjaer 76), van Nistelrooy (Forlan 90)
Subs not used: B Williams, Tierney
Booked: P Neville, Beckham

Possession	
46%	4%

Shots on target	
4	5

Shots off target	
2	7

Corners	
3	3

Offsides	
8	1

Fouls	
13	14

Man of the match
JOHN O'SHEA
More confident with every game, O'Shea controlled the threat of Hasselbaink masterfully, allowing Keane and Silvestre to push forward in search of goal. Further evidence that the young Irishman no longer falls into the up and coming category.

Premiership results
Weekend beginning 23/08/02

Birmingham City	0–1	Blackburn Rovers
Bolton Wanderers	1–2	Charlton Athletic
Liverpool	3–0	Southampton
Manchester City	1–0	Newcastle United
Middlesbrough	2–2	Fulham
Sunderland	0–1	Everton
Tottenham Hotspur	1–0	Aston Villa
West Ham United	2–2	Arsenal
West Bromwich Albion	1–3	Leeds United

Premiership table
Top 10 at the end of 24/08/02

	P	PTS
1 Leeds United	2	6
2 Liverpool	2	6
3 Fulham	2	4
4 Arsenal	2	4
5 Chelsea	2	4
6 Everton	2	4
7 Manchester United	2	4
8 Tottenham Hotspur	2	4
9 Blackburn Rovers	2	4
10 Newcastle United	2	3

Sir Alex Ferguson

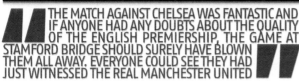
THE MATCH AGAINST CHELSEA WAS FANTASTIC AND IF ANYONE HAD ANY DOUBTS ABOUT THE QUALITY OF THE ENGLISH PREMIERSHIP, THE GAME AT STAMFORD BRIDGE SHOULD SURELY HAVE BLOWN THEM ALL AWAY. EVERYONE COULD SEE THEY HAD JUST WITNESSED THE REAL MANCHESTER UNITED

Sunderland 1
Flo 70

Manchester United 1
Giggs 7

Niall Quinn tries to get a word in as Roy Keane leaves the field

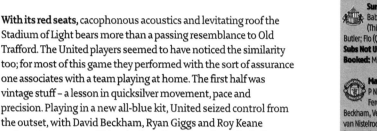

MATCHFACTS

Saturday
31 August 2002
Stadium Of Light
Attendance: **47,586**
Referee: **Uriah Rennie**

With its red seats, cacophonous acoustics and levitating roof the Stadium of Light bears more than a passing resemblance to Old Trafford. The United players seemed to have noticed the similarity too; for most of this game they performed with the sort of assurance one associates with a team playing at home. The first half was vintage stuff – a lesson in quicksilver movement, pace and precision. Playing in a new all-blue kit, United seized control from the outset, with David Beckham, Ryan Giggs and Roy Keane exchanging passes as if they had made a pact to keep the ball amongst themselves. Within seven minutes United were in front, Giggs pouncing on a header from Ole Gunnar Solskjaer before drilling low into the corner.

Rocked by the goal, the home team lost their shape. For a 20-minute period David Beckham and Juan Veron, again showing some exquisite touches, enjoyed almost total freedom, thrilling the travelling fans with their range of passing. Before the interval Giggs, Solskjaer and Keane had chances to extend United's lead, but all failed to find the target.

Sunderland made a spirited start to the second half. In the opening 15 minutes they forced two corners and – following a foul on Matthew Piper by Phil Neville – a free-kick, which was headed wide by Joachim Bjorklund. But still United appeared to be in control. Rio Ferdinand, making his Premiership debut for the Reds, was proving a formidable barrier to the Sunderland forward line of Kevin Phillips and Tore Andre Flo, while Laurent Blanc was enjoying one of his finest games yet in a United shirt.

A Sunderland goal seemed unlikely but on 70 minutes, following a surging run from Jason McAteer through the heart of the United defence, Flo put the home side level. Affronted, United went all out for a winner and threw everything at their hosts.

In the final 10 minutes a flurry of corners eventually yielded a glorious chance for van Nistelrooy, saved at close range by Thomas Sorensen, but the final drama was reserved for the last minute when Keane was sent off after tempers flared between the United skipper and his opposite number in midfield, McAteer.

Sunderland: Sorensen; Wright, Babb, Bjorklund, Gray; Piper (Thirlwell 88), McAteer, Reyna, Butler; Flo (Quinn 79), Phillips
Subs Not Used: Myhre, Kyle, McCartney
Booked: McAteer

Manchester United: Carroll; P Neville (Forlan 90), Blanc, Ferdinand, Silvestre (O'Shea); Beckham, Veron, Keane, Giggs; Solskjaer, van Nistelrooy **Subs Not Used:** B Williams, Stewart, Chadwick **Sent off:** Keane
Booked: P Neville, Beckham

Possession

50%	50%

Shots on target

6	5

Shots off target

11	6

Corners

8	6

Offsides

1	0

Fouls

16	15

Man of the match
LAURENT BLANC
Accompanied by Rio Ferdinand in defence for the first time, United's veteran centre-half put in an imperious display, ensuring that Sunderland's new £8 million signing Tore Andre Flo barely got a kick. Well, apart from the goal that is... but Laurent couldn't be blamed for that.

Premiership results
Weekend beginning 31/08/02

Birmingham City	2–1	Leeds United
Bolton Wanderers	1–0	Aston Villa
Chelsea	1–1	Arsenal
Liverpool	2–2	Newcastle United
Manchester City	3–1	Everton
Middlesbrough	1–0	Blackburn Rovers
Tottenham Hotspur	2–1	Southampton
West Bromwich Albion	1–0	Fulham
West Ham United	0–2	Charlton Athletic

Premiership table
Top 10 to the end of 31/08/02

	P	PTS
1 Tottenham Hotspur	4	10
2 Arsenal	3	7
3 Liverpool	3	7
4 Leeds United	4	6
5 Charlton Athletic	4	6
6 Manchester City	4	6
7 Chelsea	3	5
8 Manchester United	3	5
9 Middlesbrough	3	5
10 Blackburn Rovers	3	5

Sir Alex Ferguson

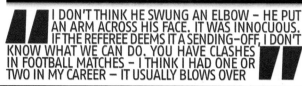

I DON'T THINK HE SWUNG AN ELBOW – HE PUT AN ARM ACROSS HIS FACE. IT WAS INNOCUOUS. IF THE REFEREE DEEMS IT A SENDING-OFF, I DON'T KNOW WHAT WE CAN DO. YOU HAVE CLASHES IN FOOTBALL MATCHES – I THINK I HAD ONE OR TWO IN MY CAREER – IT USUALLY BLOWS OVER

SEPTEMBER

Sir Alex blamed a lack of decisive finishing for the Reds' slow start to the new Premiership season, but the team soon showed why it never pays to underestimate United

Consecutive September defeats to Bolton and Leeds meant United's worst-ever Premiership start. Sir Alex bemoaned a lack of cutting edge in front of goal, resulting in 10 dropped points from the six opening games. By mid-September, West Brom sat above United and Arsenal enjoyed an ominous six-point advantage. Yet matters were partly rectified with consecutive wins against Tottenham and Charlton and fourth position by the end of the month.

With Tottenham fading, unbeaten Arsenal led the league and while they were fortunate with a last-minute winner at home to Bolton, their 4-1 romp over Leeds at Elland Road was particularly impressive. Thierry Henry and an evergreen Gianfranco Zola were the league's top scorers with six each, while Ruud van Nistelrooy had netted three times for United.

Liverpool, the only other side not to have suffered a reverse, were second with Michael Owen back on form with a marvellous hat-trick at Manchester City. The surprise team were Middlesbrough in third, with Steve McClaren's side complimented by classy new signings Geremi and Massimo Maccarone.

The first top-flight Birmingham derby game since the 1980s saw unfortunate Villa keeper Peter Enckelman touch a throw-in into his own net. Still at the bottom, Southampton, Charlton and West Ham occupied the relegation positions; after just two points from their first six games, the impish Paolo Di Canio hit two magnificent goals as the Hammers recorded their first win of the season, at Chelsea.

Barclaycard Premiership fixtures this month

Tuesday 3rd	Middlesbrough	Home
Wednesday 11th	Bolton Wanderers	Home
Saturday 14th	Leeds United	Away
Saturday 21st	Tottenham Hotspur	Home
Saturday 28th	Charlton Athletic	Away

In the Barclaycard Premiership this month

268,994
watched United play five games

United scored
5
goals

but conceded
4
goals

United travelled
556
miles to and from games

United fielded a total of
17
players

FOCUS ON RIO FERDINAND

Nearly 57,000 fans streamed into Old Trafford for the pre-season friendly against Boca Juniors eager to catch a glimpse of the world's most expensive defender in United colours. Rio Ferdinand had been signed in a blaze of publicity after his classy World Cup but limped off injured after just 28 minutes. The ankle injury kept Rio out of the first two league games of the season, but his proper Old Trafford debut, against Middlesbrough on 3rd September, was far more satisfying. The defeat against Bolton was a setback for United's new man, but next came a speedy return to his old club Leeds United. The Whites may have revelled in their win that day, but Rio held his head high. Although a cacophony of jeers greeted his appearance on the pitch, he emerged from the eye of the storm with a moral victory.

Manchester United 1
Van Nistelrooy 28 (penalty)

Middlesbrough 0

Nicky Butt stands his ground

Paul Scholes shows Gareth Southgate a clean pair of heels

This was not United at their best, or even close to it, but the resilience, resolve and focus shown by the players, especially in the closing stages, was the clearest confirmation yet that the defensive frailties of last season have been consigned to history. In American parlance, United "won ugly". The attacking display of the win over Zalaegerszeg was replaced by a more disciplined approach.

In part, this was a tribute to Middlesbrough. As in last season's clash, when Boro grabbed a surprise 1-0 win, Steve McClaren's team posed United some tough tactical questions. Confronted by a heavily manned defence, marshalled superbly by Gareth Southgate, and a midfield willing to match their own work rate, the Reds were made to toil hard for the points.

So hard, in fact, that it was 25 minutes before United registered a first threat on goal, Ryan Giggs sending a screaming left-footer inches past the angle of post and bar after first gathering the ball inside his own half. Three minutes later Giggs was involved in what proved to be the game's critical moment. He lifted a deft pass into the run of Ruud van Nistelrooy who, under pressure from Ugo Ehiogu, shot over the bar with his left foot. But the oohs of the crowd quickly turned to cheers as referee Mike Riley blew for a penalty. The Boro players were mystified, but TV replays later confirmed the centre half had tugged at his shirt. Ruud, cool as you like, buried the penalty in the roof of the net.

McClaren's men were forced to stand and watch as the Reds picked triangles around them in the second half. Too often, though, United's final ball failed to find its target, and Boro grew in confidence. Joseph-Desiré Job twice came close to snatching an equaliser, first on 88 minutes when he headed straight at Fabien Barthez, and then in injury time when only a timely block from Rio Ferdinand saved United.

But a draw would have flattered the visitors. After the match Sir Alex lamented his team's lack of a cutting edge, saying the players were guilty of overcomplicating in the final third. The result pleased him, though, as did the sight of van Nistelrooy getting his first League goal of the season.

Sir Alex Ferguson

> WE COULD HAVE DONE WITH A GOAL OR TWO MORE BUT MIDDLESBROUGH ARE VERY DIFFICULT TO PLAY AGAINST. ALL IN ALL I WAS PLEASED WITH OUR PERSISTENCE. IT LOOKED TO ME AS IF WE ARE REKINDLING THE SPIRIT OF OUR EARLY DAYS GOING BACK TO 1994 AND THIS IS GOOD TO SEE

Spot on as ever...
Ruud salutes OT
after scoring
United's winner

MATCH FACTS

Tuesday
3 September 2002
Old Trafford
Attendance: **67,508**
Referee: **Mike Riley**

Manchester Utd: Barthez;
P Neville, Silvestre, Blanc, Ferdinand;
Beckham (O'Shea 90), Veron, Butt,
Giggs; Scholes (Forlan 79), van Nistelrooy
(Solskjaer 71) **Subs not used:** Ricardo, Pugh
Booked: Veron

Middlesbrough: Schwarzer;
Stockdale, Ehiogu, Southgate,
Cooper; Queudrue (Marinelli 72),
Boateng, Geremi, Greening; Job, Maccarone
(Whelan 73)
Subs not used: Crossley, Gavin, Wilson
Booked: Southgate, Ehiogu

Possession	
53%	47%
Shots on target	
2	2
Shots off target	
9	2
Corners	
5	6
Offsides	
1	1
Fouls	
16	14

Man of the match
RIO FERDINAND

His most impressive early
outing in a United shirt.
Whether bringing the
ball out of defence or
dispossessing the Boro
strikers, Rio oozed class.
You can judge a great
player by the time he has
on the ball; when Rio's got
it, time seems to stand still.

Premiership results
Weekend beginning 31/08/02

Birmingham City	2-1	Leeds United
Bolton Wanderers	0-1	Aston Villa
Chelsea	1-1	Arsenal
Liverpool	2-2	Newcastle United
Manchester City	3-1	Everton
Middlesbrough	1-0	Blackburn Rovers
Tottenham Hotspur	2-1	Southampton
West Bromwich Albion	1-0	Fulham
West Ham United	0-2	Charlton Athletic

Premiership table
Top 10 at the end of 3/09/02

	P	PTS
1 Tottenham Hotspur	4	10
2 Arsenal	4	8
3 Liverpool	4	8
4 Manchester United	4	8
5 Leeds United	4	6
6 Chelsea	4	6
7 Charlton Athletic	4	6
8 Manchester City	4	6
9 Middlesbrough	4	5
10 Blackburn Rovers	4	5

Manchester United 0

Bolton Wanderers 1

Nolan 76

Ruud, Seba and David Beckham defend a Bolton free kick

Sir Alex Ferguson said after the match that United do not have a divine right to win but, without wishing to take anything away from a hard-working Bolton side, this was a game that the Reds should have walked away from with three points.

The difference between the sides was not effort, creativity or determination but plain luck. Neighbours Bolton arrived at Old Trafford with the memory of their shock 2-1 victory last season still fresh in their minds and believed they could win again.

United didn't play badly but the killer final ball from midfield to the front seemed to desert them. This in turn gave Bolton the opportunity to hit the Reds on the break and although Sam Allardyce's men had several strikes on goal, they could never sustain any continued pressure on a tight-looking United defence.

From the first 10 minutes of the game, a pattern was formed that United were unable to break throughout the match. The Reds were having all the play, but Bolton were creating the chances – on the half hour, Fabien Barthez made a fabulous save from Henrik Pedersen. Just before the break, Ruud van Nistelrooy was sent clear by Seba Veron but his spectacular effort flew past Jussi

MATCH FACTS

Wednesday
11 September 2002
Old Trafford
Attendance: **67,623**
Referee: **Graham Barber**

REVIEW

Manchester United: Barthez; P Neville, Ferdinand, Blanc, Silvestre; Beckham, Butt, Veron (Forlan 76), Giggs; Solskjaer, van Nistelrooy
Subs not used: Chadwick, Stewart, O'Shea, Ricardo **Booked:** P Neville

Bolton Wanderers: Jaaskelainen; Barness, Bergsson, Whitlow, Charlton; Djorkaeff (Warhurst 73), Frandsen (Holdsworth 87), Nolan, Gardner; Pedersen (Campo 90), Ricketts
Subs not used: Walters, Poole
Booked: Nolan, Holdsworth

Nicky Butt goes for the ball in a tight midfield contest

Possession		
58%		42%
Shots on target		
7		2
Shots off target		
10		3
Corners		
9		6
Offsides		
2		2
Fouls		
10		13

Man of the match
DAVID BECKHAM
Though he made the error that led to the goal – and for which he later apologised – David had no reason to reproach himself for this performance. He covered more ground than anyone else, and always looked the most likely to create an opening.

Jaaskelainen only to crash back out after hitting the underside of the bar. Replays confirmed the ball had not crossed the goal-line but on another night fate might have dealt United a kinder hand.

After the break, United dominated proceedings but were unable to make the pressure count. Then the unthinkable happened – Kevin Nolan followed his long throw into the box, the ball bounced around and with Beckham failing to clear, Nolan jumped on the loose ball and drove it under Barthez.

A frantic ending saw Barthez surge forward as an extra midfielder and Diego Forlan tried in vain to draw the match level. At the final whistle, United's frustration was evident. So was Bolton's jubilation at their second successive win at Old Trafford.

Premiership results
Matches played up to 11/09/02

Arsenal	2–1	Manchester City	
Aston Villa	2–0	Charlton Athletic	
Blackburn Rovers	2–3	Chelsea	
Fulham	3–2	Tottenham Hotspur	
Liverpool	2–2	Birmingham City	
Middlesbrough	3–0	Sunderland	
Newcastle United	2–0	Leeds United	
Southampton	1–0	Everton	
West Ham United	0–1	West Bromwich Albion	

Premiership table
Top 10 at the end of 11/09/02

	P	PTS
1 Arsenal	5	11
2 Tottenham Hotspur	5	10
3 Leeds United	5	9
4 Liverpool	5	9
5 Chelsea	5	9
6 Middlesbrough	5	8
7 Manchester United	5	8
8 Fulham	4	7
9 Aston Villa	5	6
10 Charlton Athletic	5	6

Sir Alex Ferguson

> A DEFEAT AT HOME TO BOLTON WAS NOT WHAT WE HAD PLANNED BUT WE ARE STILL IN TOUCH WITH THE LEADERS. OUR BIG PROBLEM IS A LACK OF CUTTING EDGE BUT THE TEAMWORK HAS BEEN GOOD, OVERALL WE HAVE BEEN DEFENDING WELL AND THERE HAS BEEN A RESILIENCE IN THE SIDE

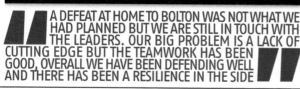

Leeds United 1
Kewell 67

Manchester United 0

Mikael Silvestre gets there first, but it wasn't to be United's day

Saturday
14 September 2002
Elland Road
Attendance: **39,622**
Referee: **Jeff Winter**

Leeds United: Robinson; Mills, Woodgate, Matteo (Radebe 45), Harte; Barmby (Bakke 45), Bowyer, Dacourt, Kewell; Smith, Viduka (McPhail 72)
Subs not used: Martyn, Kelly
Booked: Smith, Harte

Manchester United: Barthez; O'Shea, Ferdinand, Blanc, Silvestre; P Neville, Beckham, Butt (Chadwick 63), Giggs; van Nistelrooy (Forlan 71), Solskjaer
Subs Not Used: Ricardo, Pugh, Roche
Booked: Solskjaer

Possession	
57%	43%

Shots on target	
5	3

Shots off target	
2	6

Corners	
7	4

Offsides	
0	0

Fouls	
13	16

In the build-up to this match, much was made of United's impressive record against Leeds. On Saturday morning practically every paper was at pains to point out that it had been five years since the Yorkshire club had taken maximum points from the Reds. Talk about tempting fate...

Despite creating most of the game's clear-cut chances, United fell to a second 1-0 defeat inside four days, and a first loss away from home in the Premiership since a 3-1 reversal at Arsenal in November 2001.

After a fiercely contested opening 20 minutes, the Reds gradually wrestled control of the midfield, where Nicky Butt and Phil Neville, in for the injured Veron, were both operating close to the peak of their form. Ryan Giggs was prominent too, causing no end of bother when drifting in from wide to link with Solskjaer and van Nistelrooy.

The best chance of the half fell to the Dutchman when, after a swift exchange with Giggs, he muscled past three defenders and released a left-foot shot that was well saved by Paul Robinson.

As half time approached, United's football was irresistible. David Beckham, Butt and Giggs popped the ball around on the edge of the penalty area while the Leeds defence could only stand and watch, mesmerised by the pace and precision of United's passing. A goal seemed inevitable. But, despite having two strong penalty claims turned down and a couple of efforts cleared off the line, the Reds couldn't force a breakthrough.

Leeds regrouped after the interval, Terry Venables reverting to a five-man midfield to counter the threat of Giggs. The adjustments saw the balance of power shift towards the home side and, on 67 minutes, Leeds took the lead. Harry Kewell leapt unchallenged to head past Fabien Barthez from Ian Harte's left-wing cross.

The goal was a cruel blow for United – and for Rio Ferdinand, who performed well at his old club despite the barracking. But after failing to capitalise on first-half domination, the Reds had again left themselves vulnerable.

The misery was compounded by yet another injury to a midfield player – Nicky Butt had to withdraw with a hip problem midway through the second half.

Man of the match
NICKY BUTT
The focal point of all United's best work, Nicky bossed the midfield, snapping into tackles and threading passes forward for the strikers. Forced off the pitch reluctantly in the second-half after trying to play on with an injury, Leeds scored within four minutes of his substitution.

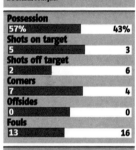

Premiership results
Weekend beginning 14/09/02

Birmingham City	3-0	Aston Villa
Bolton Wanderers	2-3	Liverpool
Charlton Athletic	0-3	Arsenal
Chelsea	3-0	Newcastle United
Everton	2-1	Middlesbrough
Manchester City	2-2	Blackburn Rovers
Sunderland	0-3	Fulham
Tottenham Hotspur	3-2	West Ham United
West Bromwich Albion	1-0	Southampton

Premiership table
Top 10 at the end of 16/09/02

	P	PTS
1 Arsenal	6	14
2 Tottenham Hotspur	6	13
3 Leeds United	6	12
4 Chelsea	6	12
5 Liverpool	6	12
6 Fulham	5	10
7 West Bromwich Albion	6	9
8 Middlesbrough	6	8
9 Birmingham City	6	8
10 Manchester United	6	8

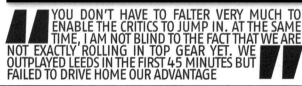

Sir Alex Ferguson

YOU DON'T HAVE TO FALTER VERY MUCH TO ENABLE THE CRITICS TO JUMP IN. AT THE SAME TIME, I AM NOT BLIND TO THE FACT THAT WE ARE NOT EXACTLY ROLLING IN TOP GEAR YET. WE OUTPLAYED LEEDS IN THE FIRST 45 MINUTES BUT FAILED TO DRIVE HOME OUR ADVANTAGE

Manchester United 1
Van Nistelrooy 63 (penalty)

Tottenham Hotspur 0

Encounters between United and Spurs are seldom 1-0 and this match may well have been a high-scoring thriller were it not for the goalkeeping masterclasses courtesy of Kasey Keller and Fabien Barthez. In front of Barthez, the United defence was looking solid again, with Silvestre and O'Shea particularly impressive.

As Sir Alex put it on the day, the critics had been relishing "our so-called demise" after two league defeats, and the way the Reds started the game suggested things were about to change. Just four minutes in, Keller was forced to intercept a cross from Phil Neville while Ruud van Nistelrooy waited ominously in the box.

Soon afterwards, a Goran Bunjevcevic effort was saved by Barthez and Beckham had a shot parried by Keller. There was good reason for Beckham's edge – this was just two days shy of his 10th anniversary of first-team football with United.

Tottenham were not without their chances and Barthez had to rush out of his area and intercept Robbie Keane with a sliding tackle as he surged towards the United goal. Barely a minute later, United had another scare: the ball was crossed deep into the box where Dean Richards' shot was brilliantly blocked by Barthez.

Ruud punishes Spurs with another perfect spot kick

MATCH FACTS

Saturday
21 September 2002
Old Trafford
Attendance: **67,611**
Referee: **Rob Styles**

On the hour mark, United were denied what appeared to be a sound penalty claim when Beckham sent van Nistelrooy clear only to see him felled by Gary Doherty. Referee Rob Styles waved play on but one minute later Doherty brought down Solskjaer in the box and this time there was no debate.

At this point Sheringham sidled up to Keller and advised him which way to go. Van Nistelrooy put the ball on the spot, Keller went to his right and the ball whizzed past to his left. It was the Dutchman's fifth goal of the season and United's first win after two successive defeats.

When Gary Neville ran on in place of Solskjaer 15 minutes from time, his return to the first team completed a productive afternoon.

Manchester United: Barthez; Silvestre, Ferdinand, O'Shea, P Neville; Veron (Forlan, 76), Beckham, Butt, Giggs (Pugh, 85); van Nistelrooy, Solskjaer (G Neville, 76) **Subs not used:** Ricardo, Stewart **Booked:** van Nistelrooy

Tottenham Hotspur: Keller; Thatcher, Richards, Doherty, Davies; Etherington, Redknapp, Bunjevcevic, Iversen (Ferdinand, 76); Sheringham (Acimovic, 85), Keane **Subs not used:** Henry, Hirschfeld, Ricketts **Booked:** Richards

Possession		
50%		50%

Shots on target		
8		3

Shots off target		
8		5

Corners		
10		5

Offsides		
2		0

Fouls		
13		9

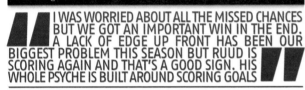

Sir Alex Ferguson

I WAS WORRIED ABOUT ALL THE MISSED CHANCES BUT WE GOT AN IMPORTANT WIN IN THE END. A LACK OF EDGE UP FRONT HAS BEEN OUR BIGGEST PROBLEM THIS SEASON BUT RUUD IS SCORING AGAIN AND THAT'S A GOOD SIGN. HIS WHOLE PSYCHE IS BUILT AROUND SCORING GOALS

Man of the match
JOHN O'SHEA

Another accomplished display from the adaptable youngster. O'Shea had played the last two games as right back but returned to his natural central defensive position here and was unflappable. Laurent Blanc, watching from the stands, must have been impressed.

Premiership results
Weekend beginning 21/09/02

Arsenal	2–1	Bolton Wanderers
Aston Villa	3–2	Everton
Blackburn Rovers	1–0	Leeds United
Fulham	0–0	Chelsea
Liverpool	2–0	West Bromwich Albion
Middlesbrough	1–0	Birmingham City
Newcastle United	2–0	Sunderland
Southampton	0–0	Charlton Athletic
West Ham United	0–0	Manchester City

Premiership table
Top 10 at the end of 21/09/02

	P	PTS
1 Arsenal	7	17
2 Liverpool	7	15
3 Chelsea	7	13
4 Tottenham Hotspur	7	13
5 Leeds United	7	12
6 Fulham	6	11
7 Middlesbrough	7	11
8 Manchester United	7	11
9 Blackburn Rovers	7	9
10 Aston Villa	7	9

Fabien Barthez goes to ground as Seba waits to clear

Charlton Athletic 1
Jensen 43

Manchester United 3
Scholes 54, Giggs 83, van Nistelrooy 90

Paul Scholes belts in the equaliser from eight yards

Supersub Ruud is congratulated by Gary and Rio

Concentration all round on the United bench

Saturday
28 September 2002
The Valley
Attendance: **26,630**
Referee: **Dermot Gallagher**

Don't be fooled by the scoreline. Charlton put up a dogged fight at The Valley and, but for an impressive second-half display from United, might easily have claimed their first Premiership victory over the Reds. That they didn't was largely down to the creative influence of Ryan Giggs. The Welshman, clearly benefiting from an injury-free run in the first team, was the architect of a fightback that saw United score three times in the second half and condemn the Addicks to a fourth consecutive home league defeat.

For much of the first half Sir Alex Ferguson's team were second best, and when Claus Jensen put the Londoners ahead just before half-time, curling a stinging shot past Fabien Barthez from the edge of the box, even the most partisan Red couldn't grumble. Earlier Paul Scholes, back after injury, had come close to breaking the deadlock but, after rounding Dean Kiely, he was forced to watch in anguish as Richard Rufus slid in to clear his goal-bound effort off the line.

Although the players wore the same white shirts in the second half, in every other aspect, United, guided by Sir Alex in his 400th Premiership match, were unrecognisable from the team who had contested the first 45 minutes. Suddenly passes started to find their target, the midfielders were snapping into tackles and up front Ole Gunnar Solskjaer and Paul Scholes, isolated in the first half, began to link promisingly. The equaliser came on 54 minutes. After a run and cross from Giggs, Scholes, arriving with the precision timing of a Swiss watchmaker, hit home from eight yards.

Once in front United began to purr. On 63 minutes, Giggs, leaping to meet a John O'Shea cross, was unlucky to see his glancing header go narrowly wide but 20 minutes later it was the Welshman who finally put United ahead, rounding Kiely to slot home after good work from substitute Ruud van Nistelrooy. Then, in the final minute, Ryan returned the compliment, sending over a cross for the Dutchman to make it 3-1 with a far-post header.

While the final score might have flattered United, the clinical finishing was in marked contrast to the recent display at Leeds. This, and the midweek Champions League win against Bayer Leverkusen, provided further evidence that the Red revival was gathering pace.

Charlton Athletic: Kiely; Young (Johansson 85), Rufus, Fortune, Powell; Robinson, Mustoe (Kishishev 87), Jensen, Konchesky, Euell, Bartlett
Subs Not Used: Rachubka, Fish, Svensson
Booked: Mustoe, Robinson

Manchester United: Barthez; O'Shea, Ferdinand, Blanc, P Neville; Beckham, Butt (G Neville 69), Forlan (van Nistelrooy 56), Giggs; Scholes, Solskjaer
Subs Not Used: Ricardo, May, Stewart
Booked: Forlan, Beckham, P Neville

Possession	
56%	44%

Shots on target	
6	2

Shots off target	
6	4

Corners	
6	3

Offsides	
0	1

Fouls	
10	14

Man of the match
RYAN GIGGS

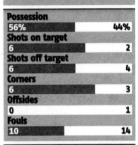

Ryan set up the first goal for Paul Scholes, scored the second himself with a finish that would have done any of the strikers proud, and laid on the third with an inch-perfect cross for Ruud van Nistelrooy. Man of the match? For this performance he probably deserved a medal too.

Premiership results
Weekend beginning 28/09/02

Bolton Wanderers	1-1	Southampton
Birmingham City	0-2	Newcastle United
Chelsea	2-3	West Ham United
Everton	2-0	Fulham
Leeds United	1-4	Arsenal
Manchester City	0-3	Liverpool
Sunderland	1-0	Aston Villa
Tottenham Hotspur	0-3	Middlesbrough
West Bromwich Albion	0-2	Blackburn Rovers

Premiership table
Top 10 at the end of 30/09/02

	P	PTS
1 Arsenal	8	20
2 Liverpool	8	18
3 Middlesbrough	8	14
4 Manchester United	8	14
5 Chelsea	8	13
6 Tottenham Hotspur	8	13
7 Leeds United	8	12
8 Blackburn Rovers	8	12
9 Fulham	7	11
10 Everton	8	11

Sir Alex Ferguson

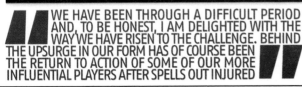

WE HAVE BEEN THROUGH A DIFFICULT PERIOD AND, TO BE HONEST, I AM DELIGHTED WITH THE WAY WE HAVE RISEN TO THE CHALLENGE. BEHIND THE UPSURGE IN OUR FORM HAS OF COURSE BEEN THE RETURN TO ACTION OF SOME OF OUR MORE INFLUENTIAL PLAYERS AFTER SPELLS OUT INJURED

OCTOBER

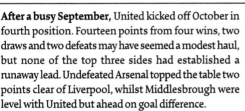

Euro 2004 qualifiers meant a reduced Premiership programme, with only three games being played, but some tough matches awaited United either side of the international fixtures

After a busy September, United kicked off October in fourth position. Fourteen points from four wins, two draws and two defeats may have seemed a modest haul, but none of the top three sides had established a runaway lead. Undefeated Arsenal topped the table two points clear of Liverpool, whilst Middlesbrough were level with United but ahead on goal difference.

International fixture demands resulted in only three Premiership games for United in October (something that must have pleased Sir Alex, who backed UEFA's call for fewer domestic matches). But many Reds, including the England contingent of Beckham, Butt, Gary Neville and Scholes, were on duty for the home nations in the Euro 2004 qualifiers.

Beckham scored in both of England's games, against Slovakia and Macedonia, which also marked Paul Scholes's 50th and 51st appearances in an England shirt. Meanwhile, Ryan Giggs captained Wales to an unforgettable 2-1 win over Italy in Cardiff.

Back in the Premiership, Southampton continued their winning run and climbed six places. Liverpool finished the month with three wins and Blackburn went into November on the back of wins against Newcastle United and Arsenal (who lost four games on the trot). West Brom failed to reverse their poor form and dropped back into the bottom three.

As the clocks turned back after the 1-1 home draw with Aston Villa, United entered winter time just eight points off the Premiership summit and with an improving injury list.

Barclaycard Premiership fixtures this month

Monday 7th	Everton	Home
Saturday 19th	Fulham	Away
Saturday 26th	Aston Villa	Home

In the Barclaycard Premiership this month

153,351 watched United play three games

United scored **5** goals

United travelled **406** miles to and from games

but conceded **2** goals

United fielded a total of **17**

FOCUS ON GARY NEVILLE

It's a testament to the flexibility of United's squad that the players can switch effortlessly between positions when tactics and injuries dictate. October's starting line-ups changed regularly, but only Gary Neville started – and finished – all three Premiership games in his usual berth. Slotting back into the team as right back after three appearances as a substitute in September, Gary couldn't wait for the chance to re-establish himself following his foot injury. "I've played in the middle for maybe 15 or 20 games over the last few seasons and I've really enjoyed it," he said. "But if my career ended tomorrow and anyone asked where I'd played, I'd have to say full back. At centre back you tend to run 30 or 40 yards forward and back, but at full back you're expected to get up and down the pitch more."

Manchester United 3
Scholes 86, 90, van Nistelrooy 89 (penalty)
Everton 0

David Moyes summed up his feelings post-match as "somewhere between gutted and disappointed," and even the staunchest Reds must have felt a flicker of pity for the Everton manager, after his battling side came within five minutes of a draw. Watching this game was like waiting for the proverbial bus: you wait 86 minutes for one precious, title-chasing goal, and then three come at once.

The first half was notable for two things: United's inventive passing play and a spine-tingling atmosphere described by one Red as the best at Old Trafford in 15 years.

The first of United's chances was created by David Beckham, who drove into the Everton box and saw his shot whistle past Richard Wright's post. United were steadily growing in confidence though; the movement was a joy to watch, a lot of it coming through a revitalised Paul Scholes. But while the Reds were impressive in attack, Everton were strong in defence, particularly the steadfast pairing of David Weir and Joseph Yobo.

The second half saw Everton gradually creep into the match, with the impressive Thomas Gravesen successful in disrupting United's midfield control.

Ruud lashes home his third goal of the Premiership season

Monday
7 October 2002
Old Trafford
Attendance: **67,629**
Referee: **Mike Riley**

It looked like the game was edging towards a goalless draw but Wayne Rooney had other thoughts when he exploded into the game with 20 minutes to go. English football's most exciting prospect grabbed the game by the scruff of the neck and ran at the United defence, but couldn't provide a finish.

Which is exactly what United did with devastating consequences. With four minutes to go Paul Scholes rifled the ball into the net from 10 yards to open the scoring.

Two minutes later the unfortunate Weir was shown a straight red after he had hauled back Solskjaer in the box. Van Nistelrooy duly netted the penalty, then Scholes finished the night off in style with a trademark 25-yard rocket.

Manchester United: Barthez; G Neville, O'Shea, Blanc, Silvestre; Beckham, Veron (Solskjaer 63), Butt (Forlan 85), Giggs; Scholes; van Nistelrooy (P Neville 90) **Subs not used:** Ricardo, Fortune

Everton: Wright; Hibbert, Yobo, Weir, Unsworth; Carsley, Gravesen, Li Tie, Pembridge; Radzinski (Rooney 74), Campbell **Subs not used:** Gerrard, Naysmith, Li Wei Feng, Ferguson **Booked:** Unsworth, Gravesen **Sent off:** Weir

Sir Alex Ferguson

WE HAD SOME FANTASTIC PASSING MOVES. OUR MOVEMENT AND ATTACKING WAS BREATHTAKING AT TIMES BUT WE COULDN'T GET THE BALL IN THE NET. WE GOT TO THE BY-LINE ON A NUMBER OF OCCASIONS BUT MADE THE WRONG DECISIONS. ONCE WE GOT IN FRONT IT WAS A DIFFERENT GAME

Possession

58%	42%

Shots on target

5	2

Shots off target

7	5

Corners

7	1

Offsides

4	0

Fouls

15	14

Man of the match
PAUL SCHOLES

Although Everton tried to stop him stamping his authority on the game, Scholes kept at it and bagged two vital late goals. As Sir Alex said afterwards, there's nobody better at scoring from midfield than Paul Scholes. Especially when it's from the edge of the penalty area.

John O'Shea and Ole Solskjaer mob Scholes after his stunning strike

Premiership results
Weekend beginning 5/10/02

Arsenal	3-1	Sunderland
Aston Villa	0-0	Leeds United
Blackburn Rovers	1-2	Tottenham Hotspur
Fulham	1-0	Charlton Athletic
Liverpool	1-0	Chelsea
Middlesbrough	2-0	Bolton Wanderers
Newcastle United	2-1	West Bromwich Albion
Southampton	2-0	Manchester City
West Ham United	1-2	Birmingham City

Premiership table
Top 10 at the end of 7/10/02

	P	PTS
1 Arsenal	9	23
2 Liverpool	9	21
3 Middlesbrough	9	17
4 Manchester United	9	17
5 Tottenham Hotspur	9	16
6 Fulham	8	14
7 Chelsea	9	13
8 Newcastle United	8	13
9 Leeds United	9	13
10 Blackburn Rovers	9	12

Fulham 1
Marlet 35

Manchester United 1
Solskjaer 62

Ole Gunnar
smashes United's
equaliser home...

United made up a point on Arsenal with this hard-fought draw but could easily have dropped all three had it not been for Fabien Barthez. The French keeper frustrated the home fans with his penalty save (and the build up to it), but for United fans it was arguably the most dramatic moment of the season so far.

The drama erupted with 20 minutes left and the game evenly poised at 1-1. Some slick passing in the Fulham midfield culminated in Steve Marlet bearing down on the United goal, with only Laurent Blanc in the vicinity. Blanc eased him off the ball at the edge of the box, just as the striker looked to be losing control. Marlet's momentum carried him forwards, down he went and referee Mike Dean pointed to the spot. It could have been Blanc's last contribution of the game but Dean produced a yellow card when it could easily have been red.

As Fulham's Steed Malbranque placed the ball on the spot, Barthez realised the Loftus Road pitch was playing havoc with his studs and started hammering the soles of his boots against the left post. Meanwhile the referee had to intervene as Rufus Brevett and Gary Neville tussled on the edge of the box. Fabien then

Fulham: Van der Sar; Ouaddou, Knight, Goma, Brevett; Finnan, Davis, Malbranque, Legwinski; Sava (Hayles 78), Marlet
Subs not used: Taylor, Inamoto, Collins, Boa Morte
Booked: Marlet

Manchester United: Barthez; Silvestre (Forlan 80), O'Shea, Blanc, G Neville; P Neville (Fortune 59), Veron, Beckham, Giggs; Scholes; Solskjaer
Subs not used: Ricardo, May, Richardson
Booked: Blanc, Barthez, Beckham

Possession	
53%	47%
Shots on target	
6	7
Shots off target	
3	7
Corners	
1	6
Offsides	
4	3
Fouls	
15	10

Man of the match
FABIEN BARTHEZ
United's No.1 kept his team in the match with a string of crucial saves, particularly a hat-trick of blocks to foil Facundo Sava and stop the Argentinian frontman from getting his latest mask out from under his shinpad. Oh, and there was one other little incident to report... but we think you know all about that one already.

...and takes his applause
from Scholes and Beckham

strolled across his goal to inspect the other post, and might well have stopped for a nice cup of tea had the referee not cautioned him for timewasting. No matter. Fabien had done enough to upset Malbranque's concentration (as he had Muzzy Izzet's last season) and easily saved the Fulham man's weak shot.

Long before all this, Marlet had given Fulham a first-half lead when he pounced on a Brevett cross. But United started the second half with much more vim and vigour, and equalised just after the hour with a typically predatory Solskjaer strike. There was a first game of the season for Quinton Fortune (on as a second-half sub for Phil Neville), and Beckham was booked for a juddering tackle on Sylvain Legwinski, but this was a day that belonged to Barthez.

Premiership results
Weekend beginning 19/10/02

Aston Villa	0–1	Southampton
Blackburn Rovers	5–2	Newcastle United
Charlton Athletic	1–0	Middlesbrough
Everton	2–1	Arsenal
Leeds United	0–1	Liverpool
Manchester City	0–3	Chelsea
Sunderland	0–1	West Ham United
Tottenham Hotspur	3–1	Bolton Wanderers
West Bromwich Albion	1–1	Birmingham City

Premiership table
Top 10 at the end of 19/10/02

	P	PTS
1 Liverpool	10	24
2 Arsenal	10	23
3 Tottenham Hotspur	10	19
4 Manchester United	10	18
5 Middlesbrough	10	17
6 Chelsea	10	16
7 Blackburn Rovers	10	15
8 Fulham	10	15
9 Everton	10	14
10 Leeds United	10	13

Sir Alex Ferguson

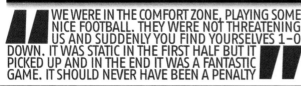

WE WERE IN THE COMFORT ZONE, PLAYING SOME NICE FOOTBALL. THEY WERE NOT THREATENING US AND SUDDENLY YOU FIND YOURSELVES 1–0 DOWN. IT WAS STATIC IN THE FIRST HALF BUT IT PICKED UP AND IN THE END IT WAS A FANTASTIC GAME. IT SHOULD NEVER HAVE BEEN A PENALTY

Manchester United 1
Forlan 77

Aston Villa 1
Mellberg 35

Diego powers in United's equaliser

There's no way past Gary and Phil Neville

It's shirt off as Old Trafford erupts

Saturday
26 October 2002
Old Trafford
Attendance: **67,619**
Referee: **Graham Poll**

UP FOR IT!

United's goal celebrations have been even more intense than usual this season, often involving several members of the team in a huge backslapping bundle, but the scenes that greeted Diego Forlan's strike in this match topped the lot. The Uruguayan's second-half header, his first goal for the Reds in open play, was the cue for the kind of jubilation usually reserved for Cup Final winners. Within seconds of the ball hitting the net, Forlan had removed his shirt and vanished – smothered by a mound of team-mates eager to congratulate him.

The goal brought relief all round: for Diego it signalled the end of an agonising wait, while for United it salvaged a point from a match in which the visitors might easily have stolen the spoils.

With a place in the next phase of the Champions League secured, Sir Alex had called for his team to step on the gas in the Premier League. But it was Villa who had the better start. In the 21st minute, Stefan Moore – put through by a Dion Dublin flick – had a shot saved by the legs of Fabien Barthez, then Dublin himself volleyed just over after the Reds failed to clear a corner.

The visitors finally scored the goal their industrious display merited on 35 minutes when Olaf Mellberg, escaping the attentions of Laurent Blanc at a corner, powered home a header. United responded with shots from Paul Scholes and David Beckham, whose left-footed curler skipped into the Stretford End off the crossbar, but could not force an equaliser before the break.

In the second half the Reds, driven on by Beckham and Scholes, gradually established supremacy. Following Forlan's 77th-minute equaliser, Sir Alex went for broke and released Blanc from his defensive duties to play as an auxiliary centre forward.

With the pressure mounting, Villa's back line – up to this point a formidably defiant unit – began to exhibit signs of stress and the Reds came close to completing a comeback victory when Solskjaer, rising to meet a Beckham cross, flicked a close-range header towards goal. The crowd rose as one, fully expecting to see the ball ripple the net, but Enckelman's reflexes were equal to the task and the Villans held on for a point.

Manchester United: Barthez; G Neville, Blanc, Ferdinand, Silvestre; Beckham, Veron, Scholes, P Neville (Fortune 60); Forlan, Solskjaer
Subs Not Used: Ricardo, O'Shea, Richardson, Roche
Booked: Beckham

Aston Villa: Enckelman; Barry, Staunton, Mellberg, Samuel; Leonhardsen (Hitzlsperger 84), Kinsella, Taylor, Delaney; Dublin (Crouch 66), Moore (Angel 66)
Subs Not Used: Postma, Allback

Possession	
62%	38%

Shots on target	
6	4

Shots off target	
8	5

Corners	
8	5

Offsides	
4	1

Fouls	
7	14

Man of the match
DAVID BECKHAM
If United's skipper was feeling the effects of the midweek trip to Athens then he did a fine job of hiding his lethargy. Beckham ran his socks off, driving his team-mates ceaselessly forward in search of victory. Makes you tired just watching him do it...

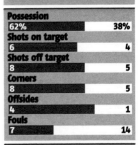

Premiership results
Weekend beginning 26/10/02

Arsenal	1-2	Blackburn Rovers
Birmingham City	0-2	Manchester City
Bolton Wanderers	1-1	Sunderland
Chelsea	2-0	West Bromwich Albion
Liverpool	2-1	Tottenham Hotspur
Middlesbrough	2-2	Leeds United
Newcastle United	2-1	Charlton Athletic
Southampton	4-2	Fulham
West Ham United	0-1	Everton

Premiership table
Top 10 at the end of 26/10/02

	P	PTS
1 Liverpool	11	27
2 Arsenal	11	23
3 Chelsea	11	19
4 Manchester United	11	19
5 Tottenham Hotspur	11	19
6 Middlesbrough	11	18
7 Blackburn Rovers	11	18
8 Everton	11	17
9 Newcastle United	10	16
10 Southampton	11	16

Sir Alex Ferguson

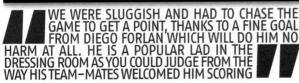

WE WERE SLUGGISH AND HAD TO CHASE THE GAME TO GET A POINT, THANKS TO A FINE GOAL FROM DIEGO FORLAN WHICH WILL DO HIM NO HARM AT ALL. HE IS A POPULAR LAD IN THE DRESSING ROOM AS YOU COULD JUDGE FROM THE WAY HIS TEAM-MATES WELCOMED HIM SCORING

NOVEMBER

As winter drew in, pundits wondered if the Premiership power base was shifting but such premature speculation didn't bother United, now with key players returning from injury

'November Spawned a Monster' – so sang the Stretford-born songsmith Morrissey. It's unlikely he could have been pre-empting a topless Diego Forlan charging around Old Trafford swinging his shirt around. No, Morrissey must have foreseen the last-ever Manchester derby at Maine Road – a traumatic event after which Sir Alex considered letting United fans into the changing rooms to voice their opinions.

The Premiership leaders for much of November were Liverpool, but as soon as pundits began to talk about the league championship finding its way back to Anfield thanks to Gerard Houllier's savvy summer signings, they started losing. That left the media to fawn over an exciting but not indomitable Arsenal side, and speculative talk of a shift in the football power base from M16 to N5.

Sixteen games into the season and Everton were riding high, having found themselves – like a kitten up a Californian Redwood – stranded in a Champions League spot and seemingly too scared to come down. Having spent little on players, what other explanation could be given? Perhaps the appointment of David Moyes might have had something to do with it.

By the close of the month, United were fifth, with just one win from seven away games but showing clear signs of an upturn in form. Compared with Leeds United, fortunes could have been much worse for as December approached, only bottom-placed West Ham had a worse home record than Leeds, under the stewardship of their new manager Terry Venables.

Barclaycard Premiership fixtures this month

Saturday 2nd	Southampton	Home
Saturday 9th	Manchester City	Away
Sunday 17th	West Ham United	Away
Saturday 23rd	Newcastle United	Home

In the Barclaycard Premiership this month

205,008
watched United play four games

United scored
9
goals

but conceded
8
goals

United travelled
447
miles to and from games

United fielded a total of
16
players

FOCUS ON JUAN SEBASTIAN VERON
United's midfield options were restricted throughout the first half of the season due to a series of injuries and operations, with Nicky Butt, David Beckham and captain Roy Keane all out for long spells. A lot of the responsibility fell on the shoulders of Seba Veron, who played his part in every game during November's league fixtures. The month started promisingly enough with a home win against Southampton, but soon went downhill with the Maine Road derby debacle. "A great honour to have participated in, but I wish I could change the result around," Seba said later about his first Manchester derby. It was an altogether different story in the last home game of the month, as Veron joined the 5–3 win over Newcastle United as a second-half substitute.

Manchester United 2
P Neville 15, Forlan 85

Southampton 1
Fernandes 18

Diego wheels away
in celebration after
snatching the winner

If October ended well for Diego Forlan, November began magnificently for the Uruguayan as he scored the winning goal against Southampton with five minutes to spare. The match was heading for what would have been United's third 1-1 league draw in a row when Forlan picked the ball up 30 yards from the visitors' goal and let fly with a stunning strike that left Antti Niemi helpless. It was the decisive act in a match contested in a Mancunian monsoon.

Last year United won this fixture 6-1, featuring a hat-trick from Ruud van Nistelrooy and a stunning strike from Phil Neville. Hampshire hearts must have sank when they saw Ruud restored to the United attack, but it was Neville who gave the Reds the lead when his shot was deflected into the net. The lead lasted just three minutes, however. Brett Ormerod found Fabrice Fernandes on the edge of the box and he stroked a classy shot past Barthez.

The rest of the half was a thrilling spectacle as play lurched from end to end. A Beckham header was cleared off the line by Oakley, while Fernandes tested Barthez once more with a rasping shot-cum-cross. Rio Ferdinand, excelling in defence, also found time to join the attack with a great run down the right wing.

Saturday
2 November 2002
Old Trafford
Attendance: **67,691**
Referee: **Uriah Rennie**

PREVIEW

THE WING MASTER

Manchester United: Barthez; G Neville, Ferdinand, Blanc, Silvestre (Solskjaer 68); Beckham, P Neville (Forlan 79),Veron, Giggs; Scholes; van Nistelrooy (O'Shea 87)
Subs not used: Ricardo, Fortune

Southampton: Niemi; Dodd, Lundekvam, M Svensson, Bridge; Fernandes, A Svensson, Marsden (Delgado 88), Oakley; Beattie, Ormerod (Delap 73)
Subs not used: Jones, Hall, Telfer
Booked: Dodd

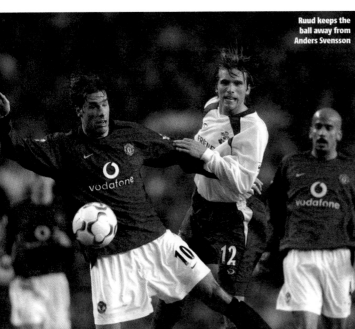

Ruud keeps the ball away from Anders Svensson

Possession	
57%	43%
Shots on target	
3	3
Shots off target	
10	6
Corners	
10	2
Offsides	
6	1
Fouls	
12	18

Man of the match
RIO FERDINAND

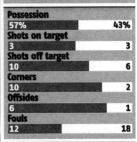

An increasing familiarity with his environment and team-mates was beginning to imbue Rio with the confidence to express himself. Against Saints, he regularly stepped out from defence, distributing his final pass with the care so often lacking in defenders.

The second half continued in much the same vein. The in-form James Beattie had a shot well saved by Barthez, while Rio was again prominent, showing a range of skills of which Juan Veron would have been proud. With the clock running down, United sacrificed Silvestre and Phil Neville in favour of Solskjaer and Forlan.

Forlan made an immediate impact, shooting just wide and then finding Beckham with an inch-perfect pass before stealing the show with his second goal in a week. And if the strike was memorable, the celebration was unforgettable. Once again the shirt came off, but this time it just wouldn't go back on again and the abiding memory of this match will be the topless South American charging after Beattie and breaking down the last Saints attack.

Premiership results
Weekend beginning 2/13/02

Birmingham City	3–1	Bolton Wanderers
Blackburn Rovers	0–0	Aston Villa
Charlton Athletic	1–1	Sunderland
Fulham	0–1	Arsenal
Leeds United	0–1	Everton
Liverpool	2–0	West Ham United
Newcastle United	2–0	Middlesbrough
Tottenham Hotspur	0–0	Chelsea
West Bromwich Albion	1–2	Manchester City

Premiership table
Top 10 at the end of 4/11/03

	P	PTS
1 Liverpool	12	30
2 Arsenal	12	26
3 Manchester United	12	22
4 Chelsea	12	20
5 Tottenham Hotspur	12	20
6 Everton	12	20
7 Blackburn Rovers	12	19
8 Newcastle United	11	19
9 Middlesbrough	12	18
10 Southampton	12	16

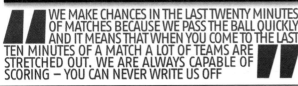

Sir Alex Ferguson

WE MAKE CHANCES IN THE LAST TWENTY MINUTES OF MATCHES BECAUSE WE PASS THE BALL QUICKLY AND IT MEANS THAT WHEN YOU COME TO THE LAST TEN MINUTES OF A MATCH A LOT OF TEAMS ARE STRETCHED OUT. WE ARE ALWAYS CAPABLE OF SCORING – YOU CAN NEVER WRITE US OFF

Manchester City 3
Anelka 5, Goater 26,50

Manchester United 1
Solskjaer 8

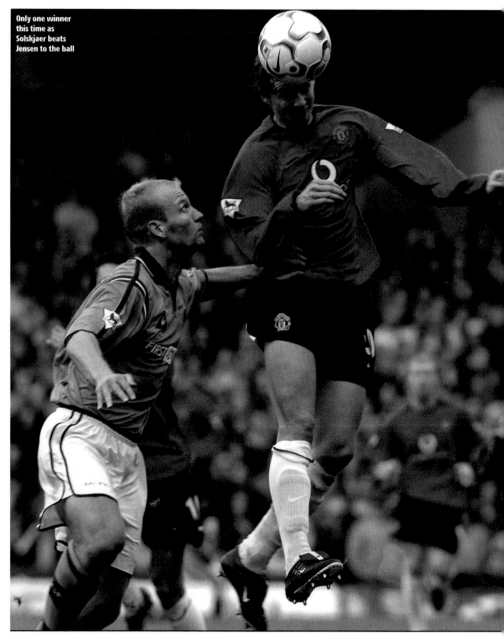

Only one winner this time as Solskjaer beats Jensen to the ball

MATCH FACTS

**Saturday
9 November 2002
Maine Road**
Attendance: **34,649**
Referee: **Paul Durkin**

★★★ **Manchester City:** Schmeichel;
Dunne, Wiekens, Mettomo; Jihai,
Berkovic (Wright-Phillips 78), Foe,
Tiatto (Horlock 88), Jensen; Anelka, Goater
Subs not used: Nash, Benarbia,
Huckerby **Booked:** Wiekens

Manchester United: Barthez;
G Neville (O'Shea 62), Blanc,
Ferdinand, Silvestre; Veron
(Forlan 62), P Neville, Giggs, Scholes;
Solskjaer, Van Nistelrooy
Subs Not Used: Ricardo, May, Fortune
Booked: Solskjaer, P Neville

Possession	
58%	42%
Shots on target	
5	5
Shots off target	
4	5
Corners	
9	0
Offsides	
5	2
Fouls	
16	14

The last league derby ever to be staged at Maine Road was a match United fans had been looking forward to all season, but it turned out to be an afternoon the supporters will want to forget – and in a hurry. Followers of the Blues, meanwhile, celebrated their victory as if they'd won the Treble, the boat race and the Grand National. But then, since it was their first derby win since 1989, they were probably entitled to.

The hosts surged into the lead after five minutes when Nicolas Anelka took advantage of sloppy United play and fed Shaun Goater, whose shot was parried by Fabien Barthez. The ball fell into the path of Anelka and a despairing dive from Rio Ferdinand couldn't prevent the opening goal. United hit straight back with an equaliser from Ole Gunnar Solskjaer. Paul Scholes won the ball in midfield, and aggressive play from Ruud van Nistelrooy caused confusion on the edge of the box, which allowed Ryan Giggs to centre for the predatory Solskjaer.

Parity wasn't to last for long though, and it was Gary Neville who handed City their second goal with an uncharacteristic error. Attempting to usher a ball out for a goal kick, he was dispossessed by Goater, who kept his cool and netted from close range. United's captain for the day was reminded of his mistake by goading City supporters until his early substitution with half an hour to go, but by then the home crowd had plenty more to crow about, as City had extended their lead with Goater's 100th goal in a Blue jersey. It was more slack play in the centre of the park that let City in, with Eyal Berkovic the architect as he found Goater with a perfectly weighted pass, and the striker (released by United 13 years earlier) made no mistake.

United now needed late goals to salvage something from the match, but for once the rescue act failed to materialise. When John O'Shea sliced wide of an open goal from two yards out with the seconds ticking away, we knew it was all over. At the final whistle, Peter Schmeichel, in the unfamiliar position of extracting pleasure from the scene of a United defeat, punched the air in delight as bragging rights went to his new charges City.

**Man of the match
PAUL SCHOLES**
With Butt and Keane
injured and David
Beckham suspended,
the midfield battle was never
going to be easy, but Scholes
never shirked a challenge and
worked valiantly to haul the
Reds back into the game.
Sadly, his tireless efforts
were ultimately in vain.

Premiership results
Weekend beginning 9/11/02

Arsenal	1–0	Newcastle United
Aston Villa	3–1	Fulham
Bolton Wanderers	1–1	West Bromwich Albion
Chelsea	3–0	Birmingham City
Everton	1–0	Charlton Athletic
Middlesbrough	1–0	Liverpool
Southampton	1–1	Blackburn Rovers
Sunderland	2–0	Tottenham Hotspur
West Ham United	3–4	Leeds United

Premiership table
Top 10 at the end of 10/11/02

	P	PTS
1 Liverpool	13	30
2 Arsenal	13	29
3 Chelsea	13	23
4 Everton	13	23
5 Manchester United	13	22
6 Middlesbrough	13	21
7 Blackburn Rovers	13	20
8 Tottenham Hotspur	13	20
9 Newcastle United	12	19
10 Leeds United	13	17

Sir Alex Ferguson

GOOD LUCK TO MANCHESTER CITY. THEY SAID A DERBY FAREWELL TO MAINE ROAD THE RIGHT WAY, BUT WE LET OURSELVES AND THE FANS DOWN WITH AN UNACCEPTABLE PERFORMANCE. WE LOST BECAUSE OF STUPID ERRORS AND A LACK OF CONCENTRATION AND YOU CAN'T AFFORD THAT

West Ham United 1
Defoe 86

Manchester United 1
Van Nistelrooy 38

Watching teams raise their game against United is hardly a new experience. Sides who have previously found it impossible to get a result under any circumstances suddenly find hitherto untapped supplies of drive and determination when the Reds visit.

Without a win in the East End so far this season, the not-so-happy Hammers were rooted at the wrong end of the Premiership, yet this battling display gave not only their fans something to shout about but their team the necessary point to lift them off the bottom of the league. For United, it was another tough 90 minutes in this injury-ravaged season.

Sir Alex's selection options were diminished once more with the loss of David Beckham, Rio Ferdinand and Gary Neville, but Wes Brown returned after three months out.

Brown was called into action early on when he was forced to break up an attack from the evergreen Paolo di Canio and sorcerer's apprentice Jermaine Defoe. The pacy opening saw both sides with the ball in the net: van Nistelrooy and Defoe's attempts were ruled offside, but just after the half-hour mark the Dutchman made it onto the scoresheet. A mistake by Trevor Sinclair saw the ball spin

David James and Ruud battle it out

Sunday
17 November 2002
Boleyn Ground
Attendance: **35,049**
Referee: **Mark Halsey**

to Quinton Fortune who released Solskjaer down the left. Ole Gunnar delivered a low cross to his strike partner Ruud, who finished cutely. Solskjaer had a chance to make it two before the break after a mistake from David James, but the Reds had to be content with a 1-0 lead at the interval.

West Ham re-emerged after the break with new purpose, and Defoe was the biggest threat, although Paul Scholes twice tested James's goal. The excellent United defence dealt with everything West Ham threw at them, but suffered a body blow with four minutes to go. Joe Cole found Defoe in a clearly offside position, but the flag stayed down, Defoe knocked the ball past Barthez and an admittedly deserved point was salvaged.

West Ham United: James; Winterburn, Dailly, Pearce, Schemmel; Sinclair, Cissé, Carrick, Cole; Defoe, di Canio
Subs not used: Van Der Gouw, Repka, Breen, Camara, Garcia
Booked: Cissé, di Canio

Manchester United: Barthez; O'Shea, Brown, Blanc, Silvestre; Scholes, Veron, Fortune, Giggs; Solskjaer, van Nistelrooy
Subs not used: Ricardo, P Neville, Forlan, Davis, Richardson **Booked:** Fortune

Possession	
50%	50%
Shots on target	
5	1
Shots off target	
9	8
Corners	
6	10
Offsides	
4	5
Fouls	
16	14

Sir Alex Ferguson

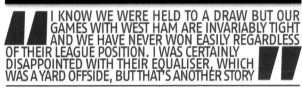

I KNOW WE WERE HELD TO A DRAW BUT OUR GAMES WITH WEST HAM ARE INVARIABLY TIGHT AND WE HAVE NEVER WON EASILY REGARDLESS OF THEIR LEAGUE POSITION. I WAS CERTAINLY DISAPPOINTED WITH THEIR EQUALISER, WHICH WAS A YARD OFFSIDE, BUT THAT'S ANOTHER STORY

Man of the match
WES BROWN

Missing since the opening game of the season, Wes made a welcome return in place of Ferdinand and performed with a steady assurance that belied his lack of fitness. Brown gave the Reds added bite at the back and his proven versatility boded well for the rest of the season.

Cissé illegally halts a swift attack by Ryan Giggs

Premiership results
Weekend beginning 16/11/02

Arsenal	3-0	Tottenham Hotspur
Birmingham City	0-0	Fulham
Blackburn Rovers	0-1	Everton
Chelsea	1-0	Middlesbrough
Leeds United	2-4	Bolton Wanderers
Liverpool	0-0	Sunderland
Manchester City	0-1	Charlton Athletic
Newcastle United	2-1	Southampton
West Bromwich Albion	0-0	Aston Villa

Premiership table
Top 10 at the end of 17/11/02

	P	PTS
1 Arsenal	14	32
2 Liverpool	14	31
3 Chelsea	14	26
4 Everton	14	26
5 Manchester United	14	23
6 Newcastle United	13	22
7 Middlesbrough	14	21
8 Blackburn Rovers	14	20
9 Tottenham Hotspur	14	20
10 Leeds United	14	17

Manchester United 5
Scholes 25, van Nistelrooy 38, 45, 53, Solskjaer 55

Newcastle United 3
Bernard 35, Shearer 52, Bellamy 75

Masterblaster...
Paul Scholes fires
home the opener

Old Trafford salutes
its hat-trick hero

Giv
Ole (
makes

Saturday
23 November 2002
Old Trafford
Attendance: **67,625**
Referee: **Steve Dunn**

REVIEW
CLEVER CLOGS

Manchester United: Barthez; O'Shea, Brown, Blanc (Roche 69), Silvestre; Solskjaer, Scholes, Fortune, Giggs; Forlan (Veron 79), van Nistelrooy (Richardson 64)
Subs Not Used: Ricardo, Chadwick
Booked: Solskjaer, van Nistelrooy

Newcastle United: Given; Griffin, Dabizas, O'Brien, Hughes; Jenas, Dyer, Speed, Bernard (Solano 72); Shearer, Bellamy **Subs Not Used:** Harper, Ameobi, Elliott, Acuna
Booked: Dabizas, Speed

Christmas arrived early for United as the Reds blew away Newcastle in a rip-roaring lunchtime match. It was about time someone was on the receiving end of a Premiership drubbing, but in the build-up to the match few Reds would have thought the visiting Magpies would be the victims.

United's scoring spree was done and dusted during a devastating half-hour spell on either side of the interval, with the opening goal the pick of the bunch. The move was started by Ruud van Nistelrooy, whose ball to Ole Gunnar Solskjaer out on the right was wonderfully controlled by the Norwegian. With his next touch Ole knocked the ball past Aaron Hughes and, with United players queuing up for the cross, he cut the ball back to Paul Scholes, who ended the move emphatically with a trademark rocket finish.

Scholes could have added to the lead with an impudent chip before Newcastle levelled against the run of play. Breaking down the left wing, Oliver Bernard left John O'Shea stricken when he blasted the ball against the defender. When the ball bounced back, Bernard attempted an early cross but instead the ball looped up and into the corner of the net.

Stung by the fluke goal, United hit back with Ruud's second United hat-trick. His first was set up by Mikael Silvestre, who twisted and turned down the left and crossed for the Dutchman to power home a header from close range. Ruud's second, in first-half injury time, was even easier. A mis-hit Diego Forlan shot landed at the feet of the No.10, who gratefully netted for 3-1.

Throughout the match United fans had been enjoying one of their favourite pastimes, Shearer-baiting, but after the restart the Geordie hero set hearts racing when he pulled it back to 3-2 with a brilliant 30-yard strike. A minute later Ruud eased any worries with a tap-in for his hat-trick, and two minutes later United declared on five goals when Ole completed the rout, allowing Sir Alex to make a few substitutions.

When Craig Bellamy pulled one back for the Geordies with 15 minutes to go, the travelling support bellowed, "We're gonna win 6-5!" Wishful thinking.

Possession	
52%	48%

Shots on target	
9	6

Shots off target	
3	3

Corners	
2	8

Offsides	
5	3

Fouls	
17	9

Man of the match
PAUL SCHOLES

It's not often someone scores a hat-trick and doesn't end up as man of the match, but that proves just how good Paul Scholes' performance was. His fierce strike kick-started United's goalfest and, pulling the strings in the centre of the park, his overall play was a joy to watch.

Premiership results
Weekend beginning 23/11/02

Aston Villa	4-1	West Ham United	
Bolton Wanderers	1-1	Chelsea	
Charlton Athletic	3-1	Blackburn Rovers	
Everton	1-0	West Bromwich Albion	
Fulham	3-2	Liverpool	
Middlesbrough	3-1	Manchester City	
Southampton	3-2	Arsenal	
Sunderland	0-1	Birmingham City	
Tottenham Hotspur	2-0	Leeds United	

Premiership table
Top 10 at the end of 24/11/02

	P	PTS
1 Arsenal	15	32
2 Liverpool	15	31
3 Everton	15	29
4 Chelsea	15	27
5 Manchester United	15	26
6 Middlesbrough	15	24
7 Tottenham Hotspur	15	23
8 Newcastle United	14	22
9 Blackburn Rovers	15	20
10 Southampton	15	20

Sir Alex Ferguson

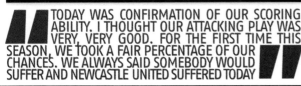

TODAY WAS CONFIRMATION OF OUR SCORING ABILITY. I THOUGHT OUR ATTACKING PLAY WAS VERY, VERY GOOD. FOR THE FIRST TIME THIS SEASON, WE TOOK A FAIR PERCENTAGE OF OUR CHANCES. WE ALWAYS SAID SOMEBODY WOULD SUFFER AND NEWCASTLE UNITED SUFFERED TODAY

DECEMBER

Christmas came twice for United fans as the resurgent Reds notched up back-to-back wins against their arch-rivals and welcomed Roy Keane back into the team after his injury lay-off

United played nine competitive games in December, more than in any other month of the season. Cup and Champions League commitments brought three victories and whilst league form improved greatly, it still varied between the stellar – consecutive victories over Liverpool and Arsenal – and the frustrating, with successive defeats away to Blackburn Rovers and Middlesbrough.

United climbed the league table, briefly going joint first before finishing the year in third – level on points with second-placed Chelsea. Liverpool, who had led the table as recently as November, slid down to 7th, their drop aided by United's gritty 2-1 win away at Anfield.

Leeds had excelled at having their manager and chairman quoted more frequently in the newspapers than any of their peers, but on the pitch, the Yorkshire club's erratic form could not be halted and the pressure on Terry Venables intensified.

Former Red Andy Cole scored his 150th Premiership goal and Everton's Wayne Rooney was awarded the BBC's Young Sports Personality of the Year award. Thierry Henry continued to be lauded by the media, with *The Guardian* comparing his influence to the eight Henrys to have ruled England.

United fans had another Christmas present to savour when their own leading influence, Roy Keane, returned to the side after a 26-game absence through injury and suspension, speaking sagaciously of his intent to return a leaner, but not meaner, player.

Barclaycard Premiership fixtures this month

Sunday 1st	Liverpool	Away
Saturday 7th	Arsenal	Home
Saturday 14th	West Ham United	Home
Sunday 22nd	Blackburn Rovers	Away
Thursday 26th	Middlesbrough	Away
Saturday 28th	Birmingham City	Home

In the Barclaycard Premiership this month

312,243
watched United play six games

United scored

10
goals

but conceded

5
goals

United travelled

386
miles to and from games

United fielded a total of

20
players

FOCUS ON DIEGO FORLAN

When it comes to choosing the big occasion, you have to applaud Diego Forlan's timing. United's Uruguayan striker ran out at Anfield on the back of two vital league goals – the equaliser against Villa and a thumping winner against Southampton – but there were surely many more shirt-off celebrations to come. Who could forget Diego's awesome volley against Senegal in the World Cup? Liverpool fans may have thought Ruud posed the bigger threat on December 1, yet it was Forlan who ruined the Merseysiders' weekend. Granted, a Jerzy Dudek gaffe gifted Diego the first goal but his emphatic finish for the second elevated him to legendary status. "It was nice to score but more important to win," said Diego. "I knew how big the United versus Liverpool games were."

Liverpool 1
Hyypia 82

Manchester United 2
Forlan 64, 67

It doesn't get any better than this... Diego enjoys his Anfield glory

A game that turned on Jerzy Dudek's catastrophic howler marked the annual assertion of United's Premiership challenge. Much had been said and written about the Reds' season being extinguished should Sir Alex's team lose to Newcastle, Basel and Liverpool; the truth, as United fans know from experience, is that no-one remembers who's top in November. Instead, an indomitable performance from an injury-hit side proved that when the going gets tough, Manchester United get going.

Liverpool opened with the belief they could dominate. Recent history – five wins over United in the last five games – and United's unfamiliar formation, suggested they might. It was folly, and after the opening half-hour, Liverpool played as though they knew it.

At first the Reds battled like underdogs, with the steadfast backline of O'Shea, Brown, Silvestre and Gary Neville working hard and cohesively, while Scholes and the impressive Quinton Fortune wrested midfield from Murphy and a lacklustre Steven Gerrard.

Jerzy Dudek has had an outstanding spell at Anfield, but had been lucky to keep his place after some poor recent form. That was nothing, though, compared to the awful error that gifted United the lead. Jamie Carragher looped a soft header to the right corner of Dudek's six-yard box, which he utterly missed and allowed through his legs. Diego Forlan rolled the ball home and ripped his shirt off in a celebration that is becoming increasingly familiar.

United now had a grip on the game, and Sir Alex barely had time to retake his seat in the dug-out when the lead was extended to two goals. Giggs's deceptive run and pass sent Forlan clear, and his instinctive snapshot jerked him back to the touchline with a broad grin across his face. A rattled Dudek perhaps should have done better, but Forlan deserved his moment, and so did Sir Alex for keeping faith in the irrepressible Uruguayan.

Liverpool rallied, with Hyypia scoring to allow the home side a last tilt at a point. Then a vicious 30-yard volley from Dietmar Hamman swerved goalbound until Fabien Barthez somehow touched the ball onto the bar. It was a magnificent save that deservedly kept all three points for United.

Liverpool: Dudek; Carragher, Henchoz, Hyypia, Traore (Riise 78); Murphy, Gerrard, Hamann, Smicer (Diouf 70); Baros (Heskey 59), Owen **Subs not used:** Kirkland, Diao **Booked:** Smicer

Manchester United: Barthez; O'Shea, Brown, G Neville, Silvestre; Solskjaer, Scholes, Fortune (P Neville 81), Giggs; Forlan (Stewart 90), van Nistelrooy (May 90) **Subs Not Used:** Ricardo, Chadwick **Booked:** van Nistelrooy, Brown, Forlan, Silvestre

Possession	
45%	**55%**

Shots on target	
4	5

Shots off target	
0	5

Corners	
2	5

Offsides	
1	1

Fouls	
13	14

Man of the match
MIKAEL SILVESTRE

Shifted into the middle of United's defence, Silvestre's sharp turn of pace and ability to spin quickly nullified Michael Owen's strengths and proved too much for Milan Baros. He shone against top quality forwards and his adaptability has provided Sir Alex with a much-needed option in the face of so many injuries.

Premiership results
Weekend beginning 30/11/02

Arsenal	3-1	Aston Villa
Birmingham City	1-1	Tottenham Hotspur
Blackburn Rovers	2-1	Fulham
Chelsea	3-0	Sunderland
Leeds United	1-2	Charlton Athletic
Manchester City	2-0	Bolton Wanderers
Newcastle United	2-1	Everton
West Bromwich Albion	1-0	Middlesbrough
West Ham United	0-1	Southampton

Premiership table
Top 10 at the end of 2/12/02

	P	PTS
1 Arsenal	16	35
2 Liverpool	16	31
3 Chelsea	16	30
4 Manchester United	16	29
5 Everton	16	29
6 Newcastle United	15	25
7 Middlesbrough	16	24
8 Tottenham Hotspur	16	24
9 Blackburn Rovers	16	23
10 Southampton	16	23

Sir Alex Ferguson

I THINK FORLAN HAS BEEN A BIT OF A HERO TO THE FANS BECAUSE THEY RECOGNISE HE DOESN'T GIVE IN. I THINK THAT IS A WONDERFUL QUALITY IN A PLAYER AND HE HAS SHOWN IT IN EVERY GAME. TODAY DIEGO'S PERSEVERANCE HAS PAID OFF BECAUSE THE FANS WILL NEVER FORGET IT

Manchester United 2
Veron 21, Scholes 73
Arsenal 0

Seba spins away after putting United ahead

Paul Scholes gets buried after his decisive strike

Sir Alex: 'Phil Neville was our foundation in midfield'

Saturday
7 December 2002
Old Trafford
Attendance: **67,650**
Referee: **Dermot Gallagher**

On the back of that magnificent victory over Liverpool, United produced yet another eye-catching display of discipline, tenacity and no little flair to comprehensively dispose of Arsène Wenger's champions at Old Trafford and blow the title race wide open.

The starting line-up may have shown some alterations from the trip to Anfield – Juan Sebastian Veron was restored to the midfield following a bout of flu, while Phil Neville stepped in for the injured Quinton Fortune – but the work ethic that underpinned United's Mersey raid was once again in evidence.

From the off the Reds were up for it, pressurising the Arsenal midfielders who, unnerved by the ankle-biting presence of Neville and Veron, were unable to settle into their usual fluency. For all that though, it was the Gunners who went closest to grabbing the lead, with Henry and Pires both failing to capitalise on head-to-head encounters with Fabien Barthez in the opening 20 minutes. Arsenal were to pay dearly for their profligacy.

In the 21st minute the Reds made the breakthrough, Veron tapping in from a Paul Scholes cross after van Nistelrooy had released the England man. Wenger claimed afterwards that Ruud's control of the ball in the run-up to the goal owed more to basketball than association football, but Dermot Gallagher was in a prime position to view the contact as accidental. The goal galvanised both the United team and support, while Arsenal's hopes took a further knock before half time when they were forced to throw third-choice stopper Stuart Taylor into the lion's den after an injury to new signing Rami Shaaban.

The start of the second half saw no let-up in tempo, with the heroic Phil Neville giving Vieira and Gilberto Silva no time on the ball. Mistakes were creeping into Arsenal's play and it was a slack throw-in by Ashley Cole which let United in for the killer second goal. Ruud picked up the loose ball and played an incisive pass to Scholes, who powered towards goal and produced a finish to match his all-round performance. The champions never looked like getting back in it, while United even had time to indulge in a spot of showboating. Another day to remember.

Manchester United: Barthez; Brown, G Neville, O'Shea, Silvestre; Giggs, P Neville, Scholes, Veron; Solskjaer, van Nistelrooy
Subs Not Used: Ricardo, May, Chadwick, Stewart, Forlan
Booked: P Neville

Arsenal: Shaaban (Taylor 43); Cole, Cygan, Keown, Luzhny; Pires (Toure 77), Gilberto, Vieira, Ljungberg; Henry, Wiltord (Bergkamp 68)
Subs Not Used: Lauren, van Bronckhorst
Booked: Cygan, Luzhny

Possession	
42%	58%

Shots on target	
4	2

Shots off target	
2	7

Corners	
6	7

Offsides	
4	2

Fouls	
16	12

Man of the match
PHIL NEVILLE
The younger Neville first played for United nearly nine years ago, but has rarely performed better. Phil dominated World Cup winners Vieira and Gilberto Silva and dictated the pace of the game. His display was the talk of United fans, and the lavish praise was richly deserved.

Premiership results
Weekend beginning 7/12/02
Aston Villa	0–1	Newcastle United
Bolton Wanderers	1–1	Blackburn Rovers
Charlton Athletic	2–0	Liverpool
Everton	1–3	Chelsea
Fulham	1–0	Leeds United
Middlesbrough	2–2	West Ham United
Southampton	2–0	Birmingham City
Sunderland	0–3	Manchester City
Tottenham Hotspur	3–1	West Bromwich Albion

Premiership table
Top 20 at the end of 9/12/02
		P	PTS
1	Arsenal	17	35
2	Chelsea	17	33
3	Manchester United	17	32
4	Liverpool	17	31
5	Everton	17	29
6	Newcastle United	16	28
7	Tottenham Hotspur	17	27
8	Southampton	17	26
9	Middlesbrough	17	25
10	Blackburn Rovers	17	24

Sir Alex Ferguson

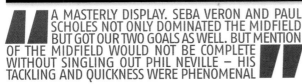

A MASTERLY DISPLAY. SEBA VERON AND PAUL SCHOLES NOT ONLY DOMINATED THE MIDFIELD BUT GOT OUR TWO GOALS AS WELL. BUT MENTION OF THE MIDFIELD WOULD NOT BE COMPLETE WITHOUT SINGLING OUT PHIL NEVILLE – HIS TACKLING AND QUICKNESS WERE PHENOMENAL

Manchester United 3
Solskjaer 15, Veron 17, Schemmel (og) 61
West Ham United 0

Ole Gunnar opens the scoring with a near post header

After gritty but vital Premiership wins over Liverpool and Arsenal, the Reds took the opportunity to turn on the style against West Ham. Though the visitors enjoyed patches of possession, United were in consummate control throughout and took just 17 minutes to wrap up the points.

Fifteen minutes had elapsed when Phil Neville, again excelling in midfield, threaded a ball to van Nistelrooy, who released Gary Neville down the right flank. Neville drove a curling cross into the near post where Solskjaer, having vacated his right midfield berth to supplement the attack, headed past James at the near post with the help of a slight deflection off Tomas Repka.

Two minutes later United's lead was doubled. Repka presented United with a free kick 30 yards from goal after following through unnecessarily on van Nistelrooy. In the absence of David Beckham, Juan Sebastian Veron assumed dead ball duties – and met his responsibilities with a flourish. Shaping as if to shoot to James' left, 'the Witch' adjusted his stance at the last second to send the ball curling into the opposite corner of the goal. It was United's first goal direct from a free kick so far this season.

Saturday
14 December 2002
Old Trafford
Attendance: **67,555**
Referee: **Rob Styles**

Hammer blow: Ryan Giggs makes another forward run

Manchester United: Barthez; G Neville, Brown, Silvestre, O'Shea (Blanc 73); Solskjaer (Beckham 46), Veron, P Neville, Giggs; Scholes (Forlan 73), van Nistelrooy
Subs not used: Ricardo, Richardson

West Ham United: James; Minto (Breen 89), Repka, Dailly, Schemmel; Sinclair, Carrick, Lomas (Moncur 85), Cole; Defoe, Pearce
Subs not used: Bywater, Camara, Ferdinand
Booked: Repka

Possession	
53%	**47%**
Shots on target	
8	**2**
Shots off target	
5	**7**
Corners	
7	**4**
Offsides	
2	**8**
Fouls	
13	**12**

Man of the match
JUAN SEBASTIAN
VERON
Yet another spellbinding show from Veron. In the absence of Roy Keane, Seba revels in the role of conducting the United orchestra. Even mixing it in the tackle these days, his passing is more decisive and that free kick showed he can bend it like Beckham too.

Before half-time the Hammers were unlucky to have a goal disallowed for offside but, with Brown and Silvestre once again supreme in central defence, their forays were easily repelled.

The second-half was a procession. As West Ham ran low on heart and steam, United's players took turns to climb aboard the showboat. Giggs, Veron and even O'Shea, again catching the eye with his attacking raids from left back, all produced touches that provoked gasps from the stands. The climax to the show came on 61 minutes when, after a move involving 22 passes, Sebastien Schemmel, perhaps in an act of mercy to his tortured team-mates, put through his own net to make it 3-0 to the Reds. In the build-up to the goal, the ball was in United's possession for over a minute.

Premiership results
Weekend beginning 14/12/02

Aston Villa	2–1	West Bromwich Albion
Bolton Wanderers	0–3	Leeds United
Charlton Athletic	2–2	Manchester City
Everton	2–1	Blackburn Rovers
Fulham	0–1	Birmingham City
Middlesbrough	1–1	Chelsea
Southampton	1–1	Newcastle United
Sunderland	2–1	Liverpool
Tottenham Hotspur	1–1	Arsenal

Premiership table
Top 10 at the end of 16/12/02

	P	PTS
1 Arsenal	18	36
2 Manchester United	18	35
3 Chelsea	18	34
4 Everton	18	32
5 Liverpool	18	31
6 Newcastle United	17	29
7 Tottenham Hotspur	18	28
8 Southampton	18	27
9 Middlesbrough	18	26
10 Blackburn Rovers	18	24

Sir Alex Ferguson

WE PLAYED SOME GOOD FOOTBALL AT TIMES, ENJOYED SOME GREAT ATTACKING PLAY AND COULD HAVE SCORED A FEW MORE – ON ANOTHER DAY RUUD VAN NISTELROOY COULD HAVE HAD A HAT-TRICK. BUT THE MAIN THING IS THAT WE ARE SHOWING THE SPIRIT TO MAKE A CHALLENGE

Blackburn Rovers 1
Flitcroft 40

Manchester United 0

United's revival suffered a setback with a Red Rose derby defeat by Blackburn. Ironically, while all the pre-match talk was of the potential danger posed by two United old boys Cole and Yorke, it was an ex-City stalwart who provided the killer blow. Not even the return of the Reds' talismanic captain could kickstart a comeback.

The visitors had the first of many chances on eight minutes when Ryan Giggs set up Ruud van Nistelrooy, whose shot was blocked by Martin Taylor. A minute later Solskjaer denied Giggs an almost certain goal, managing only to get a glancing touch to Gary Neville's cross when the Welshman was in a better position.

United fans were reminded of days gone by when Cole and Yorke linked up on 19 minutes, but the Reds continued to dominate. On the half hour, United's sometime left winger John O'Shea found Forlan in the box, but his miscued shot sliced wildly towards van Nistelrooy, who in turn failed to trouble Brad Friedel.

For all United's pressure, Blackburn edged back into the match and it was David Dunn who made the difference. The former England Under-21 captain impudently nutmegged Paul Scholes and let rip with a rasping drive, parried over by Barthez. Soon

Brad Friedel foils another attack on goal by Ruud

MATCHFACTS

Sunday
22 December 2002
Ewood Park
Attendance: **30,475**
Referee: **David Elleray**

afterwards, Scholes was tempted into bringing down Damien Duff on the corner of the box. From the free kick, Duff whipped in a cross and Garry Flitcroft powered home from a Taylor knockdown.

Blackburn started the second half brightly, which was just the cue for Roy Keane to be introduced. The substitution had an instant impact on United, and Scholes played a beautiful one-touch pass which completely sliced open the Blackburn defence and set Ruud free, but Friedel stood tall and forced the striker wide when an equaliser seemed imminent.

Keane was handed the captain's armband for the first time in four months when Giggs made way for Beckham, but not even that symbolic sight could inspire the Reds to make the breakthrough.

Sir Alex Ferguson

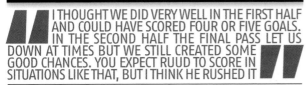

I THOUGHT WE DID VERY WELL IN THE FIRST HALF AND COULD HAVE SCORED FOUR OR FIVE GOALS. IN THE SECOND HALF THE FINAL PASS LET US DOWN AT TIMES BUT WE STILL CREATED SOME GOOD CHANCES. YOU EXPECT RUUD TO SCORE IN SITUATIONS LIKE THAT, BUT I THINK HE RUSHED IT

Blackburn Rovers: Friedel;
Neill, Johannson, Taylor, Short;
Flitcroft, Tugay, Duff, Dunn
(Gillespie 55); Yorke, Cole
Subs not used: Todd, Jansen, Kelly,
Ostenstad

Manchester Utd: Barthez;
G Neville, Brown, Silvestre, O'Shea;
Scholes, P Neville (Blanc 84);
Solskjaer, Giggs (Beckham 70);
van Nistelrooy, Forlan (Keane 59)
Subs not used: Ricardo, Richardson
Booked: G Neville

Possession	
53%	47%
Shots on target	
3	2
Shots off target	
6	8
Corners	
8	7
Offsides	
3	5
Fouls	
12	9

Man of the match
PAUL SCHOLES

Despite the defeat, this was another fine performance from Scholes. Tenacious, he also has the ability to light up any dour derby with a moment of sheer inspiration, like his second-half reverse ball on the spin to van Nistelrooy, which delighted the crowd.

Premiership results
Weekend finishing 23/12/02

Arsenal	2-0	Middlesbrough
Birmingham City	1-1	Charlton Athletic
Chelsea	2-0	Aston Villa
Leeds United	1-1	Southampton
Liverpool	0-0	Everton
Manchester City	2-3	Tottenham Hotspur
Newcastle United	2-0	Fulham
West Bromwich Albion	2-2	Sunderland
West Ham United	1-1	Bolton Wanderers

Premiership table
Top 10 at the end of 23/12/02

		P	PTS
1	Arsenal	19	39
2	Chelsea	19	37
3	Manchester United	19	35
4	Everton	19	33
5	Liverpool	19	32
6	Newcastle United	18	32
7	Tottenham Hotspur	19	31
8	Southampton	19	28
9	Blackburn Rovers	19	27
10	Middlesbrough	19	26

Blackburn scorer Flitcroft tussles with Paul Scholes

Middlesbrough 3
Boksic 43, Nemeth 47, Job 86

Manchester United 1
Giggs 60

David Beckham lets rip with a free kick

Ryan Giggs scraps for a loose ball

Ruud has a go but couldn't get on the scoresheet

Thursday
26 December 2002
The Riverside
Attendance: **34,673**
Referee: **Graham Barber**

United went to the Riverside seeking to make up lost ground on leaders Arsenal. But faced with an alert and disciplined Middlesbrough outfit, the Reds stumbled to a second successive Premiership defeat that added an unwanted helping of humbug to the Christmas festivities.

In truth, the home side were worthy of the three points. Despite the return of Roy Keane, who started his first match since hip surgery, the Reds failed to assert control in midfield, and collectively the defence, ruffled by the movement of Szilard Nemeth and Alen Boksic, had an uncertain 90 minutes.

The home side struck either side of the interval to take a 2-0 lead. Left-back Franck Queudrue intercepted a crossfield ball from Seba Veron and went on a barnstorming run from defence to the edge of the United area before threading the ball to Alen Boksic, who delicately chipped an advancing Fabien Barthez. Then, within two minutes of the restart, Nemeth muscled past John O'Shea to drive a shot into the bottom corner from 12 yards.

The Reds rallied of course, and during the final 25 minutes the match resembled a training-ground exercise of attack versus defence. United set up camp in the Middlesbrough half, probing and feeling for holes in the home side's backline, and on 60 minutes Ryan Giggs pulled a goal back, prodding home left footed from close range after a low cross from Ole Gunnar Solskjaer.

More United pressure followed and David Beckham's introduction on 72 minutes, replacing Gary Neville, saw proceedings move up a gear. The England captain hit a first-time shot narrowly wide and also saw a free-kick deflected for a corner.

Reds fans saw Ruud fall in the box under a challenge from Ugo Ehiogu, but his appeals for a penalty were turned down by referee Graham Barber, who had a good view of the incident.

In a final, desperate attempt to force an equaliser, Rio Ferdinand was introduced as a makeshift striker, but with the Reds committed to all-out attack, Boro exploited space on the break to make the points safe with a third goal tapped in at the far post by Joseph-Désiré Job.

Middlesbrough: Schwarzer; Queudrue, Ehiogu, Southgate, Parnaby; Greening, Wilson, Job, Geremi; Nemeth (Maccarone 83), Boksic (Wilkshire 63) **Subs Not Used:** Vidmar, Windass, Crossley **Booked:** Job

Manchester United: Barthez; G Neville (Beckham 72), Blanc, Brown, O'Shea (Ferdinand 83); Giggs, Keane, Veron, Scholes; van Nistelrooy, Solskjaer. **Subs Not Used:** P Neville, Ricardo, Forlan **Booked:** Scholes, Brown

Possession	
56%	44%
Shots on target	
3	4
Shots off target	
3	5
Corners	
8	5
Offsides	
4	4
Fouls	
13	7

Man of the match
WES BROWN

While the defence as a whole didn't enjoy the best of days, Wes Brown made light of Mikael Silvestre's absence and maintained his run of good form. Returning from injury a stronger player thanks to the extra training, Brown is now adding consistency to his game.

Premiership results
Games played 26/12/02

Birmingham City	1-1	Everton
Bolton Wanderers	4-3	Newcastle United
Chelsea	0-0	Southampton
Liverpool	1-1	Blackburn Rovers
Manchester City	3-1	Aston Villa
Sunderland	1-2	Leeds United
Tottenham Hotspur	2-2	Charlton Athletic
West Bromwich Albion	1-2	Arsenal
West Ham United	1-1	Fulham

Premiership table
Top 10 at the end of 26/12/02

	P	PTS
1 Arsenal	20	42
2 Chelsea	20	38
3 Manchester United	20	35
4 Everton	20	34
5 Liverpool	20	33
6 Newcastle United	19	32
7 Tottenham Hotspur	20	32
8 Middlesbrough	20	29
9 Southampton	20	29
10 Blackburn Rovers	20	28

Sir Alex Ferguson

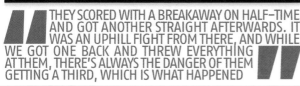

THEY SCORED WITH A BREAKAWAY ON HALF-TIME AND GOT ANOTHER STRAIGHT AFTERWARDS. IT WAS AN UPHILL FIGHT FROM THERE, AND WHILE WE GOT ONE BACK AND THREW EVERYTHING AT THEM, THERE'S ALWAYS THE DANGER OF THEM GETTING A THIRD, WHICH IS WHAT HAPPENED

Manchester United 2
Forlan 37, Beckham 73

Birmingham City 0

Beck on target: David's goal was the perfect return from injury

Saturday
28 December 2002
Old Trafford
Attendance: **67,640**
Referee: **Mike Dean**

REVIEW
A SEASON TO BE JOLLY

Manchester United: Barthez; O'Shea, Ferdinand, Brown, Silvestre; Beckham, Keane (Giggs 85), Veron, Scholes (Richardson 74); Solskjaer (P Neville 76), Forlan
Subs Not Used: Ricardo, G Neville
Booked: Brown

Birmingham City: Vaesen; Kenna, Cunningham (Powell 63), Johnson, Sadler (Woodhouse 68); Devlin, Cissé, Savage, Lazaridis (Horsfield 51); Kirovski, Morrison **Subs Not Used:** Bennet, Hughes
Booked: Kenna, Cissé

After United's festive setbacks, Sir Alex Ferguson had deemed this match a no-lose situation, and an assured performance from his players showed it was message understood. Goalkeeping heroics, defensive grit, midfield artistry and attacking industry combined to ensure Steve Bruce's return to Old Trafford wasn't to be a winning one.

Sir Alex shuffled his pack once more, with Blanc, Giggs and Gary Neville dropping out and van Nistelrooy missing through injury. O'Shea switched to right back, Ferdinand returned to the heart of the defence and David Beckham started for the first time since his rib injury.

With Keane and Savage going head-to-head, the midfield battle was always going to be key but a biting return to form from the captain provided the space for Veron, Beckham and Scholes to work their magic. However, a sackful of chances were squandered before the guy from Uruguay popped up once more.

On another day Scholes could have had a hat-trick, while the marauding Silvestre, Ferdinand and O'Shea all had gilt-edged chances to get on the score-sheet, although Rio's second half miss from a yard out is one he'll find hard to live down.

Just when Reds fans were wondering what it would take to break the deadlock, the answer arrived in style just before half time. It started with an audacious dummy from O'Shea deep in his own half. The Irishman switched to Scholes who then worked the ball to Veron, and a deep cross from Silvestre found the head of Beckham whose knockback into the danger area was met on the half-volley by the prolific Forlan.

Given United's dominance, the goal should have been the sign for the floodgates to open after the break, but the visitors could have grabbed a shock equaliser or even more were it not for a succession of world-class stops from Barthez.

Finally, the game was settled thanks to a magical lob from Beckham which dropped into the net while keeper Nico Vaesen was comically back-pedalling to no avail – all created by a defence-splitting pass from the Little Witch.

Possession

62%	38%

Shots on target

6	2

Shots off target

14	4

Corners

13	4

Offsides

0	4

Fouls

13	11

Man of the match
DAVID BECKHAM

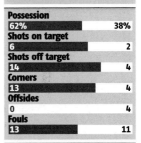

Beckham announced his full return to Manchester United's first team with a goal, an assist and a special performance that just about topped those of his midfield partners Veron and Keane. And the goal which settled nerves all round M16 was fit to win any match. Welcome back, David.

Premiership results

Weekend beginning 28/12/02

Arsenal	1–1	Liverpool
Aston Villa	1–0	Middlesbrough
Blackburn Rovers	2–2	West Ham United
Charlton Athletic	1–0	West Bromwich Albion
Everton	0–0	Bolton Wanderers
Fulham	0–1	Manchester City
Leeds United	2–0	Chelsea
Newcastle United	2–1	Tottenham Hotspur
Southampton	2–1	Sunderland

Premiership table

Top 10 at the end of 29/12/02

	P	PTS
1 Arsenal	21	43
2 Chelsea	21	38
3 Manchester United	21	38
4 Newcastle United	20	35
5 Everton	21	35
6 Liverpool	21	34
7 Southampton	21	32
8 Tottenham Hotspur	21	32
9 Manchester City	21	30
10 Middlesbrough	21	29

Sir Alex Ferguson

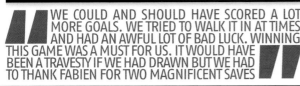

" WE COULD AND SHOULD HAVE SCORED A LOT MORE GOALS. WE TRIED TO WALK IT IN AT TIMES AND HAD AN AWFUL LOT OF BAD LUCK. WINNING THIS GAME WAS A MUST FOR US. IT WOULD HAVE BEEN A TRAVESTY IF WE HAD DRAWN BUT WE HAD TO THANK FABIEN FOR TWO MAGNIFICENT SAVES "

JANUARY

No New Year's hangovers for United as they took maximum points from three games and continued to climb the table, showing that never-say-die attitude the Reds are famous for

January may be the only month without European football, but with the FA Cup occupying two weekends, United's Premiership obligations were reduced to three games. With two of these at home, and cup ties having taken the number of matches played at Old Trafford to eight between December 7 and January 7, a new pitch – the second of the season – had to be laid at the end of the month.

Although they secured a maximum nine points in the Premiership, the Reds had developed a habit of leaving it late. Paul Scholes hit a dramatic last-minute winner against Sunderland and Diego Forlan did likewise in the vital clash with Chelsea.

Yet leaders Arsenal had their anxious moments too: 3-0 up against Chelsea with five minutes left, Claudio Ranieri's side then scored twice in one minute, but couldn't snatch an unlikely leveller. Thierry Henry continued to be the league's top scorer, closely followed by Southampton's James Beattie.

Beattie's team, along with Everton and Charlton, all boasted top eight positions by the end of January, when many would have expected them to have been scrapping against relegation. Instead, Sunderland, West Ham and West Brom made those unwanted spots their own. A snap-shot of Sunderland's season came when local lad Michael Proctor scored two own goals in three minutes against Charlton.

United finished January in second position, six points behind Arsenal but with a game in hand. The title race was on in earnest.

Barclaycard Premiership fixtures this month

Wednesday 1st	Sunderland	Home
Saturday 11th	West Bromwich Albion	Away
Saturday 18th	Chelsea	Home

In the Barclaycard Premiership this month

162,344
watched United play three games

United scored

7
goals

but conceded

3
goals

United travelled

166
miles to and from games

United fielded a total of

17
players

FOCUS ON PAUL SCHOLES

United's impressive winning run during January would have been much harder work were it not for Paul Scholes: a last-gasp winner against Sunderland, the goal that put the Reds ahead of West Brom and that leveller against Chelsea. Three goals in three games is a striker's form, yet these all came from midfield – although you always fancy United's No.18 to score from anywhere. More strikes in the cups boosted Paul's haul to seven goals in six outings, three of them coming when he played up front in both legs of the league cup semis against Blackburn (only the post denied him the chance of stretching his run further, against West Ham in the FA Cup). "Scoring for six games in a row did surprise me a bit," Paul admitted modestly. "I was just lucky to get in the right positions at the right time."

Manchester United 2
Beckham 81, Scholes 90

Sunderland 1
Veron (og 5)

Paul Scholes unleashes another piledriver

2003 got off to a nerve-jangling start as the Reds finally secured three crucial points, but only after breaking the heart of a keeper intent on doing United's rivals a favour.

The Old Trafford faithful looked on in disbelief as the relegation-threatened visitors went ahead after just five minutes. A Thirwell free kick was punched by Barthez straight to McCann, whose shot was headed by Veron into his own net. The setback didn't alter United's game plan and Scholes was immediately denied when his drive bounced off one post, pinged against the other and fell into the arms of a disbelieving but grateful Macho.

Sunderland made an early change when McCann limped off and soon after Barthez was forced off with a groin injury, which gave a rare chance to Roy Carroll. The Irishman wasn't called into action too often as United hunted for an equaliser, but half time came with statistics telling two different stories. United had 16 goal attempts to Sunderland's one, but theirs was decisive.

The Reds came out for the second half no doubt with their ears stinging, and Solskjaer immediately tested Macho with a long-range drive, followed by an equally impressive strike from Veron,

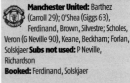

**Wednesday
1 January 2003
Old Trafford**
Attendance: **67,609**
Referee: **Graham Poll**

Manchester United: Barthez (Carroll 29); O'Shea (Giggs 63), Ferdinand, Brown, Silvestre; Scholes, Veron (G Neville 90), Keane, Beckham; Forlan, Solskjaer **Subs not used:** P Neville, Richardson
Booked: Ferdinand, Solskjaer

Sunderland: Macho; McCartney, Babb, Craddock, Wright; McCann (Williams 14), Thirlwell, Kilbane, Stewart (Oster 84); Flo (Proctor 72), Phillips
Subs not used: Bjorklund, Sorensen
Booked: Wright

Possession	
61%	39%
Shots on target	
14	0
Shots off target	
17	3
Corners	
10	2
Offsides	
0	1
Fouls	
12	14

Man of the match
DAVID BECKHAM
His second man of the match display in five days, as Beckham single-handedly set about breaking down Sunderland's resolve. His energy-sapping effort was reminiscent of his heroics in the World Cup qualifier between England and Greece.

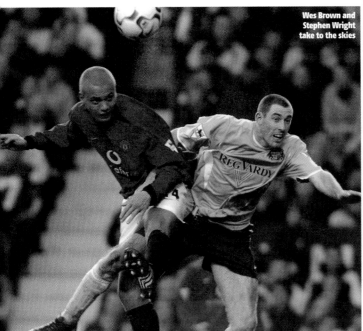

Wes Brown and Stephen Wright take to the skies

tipped over the bar by the Black Cat in goal. The game took on a frantic rhythm, with Beckham all over the park creating openings, only to be foiled each time by the brilliant Macho. Ferdinand, who had just picked up his first league booking in over three years, was denied by the Austrian stopper, and he was to intercept three more Beckham crosses in the space of five minutes.

But when all was looking lost, United created another match-winning finale. With 10 minutes to go Beckham expertly controlled a route-one pass from Ferdinand, and lifted the ball over his nemesis for the equaliser. Then, with the clock ticking down, Silvestre hooked the ball into the box and Scholes blasted a power header past Macho to send Old Trafford into delirium.

Premiership results
Matches played up to 1/01/03

Arsenal	3-2	Chelsea
Aston Villa	2-0	Bolton Wanderers
Blackburn Rovers	1-0	Middlesbrough
Everton	2-2	Manchester City
Leeds United	2-0	Birmingham City
Newcastle United	1-0	Liverpool
Southampton	1-0	Tottenham Hotspur

Sir Alex Ferguson

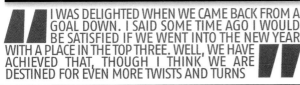

> I WAS DELIGHTED WHEN WE CAME BACK FROM A GOAL DOWN. I SAID SOME TIME AGO I WOULD BE SATISFIED IF WE WENT INTO THE NEW YEAR WITH A PLACE IN THE TOP THREE. WELL, WE HAVE ACHIEVED THAT, THOUGH I THINK WE ARE DESTINED FOR EVEN MORE TWISTS AND TURNS

Premiership table
Top 10 at the end of 1/01/03

	P	PTS
1 Arsenal	22	46
2 Manchester United	22	41
3 Chelsea	22	38
4 Newcastle United	21	38
5 Everton	22	36
6 Southampton	22	35
7 Liverpool	22	34
8 Blackburn Rovers	22	32
9 Tottenham Hotspur	22	32
10 Manchester City	22	31

West Bromwich Albion 1
Koumas 6

Manchester United 3
Van Nistelrooy 8, Scholes 23, Solskjaer 55

Ruud challenges Baggies keeper Russell Hoult

Paul Scholes: put United ahead in the first half

Before the visit to West Brom, David Beckham had indicated the need for the team to improve its away form, and described how all fans love coming to see the Reds play. After the game, two Albion fans leaving the ground admitted this was the first time their team had been outclassed all season and that United were, far and away, the best team they had seen. So 1-0 to Beckham, and 3-1 to United.

The home side hotwired this match when they flew into a shock lead. Rio Ferdinand's attempted clearance sliced into the path of Jason Koumas, who unerringly slammed the ball home with just six minutes gone. Some 23,000 Baggies deliriously boing-boinging in celebration shook this corner of the Black Country to the core.

But their bouncing ball impressions were instantly punctured by a United equaliser. An error from Neil Clement direct from the restart was punished by Beckham, whose pass to Ruud van Nistelrooy was despatched through Russell Hoult's legs by the Dutchman. Cue the massed United choir to roar into voice, clearly enjoying a rare 3pm Saturday away fixture.

United made it 2-1 midway through the first half when Paul Scholes pounced on a Roy Keane cross and drilled home from six yards out. The Reds were rampant with the captain everywhere, spraying 40-yard passes one minute, breaking up Albion attacks the next, and berating unfortunate team-mates whenever he deemed it necessary. Which, thankfully, wasn't often.

After the break, Albion tried to catch United on the counter whenever one of the many and varied visiting attacks broke down. Koumas and ex-Red Ronnie Wallwork did threaten, but United were always in control and the game was settled just 10 minutes into the second half. Ole Gunnar Solskjaer took his habitual place on the scoresheet when he finished off a fine attacking move, sweeping in a deep cross from the excellent Gary Neville.

The Hawthorns may be the highest League ground in England, but at full time Albion slipped to rock bottom in the Premiership as news filtered through of a valuable point for West Ham. For United, both on the pitch and off, the afternoon could only be described as high and mighty.

Sir Alex Ferguson

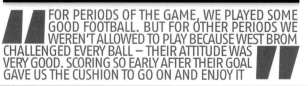

FOR PERIODS OF THE GAME, WE PLAYED SOME GOOD FOOTBALL. BUT FOR OTHER PERIODS WE WEREN'T ALLOWED TO PLAY BECAUSE WEST BROM CHALLENGED EVERY BALL – THEIR ATTITUDE WAS VERY GOOD. SCORING SO EARLY AFTER THEIR GOAL GAVE US THE CUSHION TO GO ON AND ENJOY IT

The travelling Reds take their salute from Gary and Ole Gunnar

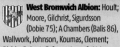

Saturday
11 January 2003
The Hawthorns
Attendance: **27,129**
Referee: **Neale Barry**

West Bromwich Albion: Hoult; Moore, Gilchrist, Sigurdsson (Dobie 75); A Chambers (Balis 86), Wallwork, Johnson, Koumas, Clement; Dichio, Roberts **Subs not used:** McInnes, J Chambers, Murphy

Manchester United: Barthez; G Neville, Ferdinand, Brown, Silvestre; Beckham, Keane (O'Shea 81), P Neville, Solskjaer (Forlan 68); Scholes; van Nistelrooy
Subs not used: Blanc, Ricardo, Richardson
Booked: Scholes

Possession
| 47% | 53% |

Shots on target
| 6 | 2 |

Shots off target
| 6 | 7 |

Corners
| 6 | 2 |

Offsides
| 7 | 2 |

Fouls
| 9 | 12 |

Man of the match
ROY KEANE

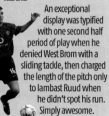

An exceptional display was typified with one second half period of play when he denied West Brom with a sliding tackle, then charged the length of the pitch only to lambast Ruud when he didn't spot his run. Simply awesome.

Premiership results
Weekend beginning 11/01/03

Birmingham City	0-4	Arsenal
Bolton Wanderers	0-0	Fulham
Chelsea	4-1	Charlton Athletic
Liverpool	1-1	Aston Villa
Manchester City	2-1	Leeds United
Middlesbrough	2-2	Southampton
Sunderland	0-0	Blackburn Rovers
Tottenham Hotspur	4-3	Everton
West Ham United	2-2	Newcastle United

Premiership table
Top 10 at the end of 12/01/03

	P	PTS
1 Arsenal	23	49
2 Manchester United	23	44
3 Chelsea	23	41
4 Newcastle United	22	39
5 Southampton	23	36
6 Everton	23	36
7 Liverpool	23	35
8 Tottenham Hotspur	23	35
9 Manchester City	23	34
10 Blackburn Rovers	23	33

Manchester United 2
Scholes 39, Forlan 90

Chelsea 1
Gudjohnsen 30

Chelsea arrived in Manchester with an enviable record – of the Premiership encounters between the two sides at Old Trafford, they had won three to United's two, with the rest shared. And as soon as the match kicked off it was clear that Claudio Ranieri's men were out for all three points.

The Blues dominated from the whistle, but it took them until the half-hour mark to take the lead, when Eidur Gudjohnsen broke free and skilfully scooped Emmanuel Petit's clever pass over Fabien Barthez. But, despite the fact that the Reds had not managed a single effort on goal by that point, it took them just nine minutes to redress the balance. There's no doubt, however, it was an opportunity gift-wrapped by the Chelsea defence.

Frank Lampard gave his keeper Carlo Cudicini an awkward backpass and his clearance fell to the one person on the pitch he wouldn't have chosen – David Beckham. United's No.7 sent a wickedly curling cross into the area which was met by an unstoppable header from Paul Scholes for the equaliser.

United appeared after the break looking more determined and laid siege to the Chelsea goal. Ole Gunnar Solskjaer fired against

Better late than never: Diego does it again

Saturday
18 January 2003
Old Trafford
Attendance: **67,606**
Referee: **Paul Durkin**

REVIEW

KEANO

the post following a blistering run from Ryan Giggs, then Roy Keane found himself unmarked in the box but was unable to hit the target. A trademark Ruud van Nistelrooy header had Cudicini stretching to keep the ball out of the net by his fingertips, and the Dutchman's replacement, Diego Forlan, brought another fine save.

With the clock ticking away it looked destined to end honours even as Chelsea, who seemed happy to see out the match in their own half, kept United at bay. But with seconds remaining, Forlan ran on to Seba Veron's killer pass and produced an explosive finish, maintaining his knack of scoring winning goals in United's big matches. "We've left it late so many times you almost get used to it," laughed Sir Alex. But then that's the beauty of being a Red.

Sir Alex Ferguson

DIEGO HAS SCORED SOME IMPORTANT GOALS THIS SEASON BUT THIS ONE COULD BE ABSOLUTELY VITAL. NEITHER CHELSEA OR OURSELVES WOULD HAVE BENEFITTED FROM A DRAW AND YES, WE LEFT IT LATE. I DIDN'T THINK A GOAL WAS COMING BUT WE NEVER GIVE UP AT MANCHESTER UNITED

Manchester United: Barthez; G Neville, Ferdinand, Brown, Silvestre (Veron 85); Beckham, Keane, Scholes, P Neville (Giggs 45); van Nistelrooy (Forlan 71), Solskjaer
Subs not used: Carroll, O'Shea

Chelsea: Cudicini; Gallas, Melchiot, Desailly, Le Saux; Gronkjaer (de Lucas 56), Petit, Lampard, Babayaro; Hasselbaink (Zola 16), Gudjohnsen (Zenden 84)
Subs not used: de Goey, Morris

Possession
52%	48%

Shots on target
5	3

Shots off target
3	5

Corners
6	6

Offsides
3	5

Fouls
10	10

Man of the match
PAUL SCHOLES

Manchester's answer to Zinedine Zidane. With five goals in five games under his belt, Scholes was one of United's most dangerous players. Chelsea had to put up with his late runs into the box, constant support for the front two and clever movement outside the area.

The equaliser: Roy Keane congratulates Paul Scholes

Premiership results
Weekend beginning 18/01/03
Arsenal	3-1	West Ham United
Aston Villa	0-1	Tottenham Hotspur
Blackburn Rovers	1-1	Birmingham City
Charlton Athletic	1-1	Bolton Wanderers
Everton	2-1	Sunderland
Fulham	1-0	Middlesbrough
Leeds United	0-0	West Bromwich Albion
Newcastle United	2-0	Manchester City
Southampton	0-1	Liverpool

Premiership table
Top 10 at the end of 19/01/03
		P	PTS
1	Arsenal	24	52
2	Manchester United	24	47
3	Newcastle United	24	45
4	Chelsea	24	41
5	Everton	24	39
6	Liverpool	24	38
7	Tottenham Hotspur	24	38
8	Southampton	24	36
9	Blackburn Rovers	24	34
10	Manchester City	24	34

FEBRUARY

As the league programme reached its final third, a determined United entered familiar territory – the 'business end' of the season – and set out to keep the pressure on leaders Arsenal

February was a frustrating month for United fans. While the Reds remained unbeaten in the league, the 1-1 draws at home to neighbours City (two days after the 45th anniversary of the Munich disaster) and away to Bolton Wanderers came either side of an early FA Cup exit against Arsenal. Domestic performances lacked the sparkle shown in the Champions League, especially in those memorable wins over Juventus.

When Middlesbrough postponed their game against Newcastle due to the icy conditions around the Riverside Stadium, Sir Bobby Robson – who celebrated his 70th birthday this month – was annoyed and unconvinced by the decision. Some Geordies went to the re-arranged match prepared for the elements, only to be refused entry.

Manchester City's new striker Robbie Fowler failed to score on his home debut as City were beaten by relegation candidates West Brom. Blues fans who had hoped for telepathy between Fowler and Nicolas Anelka quipped that telephony may have been a more suitable mode of communication. Elsewhere, Newcastle signed Jonathan Woodgate as debt-riddled Leeds continued to offload their best players.

Roy Keane divided public opinion in Ireland by announcing his retirement from international football, as a result of his continuing hip problems.

United finished February in second place, five points behind an Arsenal side who thumped City 5-1 at Maine Road on the last Saturday of the month. It would take some effort to catch them now...

Barclaycard Premiership fixtures this month

Saturday 1st	Southampton	Away
Tuesday 4th	Birmingham City	Away
Sunday 9th	Manchester City	Home
Saturday 22nd	Bolton Wanderers	Away

In the Barclaycard Premiership this month

156,615
watched United play four games

United scored
5
goals

but conceded
2
goal

United travelled
677
miles to and from games

United fielded a total of
17
players

FOCUS ON OLE GUNNAR SOLSKJAER

Ole Solskjaer turned 30 at the end of this month, providing a wake-up call for those who continue to label him the "baby-faced assassin". His deadly eye for goal hasn't faded over the years, as Bolton Wanderers found out to their cost just one week short of his birthday. Sam Allardyce's battlers had, if truth be told, pummelled United at the Reebok Stadium and were looking good value for their 1–0 lead, after Bruno N'Gotty had opened the scoring on the hour. Wanderers should have put the game out of sight on numerous occasions but anyone connected with Bayern Munich will tell you that United are never finished, particularly with Ole on the field. With seconds remaining David Beckham whipped in a cross which was forced home by Solskjaer, adding another point to United's total and denying Bolton a historic league double.

Southampton 0

Manchester United 2
Van Nistelrooy 15, Giggs 22

**On target again:
Ryan Giggs takes
his team-mates'
congratulations**

Saturday
1 February 2003
St Mary's Stadium
Attendance: **32,085**
Referee: **Philip Dowd**

United's mastery of the one-two was perfectly illustrated in this trip to the south coast. Here's how it works: opposing side starts brightly, goes close on a couple of occasions, falls prey to a double blast of attacking menace, game all but tied up. Opposing manager blasts lack of concentration, United go home with three points.

Southampton started this game the brighter, and it was no surprise to see Fabrice Fernandes test United early on. The gifted Frenchman stepped in from the right and let rip with a fierce drive, forcing his compatriot Fabien Barthez to tip over the bar. Almost 10 minutes later, Michael Svensson had an even clearer chance, heading wide when he really should have opened the scoring.

On 15 minutes, United did just that. Mikael Silvestre found David Beckham on the right, with Gary Neville thundering down the wing on the overlap. Beckham paused, waiting for the optimum moment, then lobbed two defenders to set Neville free. The right-back launched a perfect cross to find van Nistelrooy on the six-yard line waiting to sweep home.

It took United just seven minutes to double their lead with a textbook counter-attack. The goal was created by Beckham with an inch-perfect ball down the right wing to Solskjaer, whose rifled ball into the box was dummied by Veron and struck home by Ryan Giggs at the second time of asking.

On the half-hour mark, Saints had a strong shout for a penalty when Jo Tessem was bundled over in the box but referee Philip Dowd wasn't convinced. With six first-half minutes remaining, Barthez was carried off on a stretcher after falling awkwardly, to be replaced by Roy Carroll.

Two goals down at half-time, it was up to Southampton to chase the game, but the strike partnership of Tessem and the in-form James Beattie struggled to make an impact. Faced with a defensive four marshalled by an outstanding Rio Ferdinand, the closest Beattie got to an opening was a vain chase for a loose ball after Carroll had spilled, but for once in recent games it wasn't his day. It wasn't Antti Niemi's either. He became the second keeper to be carried off after saving bravely at the feet of van Nistelrooy.

Southampton: Niemi (Jones 86); Telfer, Lundekvam, M Svensson, Benali; Fernandes, Oakley, A Svensson, Marsden; Beattie, Tessem (Davies 70) **Subs not used:** Williams, Arias, Ormerod
Booked: Benali, A Svensson

Manchester United: Barthez (Carroll 37); G Neville, O'Shea, Ferdinand, Silvestre; Beckham (Scholes 69), Veron, Keane, Giggs; van Nistelrooy (Forlan 88), Solskjaer **Subs not used:** P Neville, Brown

Possession	
52%	48%
Shots on target	
5	2
Shots off target	
5	9
Corners	
6	7
Offsides	
3	1
Fouls	
14	15

Man of the match
RIO FERDINAND
Much of the pre-match talk focused on England call-up James Beattie but he wasn't given a sniff under the close attention of an imperious Rio Ferdinand. United's centre back strolled through the match, showing Beattie exactly what sort of qualities are needed at the highest level.

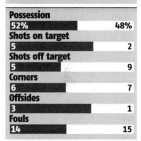

Premiership results
Weekend beginning 1/02/03

Arsenal	2-1		Fulham
Aston Villa	3-0		Blackburn Rovers
Bolton Wanderers	4-2		Birmingham City
Chelsea	1-1		Tottenham Hotspur
Everton	2-0		Leeds United
Manchester City	1-2		West Bromwich Albion
Sunderland	1-3		Charlton Athletic
West Ham United	0-3		Liverpool

Premiership table
Top 10 at the end of 2/02/03

	P	PTS
1 Arsenal	26	56
2 Manchester United	25	50
3 Newcastle United	25	48
4 Chelsea	26	45
5 Everton	26	45
6 Liverpool	26	42
7 Southampton	26	39
8 Charlton Athletic	26	39
9 Tottenham Hotspur	26	39
10 Manchester City	26	37

Sir Alex Ferguson

SOUTHAMPTON ISN'T THE EASIEST PLACE TO GO, AS WE HAVE DISCOVERED ON MORE THAN ONE OCCASION IN RECENT SEASONS. BUT THIS TRIP TURNED OUT TO BE MUCH HAPPIER. WE PLAYED WELL – I SAID WE HAD TO GET OUR AWAY FORM RIGHT AND WE HAVE STARTED TO DO THAT NOW

Birmingham City 0

Manchester United 1

Van Nistelrooy 56

All rise: David Beckham tries another curler

Just one exquisite demonstration of the ancient and noble art of goalscoring was enough to tip the scales United's way in this thriller against Steve Bruce's Birmingham City at St Andrews. Ruud van Nistelrooy provided the magic moment that was to give him his 26th goal of the season and keep United hot on the heels of Arsenal at the summit of the Premiership.

Birmingham had given a good account of themselves during a first half in which neither side could claim superiority. United led in terms of sophistication, but the Brummies matched them with true grit and not a little guile from French star Christophe Dugarry.

The early moments of the second spell saw United begin to turn the screw, with van Nistelrooy twice giving a hint of what was looming. Then, with 56 minutes on the clock, the Dutch master inflicted the blow that was to prove decisive.

Mikael Silvestre, overlapping on the left for the umpteenth time, lost his footing as he attempted to dispatch another teasing cross into the area. Fortunately for United, he recovered instantly to complete his contribution. The ball landed at the feet of van Nistelrooy who, with his back to the goal, wasn't ideally positioned

Tuesday
4 February 2003
St Andrews
Attendance: **29,475**
Referee: **Steve Dunn**

Birmingham City: Vaesen;
Kenna (Devlin 84), Cunningham,
Upson, Clapham; Johnson,
Clemence, Savage; Morrison (Kirovski 78),
John (Lazaridis 63), Dugarry
Subs not used: Bennett, Swierczewski
Booked: Johnson

Manchester United: Carroll,
G Neville, Ferdinand, Brown,
Silvestre; Beckham, Veron, Keane,
Giggs; Scholes; van Nistelrooy (Solskjaer 82)
Subs not used: P Neville, Butt, Ricardo,
Forlan **Booked:** Keane

Possession	
54%	**46%**
Shots on target	
3	1
Shots off target	
10	3
Corners	
5	3
Offsides	
4	2
Fouls	
16	10

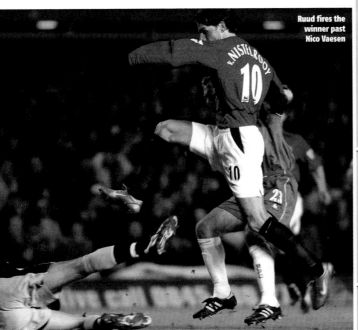

Ruud fires the
winner past
Nico Vaesen

Man of the match
JUAN SEBASTIAN VERON
Another glowing display
from United's favourite
Argentinian international.
Seba's virtuosity and silky
control on the ball were a
pivotal feature of the
team's performance and
continued to enhance the man
from La Plata's growing
reputation as one of the classiest
midfielders in the Premiership.

to make a strike. That, of course, didn't dissuade United's leading
scorer from trying add to his mountain of goals. There appeared to
be no danger, with Birmingham well represented in the area, but
in one mesmerising movement 'Ruuuuuud' turned on a guilder
before ramming a low shot past City keeper Nico Vaesen.

It was the pivotal incident in the contest, for after that
Birmingham, perhaps sensing the inevitability of the situation,
failed to provide the level of industry and mobility that had been
a feature earlier in the evening. That's not to say they didn't keep
plugging away – Steve Bruce would never let that happen – but the
zip in their work had diminished. Van Nistelrooy could have made
it two later on, but his marvellous goal was to prove enough.

Premiership table
Top 10 at the end of 4/02/2003

	P	PTS
1 Arsenal	26	56
2 Manchester United	26	53
3 Newcastle United	25	48
4 Chelsea	26	45
5 Everton	26	45
6 Liverpool	26	42
7 Southampton	26	39
8 Charlton Athletic	26	39
9 Tottenham Hotspur	26	39
10 Manchester City	26	37
11 Aston Villa	26	35
12 Blackburn Rovers	26	34
13 Leeds United	26	31
14 Middlesbrough	25	30
15 Fulham	25	27
16 Birmingham City	26	26
17 Bolton Wanderers	26	24
18 West Bromwich Albion	25	20
19 West Ham United	26	20
20 Sunderland	26	19

Sir Alex Ferguson

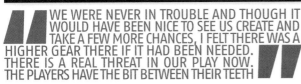

WE WERE NEVER IN TROUBLE AND THOUGH IT
WOULD HAVE BEEN NICE TO SEE US CREATE AND
TAKE A FEW MORE CHANCES, I FELT THERE WAS A
HIGHER GEAR THERE IF IT HAD BEEN NEEDED.
THERE IS A REAL THREAT IN OUR PLAY NOW.
THE PLAYERS HAVE THE BIT BETWEEN THEIR TEETH

Manchester United 1
Van Nistelrooy 18

Manchester City 1
Goater 86

The fall guy: Ruud puts United ahead

David Beckham gets stopped in his tracks

Midfield general: Roy Keane goes for a 50/50 ball

Sunday
9 February 2003
Old Trafford
Attendance: **67,646**
Referee: **Alan Wiley**

Before this 128th Manchester derby, *United Review* outlined the six tribes of football fan, ranging from The Believer to The Pessimist. Come the final whistle, The Believer would remind you that United had just stretched their unbeaten home record to 20 games in all competitions and picked up a point that could be crucial at the end of the season. The Pessimist, however, would have thrown his programme in the canal and locked himself in his shed.

It had all started so well, too. United's first half dominance should have brought more than the one goal – an 18th-minute strike by Ruud van Nistelrooy after a great cross from Ryan Giggs which foxed City keeper Carlo Nash (a late stand-in for Peter Schmeichel who was injured in the warm-up).

The Reds were rampant, spurred on by a buzzing Roy Keane clearly enjoying his first derby action for two seasons. Wes Brown and Rio Ferdinand were proving more than a match for Nicolas Anelka and Robbie Fowler, a potential strike force that would have brought the The Pessimist out in a cold sweat. In actual fact, Fowler was evidently short of match fitness and looked unlikely to last the full 90 minutes. How the home team would come to rue his eventual departure.

The second half saw the Blues edge back into the game, with Eyal Berkovic enjoying the freedom of the pitch. Yet United could have put the game out of reach – both van Nistelrooy and Giggs passed up gilt-edged chances to make amends for November's Maine Road debacle after chasing long balls, firstly from Ferdinand then from David Beckham.

The game turned on 86 minutes when, as the Blues were preparing to take a free kick on the edge of United's box, Keegan swapped Fowler and Berkovic for Shaun Goater and Ali Benarbia. As the Goat took his place in the danger area, Benarbia squared the ball to fellow sub Shaun Wright-Phillips who hoisted the ball into the box where Goater was waiting to cement his place in derby legend, just nine seconds after coming on. He then had a goal ruled out in stoppage time, after a handball by Anelka. If that had counted, even Mr Believer's faith would have been tested.

Manchester United: Carroll; G Neville, Ferdinand, Brown, Silvestre; Beckham, Veron (Butt 77), Keane, Scholes; Giggs (Solskjaer 89), van Nistelrooy
Subs not used: Ricardo, O'Shea, P Neville
Booked: G Neville

★★★ **Manchester City:** Nash; Sommeil, Howey, Distin; Jihai, Foe, Horlock (Wright-Phillips 66), Jensen, Berkovic (Benarbia 86); Anelka, Fowler (Goater 86) **Subs not used:** Dunne, Stuhr-Ellegaard **Booked:** Foe

Possession
56%	44%

Shots on target
4	4

Shots off target
7	3

Corners
10	4

Offsides
2	5

Fouls
11	13

Man of the match
RIO FERDINAND
Another strong performance from a defender in top-class form. Anelka and Fowler were desperate to make an impact on this match, given their previous home addresses, but they had to get past Ferdinand and Wes Brown first. The Goat was another matter, though...

Premiership results

Premiership table

Sir Alex Ferguson

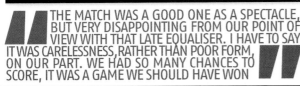

"THE MATCH WAS A GOOD ONE AS A SPECTACLE, BUT VERY DISAPPOINTING FROM OUR POINT OF VIEW WITH THAT LATE EQUALISER. I HAVE TO SAY IT WAS CARELESSNESS, RATHER THAN POOR FORM, ON OUR PART. WE HAD SO MANY CHANCES TO SCORE, IT WAS A GAME WE SHOULD HAVE WON"

Bolton Wanderers 1
N'Gotty 61

Manchester United 1
Solskjaer 90

A fixture coming on the back of big games against Manchester City, Arsenal and Juventus, in the Champions League, could well be looked on as a case of 'after the Lord Mayor's Show', but there's definitely nothing second-rate about encounters between United and these near-neighbours. Close proximity has always ensured a heated local rivalry, which stretches as far back as the early 1890s and shows little sign of cooling. United and Bolton have fought out many memorable matches in both league and cup over the years and this one, at a sunbathed but bitterly cold Reebok Stadium, was another that will be recalled long into the future.

Not that it was the type of game to find a home in the file marked 'Classics', because it never got remotely close to those heady standards. Nevertheless, it was an enthralling contest and one that appeared to be heading towards Wanderers' second 1-0 win over United this season until the Reds thankfully pulled off yet another late, late show.

Sir Alex's men hadn't been anywhere near their best against a determined, industrious and lively home side, but anyone who writes United off, even in added time, does so at their peril.

Bolton try their best to restrain Ole Gunnar Solskjaer...

**Saturday
22 February 2003
Reebok Stadium**
Attendance: **27,409**
Referee: **Andy D'Urso**

So it proved again. Wanderers' supporters were holding their breath in anticipation of another great win after they went ahead on 61 minutes. A flighted free kick from Youri Djorkaeff bounced off Bruno N'Gotty's back and went in off a post. For once, Fabien Barthez had misjudged the danger posed by a set piece.

But even though Bolton continued to match their visitors in every facet of the game, and outstrip them in some, the feeling persisted that United would eventually claim something. And that's how it turned out when, in the final minute of normal time, Ole Gunnar Solskjaer got on the end of David Beckham's right-wing cross to squeeze home the equaliser. In truth, it was probably more than United deserved.

Bolton Wanderers: Jaaskelainen; N'Gotty, Laville, Bergsson, Charlton; Mendy (Barness 82), Okocha, Campo, Gardner; Pedersen (Salva 58), Djorkaeff (Nolan 85) **Subs Not Used:** Poole, Andre **Booked:** Campo

Manchester United: Barthez; G Neville, Ferdinand, Brown (P Neville 74), O'Shea; Beckham, Keane, Veron (Butt 81), Giggs (Forlan 57); van Nistelrooy, Solskjaer
Subs Not Used: Ricardo, Fletcher
Booked: Keane

Possession		
60%		40%
Shots on target		
2		5
Shots off target		
4		8
Corners		
5		8
Offsides		
6		2
Fouls		
11		14

Sir Alex Ferguson

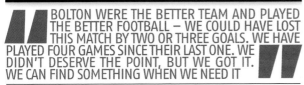

> BOLTON WERE THE BETTER TEAM AND PLAYED THE BETTER FOOTBALL – WE COULD HAVE LOST THIS MATCH BY TWO OR THREE GOALS. WE HAVE PLAYED FOUR GAMES SINCE THEIR LAST ONE. WE DIDN'T DESERVE THE POINT, BUT WE GOT IT. WE CAN FIND SOMETHING WHEN WE NEED IT

But he grabbed a point for United on 90 minutes

Man of the match
FABIEN BARTHEZ

A very busy afternoon for the French no.1. Wanderers tried every trick in the book to bypass him, but Barthez stood firm on all but one occasion. In fact, his impressive contribution was every inch as important as Solskjaer's last-gasp equaliser, helping to secure a point from a less-than-perfect performance.

Premiership results
Weekend beginning 22/02/03

Birmingham City	2-1	Liverpool
Charlton Athletic	3-0	Aston Villa
Chelsea	1-2	Blackburn Rovers
Everton	2-1	Southampton
Leeds United	0-3	Newcastle United
Manchester City	1-5	Arsenal
Sunderland	1-3	Middlesbrough
Tottenham Hotspur	1-1	Fulham
West Bromwich Albion	1-2	West Ham United

Premiership table
Top 10 at the end of 24/02/03

		P	PTS
1	Arsenal	28	60
2	Manchester United	28	55
3	Newcastle United	27	52
4	Chelsea	28	48
5	Everton	28	48
6	Charlton Athletic	28	45
7	Liverpool	28	43
8	Tottenham Hotspur	28	43
9	Blackburn Rovers	28	40
10	Southampton	28	39

MARCH

In a month when Blackburn Rovers completed a league double over Arsenal and two ex-England managers bit the bullet, United quietly collected maximum points in the Premiership

After the disappointment, rather than despair, of the Worthington Cup final defeat to Liverpool, a downbeat mood prevailed amongst Reds and with Arsenal eight points clear in the league, it seemed implausible that some had talked of a Quadruple only weeks earlier. But when hope seemed lost, Blackburn completed their season's double over the Gunners. For the second time in the league, United won a game in hand and the gap shrunk to two points.

At the bottom, Howard Wilkinson and Terry Venables were both relieved of their managerial duties. Wilkinson hadn't even spent six months at Sunderland, something Venables just about managed at Leeds. Sunderland and West Brom seemed confirmed candidates for the drop as Bolton and West Ham opened up a nine point gap above them.

Five or six teams were still in danger of slipping into the third relegation spot, including Leeds with their woeful form. Chairman Peter Ridsdale installed Peter Reid as caretaker manager but it was to be his last appointment – he bowed to intense pressure from Leeds fans and resigned a few days later.

Ruud van Nistelrooy headed the goalscorers' chart with 33 in all competitions, five ahead of Arsenal's Thierry Henry who had netted more league goals.

United remained the only English team in Europe by the end of March after Arsenal, Newcastle and Liverpool were eliminated. Perhaps Arsenal fans were tempting fate when they sang, "We'll be back again in May" at Old Trafford after February's FA Cup win.

Barclaycard Premiership fixtures this month

Wednesday 5th	Leeds United	Home
Saturday 15th	Aston Villa	Away
Saturday 22nd	Fulham	Home

In the Barclaycard Premiership this month

177,934
watched United play three games

United scored
6
goals

but conceded
1
goal

United travelled
172
miles to and from games

United fielded a total of
16
players

FOCUS ON DAVID BECKHAM

After the stormy month of February and more front page splashes, March gave Beckham an opportunity to get back to football matters. Depending on your point of view, the Reds either put the Worthington Cup final defeat behind them or used it as an inspiration, and won all three league matches this month. Beckham was instrumental in all of them. Two crosses from that right boot set up the goals in the home tie with Leeds United, securing a 2–1 win, and he turned matchwinner away to Aston Villa, grabbing an early goal that was enough to guarantee three points. He may have scored more sexy goals, but in the long run few will have been more important. Beckham ended the month on the cover of *United Review* for the Fulham game and had one simple message for the fans: "We can catch Arsenal."

Manchester United 2
Radebe (o.g.) 21, Silvestre 79

Leeds United 1
Viduka 64

With hopes of another trophy treble dashed at the Millennium Stadium, United returned to Premiership action eager to claw back lost ground on Arsenal. It may not be considered a priority these days but, as a tasty *hors d'oeuvre* to the desired end-of-season silverware banquet, victory in the Worthington Cup final would have provided a timely confidence boost for the run-in. So how would the Reds respond to that Cymru koshing?

On the face of it, the fates appeared to have done Sir Alex's team a favour. On top of their financial worries, Leeds came to Old Trafford with several of their big names unavailable. But that wasn't going to prevent them from attempting to throw a spanner into the works of United's title bid.

Nobody was in any doubt that with Arsenal stretching their lead to eight points the previous weekend, United really couldn't afford any slip-ups. So it was encouraging to see the Reds start well. In the early stages Juan Sebastian Veron was unlucky not to give United the lead, letting rip with a fierce drive from 30 yards which had goal written all over it – only for the guidance system to fail at the last minute and send the ball into the side-netting.

He stoops, he scores: Mikael Silvestre nods in United's second

Wednesday
5 March 2003
Old Trafford
Attendance: **67,626**
Referee: **Graham Poll**

But on 21 minutes, a David Beckham cross from the right wing caused mass panic in the Leeds defence. Nicky Butt bravely got in a header which keeper Paul Robinson managed to parry. Ruud van Nistelrooy and Lucas Radebe were both in the vicinity and the ball struck the South African international before crossing the line.

Things didn't go entirely United's way though, and when Mark Viduka leapt to head the equaliser in the 64th minute it appeared that two vital points were in danger of being jettisoned. But help, in the unlikely figure of Mikael Silvestre, was at hand.

With 11 minutes to go the Frenchman, nipping in undetected by the Leeds defence, stooped to head the winner from a quickly-taken Beckham free-kick.

Sir Alex Ferguson

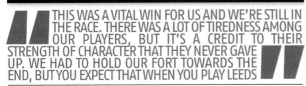

THIS WAS A VITAL WIN FOR US AND WE'RE STILL IN THE RACE. THERE WAS A LOT OF TIREDNESS AMONG OUR PLAYERS, BUT IT'S A CREDIT TO THEIR STRENGTH OF CHARACTER THAT THEY NEVER GAVE UP. WE HAD TO HOLD OUR FORT TOWARDS THE END, BUT YOU EXPECT THAT WHEN YOU PLAY LEEDS

Manchester United: Barthez; O'Shea, Ferdinand, Keane, Silvestre; Beckham, Butt, Veron (P Neville 56) Fortune (Giggs 64); Scholes; van Nistelrooy (G Neville 90)
Subs not used: Carroll, Fletcher
Booked: Scholes

Leeds United: Robinson; Mills, Radebe, Lucic, Harte; Okon, Johnson, Bravo (McPhail 85); Smith, Viduka, Barmby (Milner 85)
Subs not used: Martyn, Cansdell-Sherriff, Kilgallon **Booked:** Smith

Possession	
55%	45%
Shots on target	
4	4
Shots off target	
13	1
Corners	
6	3
Offsides	
3	2
Fouls	
16	17

Man of the match
JOHN O'SHEA
Another polished performance. O'Shea scarcely put a foot wrong in his role as Gary Neville's right-back deputy, and even found time to wow the crowd with a brilliantly-executed turn to get himself out of a tight spot on the touchline.

Premiership results
Weekend beginning 1/03/03

Arsenal	2–0	Charlton Athletic
Aston Villa	0–2	Birmingham City
Blackburn Rovers	1–0	Manchester City
Fulham	1–0	Sunderland
Middlesbrough	1–1	Everton
Newcastle United	2–1	Chelsea
Southampton	1–0	West Bromwich Albion
West Ham United	2–0	Tottenham Hotspur

Premiership table
Top 10 at the end of 5/03/03

	P	PTS
1 Arsenal	28	60
2 Manchester United	28	55
3 Newcastle United	27	52
4 Chelsea	28	48
5 Everton	28	48
6 Charlton Athletic	28	45
7 Liverpool	28	43
8 Tottenham Hotspur	28	43
9 Blackburn Rovers	28	40
10 Southampton	28	39

David Beckham had a hand in both goals

Aston Villa 0

Manchester United 1
Beckham 12

David Beckham
nicks in to put
United ahead

Fabien Barthez had
to resist a siege
on his goal

Ryan Giggs shields
the ball from
Moustapha Hadji

Saturday
15 March 2003
Villa Park
Attendance: **42,602**
Referee: **Mike Dean**

In 2002 **Manchester** declared itself Britain's second city, much to the annoyance of Birmingham's city fathers who had long claimed the title. Just to rub Brummie noses in it, the Midlands has been a happy hunting ground for United this season, with the Reds gaining maximum points from three trips down the M6. But as in the game against Birmingham City, Sir Alex's troops were made to work hard and settled for a single-goal victory.

United got off to a flyer, with Villa's stand-in keeper Stefan Postma saving at point-blank range from David Beckham. Moments later Ruud van Nistelrooy had the ball in the net, only to see the goal ruled out following a late flag from the linesman. A minute later and United's early efforts were rewarded as the No.7 made amends for his previous miss. Paul Scholes got things going with a pass to Ryan Giggs, who sent the ball into the danger area where Beckham, showing sharper reflexes than Alan Wright, nicked in for the opening goal.

Villa were hellbent on putting up a fight for fans smarting from their own recent derby miseries, and they peppered Fabien Barthez's goal in search of an equaliser. Gareth Barry was providing the industry and Mustapha Hadji the artistry, with the Moroccan going close with one long-range header and two vicious drives. Beckham could have bagged his own hat-trick, miscuing his third attempt from six yards out, while Vassell, Hendrie and Hitzlsperger added to Villa's chances. United's defence – with Rio Ferdinand and Mikael Silvestre looking solid – stood firm.

Both teams had early chances after the break, the best of which fell to Dublin, whose header was kept out by Barthez. Goalmouth action wasn't confined to the United end, though, and Giggs came close when his superb free-kick rattled the bar. Beckham and Scholes gave another airing to their party trick, linking up directly from a corner, but Scholes' volley was deflected wide. The Reds should have sewn the game up when van Nistelrooy broke, with Ole Gunnar Solskjaer and Beckham in support, but the Dutchman opted to go it alone, leaving his manager fuming. No matter, as the Reds withstood late pressure for three vital points.

Aston Villa: Postma; Samuel, Mellberg, Johnsen, Wright; Hendrie, Hitzlsperger, Hadji, Barry; Vassell, Dublin (Cooke 79)
Subs not used: Enckelman, Crouch, Kinsella, Edwards **Booked:** Wright, Hadji

Manchester United: Barthez; Neville, Ferdinand, O'Shea, Silvestre; Beckham, Butt, Scholes, Giggs; van Nistelrooy, Solskjaer
Subs not used: P Neville, Blanc, Ricardo, Forlan, Fletcher
Booked: Scholes

Possession	
49%	51%
Shots on target	
8	5
Shots off target	
13	9
Corners	
6	6
Offsides	
2	5
Fouls	
13	10

Man of the match
RIO FERDINAND

Centre halves need to be on top of their game when Dion Dublin is around, but the ex-United striker's power play proved meat and drink for Rio Ferdinand, again enjoying an excellent match and helping the Reds to another clean sheet, to the delight of his manager.

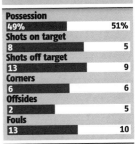

Premiership results
Weekend beginning 15/03/03

Blackburn Rovers	2-0	Arsenal
Charlton Athletic	0-2	Newcastle United
Everton	0-0	West Ham United
Fulham	2-2	Southampton
Leeds United	2-3	Middlesbrough
Manchester City	1-0	Birmingham City
Sunderland	0-2	Bolton Wanderers
Tottenham Hotspur	2-3	Liverpool
West Bromwich Albion	0-2	Chelsea

Premiership table
Top 10 at the end of 16/03/03

	P	PTS
1 Arsenal	30	63
2 Manchester United	30	61
3 Newcastle United	30	58
4 Chelsea	30	51
5 Everton	30	50
6 Liverpool	30	49
7 Blackburn Rovers	30	46
8 Charlton Athletic	30	45
9 Southampton	30	43
10 Tottenham Hotspur	30	43

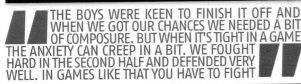

Sir Alex Ferguson

THE BOYS WERE KEEN TO FINISH IT OFF AND WHEN WE GOT OUR CHANCES WE NEEDED A BIT OF COMPOSURE. BUT WHEN IT'S TIGHT IN A GAME THE ANXIETY CAN CREEP IN A BIT. WE FOUGHT HARD IN THE SECOND HALF AND DEFENDED VERY WELL. IN GAMES LIKE THAT YOU HAVE TO FIGHT

Manchester United 3

Van Nistelrooy 45 (pen), 68, 90

Fulham 0

Referee Steve Bennett had three goal celebrations to deal with

On a day that United broke the Premiership's highest attendance record yet again, Ruud van Nistelrooy gave Old Trafford's paying customers full value for their coin. The Dutchman struck all three goals, opening his account with a penalty on the stroke of half-time and bringing the curtain down with a deflected volley from close range in second-half injury time.

But it was his second goal, a rampaging run that began inside his own half and ended in joy in front of the Stretford End, that elevated this, his fourth hat-trick in a red shirt, above routine matchball-snaffling and into the realms of sporting fantasy.

The match was a belter: incident-packed and breathless. For once it was United who made the early running. Paul Scholes proved Fulham's tormentor , linking play and spreading passes right and left with a casual, almost absent-minded, excellence.

For all United's early dominance though, it was Fulham who came closest to a goal on 25 minutes through Martin Djetou. But just before the interval, the Reds finally made the breakthrough, van Nistelrooy scoring from the spot after Djetou had been penalised for a tug on Ole Gunnar Solskjaer.

Ruud converts his sixth penalty of the season

MATCHFACTS

Saturday
22 March 2003
Old Trafford
Attendance: **67,706**
Referee: **Steve Bennett**

Manchester United: Barthez; G Neville, Ferdinand, Brown, O'Shea; Beckham, Butt, Scholes, Giggs; Solskjaer, van Nistelrooy
Subs not used: Blanc, Ricardo, Forlan, Fortune, Fletcher
Booked: G Neville, Ferdinand

Fulham: Taylor; Ouaddou, Melville, Knight, Harley; Malbranque, Legwinski, Djetou, Boa Morte; Saha, Marlet
Subs not used: Herrera, Inamoto, Clark, Sava, Wome **Booked:** Melville

Possession
| 55% | 45% |

Shots on target
| 11 | 3 |

Shots off target
| 7 | 6 |

Corners
| 9 | 5 |

Offsides
| 4 | 0 |

Fouls
| 13 | 15 |

Man of the match
RUUD VAN NISTELROOY

Although this was a team performance, that show-stopping second goal and the emphatic, icy-veined calm with which he dispatched his penalty saw Ruud emerge as the game's stand-out performer.

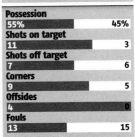

In the second half United's grip on the game tightened, with Solskjaer and van Nistelrooy going close. Then, on 65 minutes, Ruud made his move. Collecting the ball in the centre-circle, he shrugged off Sylvain Legwinski's challenge, outpaced two covering defenders and powered towards goal. A jink to the left took care of Melville, Fulham's remaining defender, and Maik Taylor was still calculating his angles when the Dutchman, contorting his body to apply a right-footed finish, beat him with a precise shot into the far corner. The ball seemed to dawdle before crossing the line, like a ham actor trying to steal the scene. But it was Ruud who took the accolades; fans bellowed his name while joyous team-mates formed a disorderly queue to slap his back.

Premiership results
Weekend beginning 22/03/03

Arsenal	2-1	Everton
Birmingham City	1-0	West Bromwich Albion
Bolton Wanderers	1-0	Tottenham Hotspur
Chelsea	5-0	Manchester City
Liverpool	3-1	Leeds United
Middlesbrough	1-1	Charlton Athletic
Newcastle United	5-1	Blackburn Rovers
Southampton	2-2	Aston Villa
West Ham United	2-0	Sunderland

Premiership table
Top 10 at the end of 24/03/03

	P	PTS
1 Arsenal	31	66
2 Manchester United	31	64
3 Newcastle United	31	61
4 Chelsea	31	54
5 Liverpool	31	52
6 Everton	31	50
7 Charlton Athletic	31	46
8 Blackburn Rovers	31	46
9 Southampton	31	44
10 Tottenham Hotspur	31	43

Sir Alex Ferguson

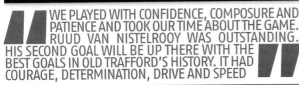

WE PLAYED WITH CONFIDENCE, COMPOSURE AND PATIENCE AND TOOK OUR TIME ABOUT THE GAME. RUUD VAN NISTELROOY WAS OUTSTANDING. HIS SECOND GOAL WILL BE UP THERE WITH THE BEST GOALS IN OLD TRAFFORD'S HISTORY. IT HAD COURAGE, DETERMINATION, DRIVE AND SPEED

APRIL

The last full month of the Premiership saw United facing two main title rivals in successive games – would the Reds find that end-of-season top gear just when it was most needed?

It was onwards and upwards as United's excellent run of league results continued. Possible title rivals Newcastle were destroyed 6-2 with Sir Alex describing the performance as, "the sort of day you might get once every three years". In an even bigger game, United were superior to Arsenal for long periods in a 2-2 draw at Highbury, where tickets sold for up to £375 on the black market. Problems over the building of a new ground mean that Highbury's limited capacity will be a tout's dream for years to come.

Liverpool, Blackburn and Spurs were all well beaten by a United side that became title favourites only months after Arsenal had been declared the greatest team since Real Madrid in the 1950s. The Gunners' nerves became evident when Arsène Wenger ripped off his tie in frustration as his side slipped up against Bolton.

West Brom and Sunderland finally had relegation confirmed – new Mackems' manager Mick McCarthy was unable to prevent his team going down. Bolton and West Ham delayed their fate, however, by picking up points – the latter under caretaker boss Trevor Brooking after Glenn Roeder suffered a mild stroke.

Thierry Henry was voted the PFA Player of the Year ahead of Ruud van Nistelrooy and Paul Scholes. Jermaine Jenas grabbed the young player award in front of John O'Shea and wonderboy Wayne Rooney. If that wasn't surprising enough, Scholes was the only United player to make it into the divisional team that included four Arsenal stars. Go figure that one out.

Barclaycard Premiership fixtures this month

Saturday 5th	Liverpool	Home
Saturday 12th	Newcastle United	Away
Wednesday 16th	Arsenal	Away
Saturday 19th	Blackburn Rovers	Home
Sunday 27th	Tottenham Hotspur	Away

In the Barclaycard Premiership this month

261,666
watched United play five games

United scored
17
goals

but conceded
5
goals

United travelled
1,166
miles to and from games

United fielded a total of
19
players

FOCUS ON RUUD VAN NISTELROOY

Unstoppable. Ruud van Nistelrooy led the line in eight games for club and country throughout April, and scored in every one of them. Incredibly, there had been grumblings among short-sighted United fans about van Nistelrooy's scoring record, claiming he hadn't delivered the goods against the big teams. Answering the critics in style doesn't even come into it. Ruud kicked the month off with a brace of penalties against Liverpool, scored home and away against the mighty Real Madrid, added one of the six against Newcastle United and netted vital strikes against Blackburn Rovers, Arsenal and Tottenham Hotspur. The goal at Highbury in particular was one to savour – a powerful run and stunning finish which sent a message saying: "If it's big game players you're after, look no further".

Manchester United 4
Van Nistelrooy 5 (pen), 65 (pen), Giggs 79, Solskjaer 90

Liverpool 0

Gary Neville hugs Old Trafford's penalty king

Mikael Silvestre foils a Liverpool attack

Mindful of the difficulties posed by Liverpool of late, Sir Alex had some uncomplicated advice for his players in the build-up to this game. It was, quite simply, to score first. Ruud van Nistelrooy, to whose formidable list of attributes we can now add a burgeoning understanding of Glaswegian, got the message loud and clear.

The Dutchman put United ahead after just five minutes, smashing home a spot-kick awarded when, after collecting a delicate through ball from Paul Scholes, his progress towards goal had been halted by a tug from Sami Hyypia. For his act of desperation, the Liverpool captain saw red.

Despite being reduced to 10 men, the visitors enjoyed lengthy periods of possession in the first half, even causing a flutter or two in the United defence, but steadily the Reds began to exploit the extra man and in the 65th minute went further ahead. Another penalty, this time for a foul on Scholes by Liverpool substitute Igor Biscan, was rammed home by van Nistelrooy, the Dutchman's ninth successive conversion in the Premiership. Jerzy Dudek guessed right, but would never have beaten the pace of the shot.

With the match over as a contest Sir Alex withdrew both Phil Neville, impeccable in midfield, and Mikael Silvestre and invited David Beckham and John O'Shea to the party. Both brought renewed vigour to United, the young Irishman catching the eye with his languid elegance and cementing his reputation as Old Trafford's nutmeg king.

Liverpool's resistance was weakened further on 78 minutes. Ryan Giggs, left out of the starting line-up due to a heavy cold, stretched to meet a Beckham cross and directed the ball into the roof of the net for his first Premiership goal at Old Trafford for two years. Ole Gunnar Solskjaer, no stranger to late goals against Liverpool, completed the rout in the final minute, driving a right-footed shot from the edge of the area inside Dudek's near post.

This was United's first league double over the Merseysiders for six years, and having ended such an unwanted sequence in style, those present transformed Old Trafford into a sea of grinning faces as referee Mike Riley blew the final whistle.

Sir Alex Ferguson

IF YOU'RE ASKED AT THE START OF THE SEASON WOULD YOU RATHER HAVE TWO LEAGUE VICTORIES OVER LIVERPOOL OR THE LEAGUE CUP, WHAT WOULD THE ANSWER BE? IT'S ALWAYS A DISAPPOINTMENT TO LOSE TO THEM – BUT TO HAVE THE LEAGUE DOUBLE IS VERY SATISFYING

Ruud puts United one up after five minutes

MATCHFACTS

**Saturday
5 April 2003
Old Trafford**
Attendance: **67,639**
Referee: **Mike Riley**

Manchester United: Barthez; G Neville, Ferdinand, Brown, Silvestre (O'Shea 66); Solskjaer, Keane, P Neville (Beckham 66), Giggs; Scholes (Butt 79); van Nistelrooy
Subs not used: Ricardo, Forlan
Booked: Silvestre

Liverpool: Dudek; Carragher, Hyypia, Traore, Riise; Diouf (Smicer 71), Hamann, Gerrard, Murphy (Cheyrou 80); Heskey, Baros (Biscan 6)
Subs not used: Arphexad, Mellor
Booked: Diouf, Murphy, Gerrard
Sent off: Hyypia

Possession	
64%	36%
Shots on target	
7	0
Shots off target	
6	4
Corners	
10	4
Offsides	
2	0
Fouls	
16	19

Man of the match
OLE GUNNAR SOLSKJAER

Ruud van Nistelrooy's penalties understandably grabbed the headlines, but it was Solskjaer's performance – in particular his movement, notably down the right-hand side – that was crucial in setting the tenor of the match. His goal, in the final minute, was a fitting reward for his efforts.

Premiership results
Weekend beginning 5/04/03

Aston Villa	1-1	Arsenal
Bolton Wanderers	2-0	Manchester City
Charlton Athletic	1-6	Leeds United
Everton	2-1	Newcastle United
Fulham	0-4	Blackburn Rovers
Middlesbrough	3-0	West Bromwich Albion
Southampton	1-1	West Ham United
Sunderland	1-2	Chelsea
Tottenham Hotspur	2-1	Birmingham City

Premiership table
Top 10 at the end of 7/04/03

	P	PTS
1 Arsenal	32	67
2 Manchester United	32	67
3 Newcastle United	32	61
4 Chelsea	32	57
5 Everton	32	53
6 Liverpool	32	52
7 Blackburn Rovers	32	49
8 Tottenham Hotspur	32	46
9 Charlton Athletic	32	46
10 Middlesbrough	32	45

Newcastle United 2
Jenas 21, Ameobi 89

Manchester United 6
Solskjaer 32, Scholes 34, 38, 52, Giggs 44, van Nistelrooy 58 (pen)

With five minutes to go in this fixture, Sir Alex Ferguson rose to demand another goal. Nothing remarkable about that except, by this stage, the Reds were already 6-1 up! Though his team were unable to fulfil his request, the full-beam smile that lit up his post-match interviews indicated the manager's satisfaction.

United were magnificent, irresistible, rampant. Despite the absence of David Beckham and the setback of an early goal – a 21st-minute cracker from Jermaine Jenas – the Reds took the game to the home team, dominating with a combination of high-speed passing and movement.

Ole Solskjaer drew United level on 32 minutes, springing the offside trap to swivel and shoot past Shay Given from a Ryan Giggs pass. Lifted by the equaliser, the Reds went on the rampage, scoring a further three goals in a devastating 12-minute blitz.

Paul Scholes, enhancing his credentials as the Premiership's only credible Zinedine Zidane impersonator, scored two of them. His first, a thumping, low volley on 34 minutes, came after a slick one-two with Solskjaer; his second, four minutes later, followed fleet footwork from Giggs and Wes Brown, who combined to tee

Ole Gunnar Solskjaer puts United level

MATCHFACTS

Saturday
12 April 2003
St James's Park
Attendance: **52,164**
Referee: **Steve Dunn**

him up from 18 yards. And Geordie chins dropped even further a minute from half-time when John O'Shea's shot, an angled screamer from 15-yards, rebounded off the underside of the bar for Giggs to make it 4-1.

Newcastle supporters dreaming of a second-half comeback had little time to indulge their fantasies. Within 12 minutes of the restart United added two more goals. On 52 minutes Scholes tapped in at the far post to complete his hat-trick and take his season's tally to a personal best 17. Then, five minutes later, Diego Forlan, on at half-time for the injured Giggs, was upended in the box by Titus Bramble to give Ruud van Nistelrooy a crack from the penalty spot. No prizes for guessing what happened next.

Newcastle United: Given; Hughes, Bramble, Woodgate, Bernard; Solano (Ameobi 66), Dyer, Jenas, Robert (Viana 15) (LuaLua 66); Shearer, Bellamy
Subs Not Used: Griffin, Harper
Booked: Shearer

Manchester United: Barthez; O'Shea (G Neville 49), Ferdinand, Brown (Blanc 65), Silvestre; Solskjaer, Keane, Scholes, Butt; Giggs (Forlan 45), van Nistelrooy
Subs Not Used: P Neville, Ricardo

Possession		
48%		**52%**
Shots on target		
11		7
Shots off target		
4		8
Corners		
6		6
Offsides		
2		4
Fouls		
9		8

Sir Alex Ferguson

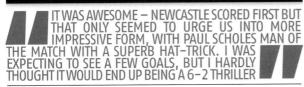

IT WAS AWESOME – NEWCASTLE SCORED FIRST BUT THAT ONLY SEEMED TO URGE US INTO MORE IMPRESSIVE FORM, WITH PAUL SCHOLES MAN OF THE MATCH WITH A SUPERB HAT-TRICK. I WAS EXPECTING TO SEE A FEW GOALS, BUT I HARDLY THOUGHT IT WOULD END UP BEING A 6–2 THRILLER

Man of the match
PAUL SCHOLES

For several seasons football's great and good have operated a rota to heap praise on Paul Scholes, championing his potential to emerge as one of the most influential players in the game. That potential is now being spectacularly fulfilled.

United ruin Shay Given's day – again

Premiership results
Weekend beginning 12/04/03

Birmingham City	2–0	Sunderland
Blackburn Rovers	1–0	Charlton Athletic
Chelsea	1–0	Bolton Wanderers
Leeds United	2–2	Tottenham Hotspur
Liverpool	2–0	Fulham
Manchester City	0–0	Middlesbrough
West Bromwich Albion	1–2	Everton
West Ham United	2–2	Aston Villa

Premiership table
Top 10 at the end of 14/04/03

	P	PTS
1 Manchester United	33	70
2 Arsenal	32	67
3 Newcastle United	33	61
4 Chelsea	33	60
5 Everton	33	56
6 Liverpool	33	55
7 Blackburn Rovers	33	52
8 Tottenham Hotspur	33	47
9 Middlesbrough	33	46
10 Charlton Athletic	33	46

Arsenal 2
Henry 51, 62

Manchester United 2
Van Nistelrooy 24, Giggs 63

Acrobatics from
Ruud as Stuart
Taylor tries to block

So, did the earth move for you? If you'd been reading the tabloids in the build-up to 'the big one' you'd have been forgiven for thinking Highbury was about to career wildly off the Richter scale prior to the 'crunch', 'shakedown', or whichever adjective you like.

The game didn't disappoint either, even if once the dust had settled on Sol Campbell's elbowing of Ole Gunnar Solskjaer and subsequent dismissal, it was as-you-were at the top of the table.

Ruud van Nistelrooy, having mustered just a single shot on target in four previous matches against the Gunners, opened his account and the scoring on 24 minutes, with a surging run and adroit chip over Stuart Taylor from Paul Scholes' superb first-time ball. Remarkably, Leeds are now the only Premiership side he has failed to find the net against in his first two seasons.

Though Arsenal had their fair share of possession, and were soon level after the break through Henry's deflection from an Ashley Cole shot, United looked a completely different side to the one undone by the Gunners in the Cup, with Rio Ferdinand, Ryan Giggs and van Nistelrooy keen to exorcise their demons.

If anything, it was Arsenal who struggled to maintain their

**Wednesday
16 April 2003
Highbury**
Attendance: **38,164**
Referee: **Mark Halsey**

Arsenal: Taylor; Cole, Lauren, Keown, Campbell; Ljungberg, Silva, Vieira (Edu 34), Pires (Kanu 79); Bergkamp (Wiltord 75), Henry
Subs not used: Warmuz, Luzhny
Sent off: Campbell

Manchester United: Barthez; O'Shea (G Neville 45), Ferdinand, Brown, Silvestre; Butt, Keane, Giggs, Scholes; Solskjaer, van Nistelrooy
Subs not used: P Neville, Beckham, Ricardo, Fortune
Booked: Keane, Butt

Possession

42%	58%

Shots on target

2	4

Shots off target

4	4

Corners

2	6

Offsides

3	0

Fouls

15	15

Gary Neville and Ryan Giggs celebrate United's equaliser

**Man of the match
RYAN GIGGS**

Not only was Giggs involved in a smart one–two in the build up to the opener, he was in the right place at the right time to head home the equaliser. These contributions gave him the nod on a night when United heroes were plentiful.

poise this time. Campbell's controversial rush of blood to the head aside, a truly horrible free kick from Henry was a candidate for the skew of this, or any other season, ending up in the stand on the opposite side of the pitch.

United's joy was unconfined at Giggs' riposte to Henry's second – and rather offside-looking strike on 62 minutes – a neat downward header from Solskjaer's Beckham-esque cross silencing the North London faithful within a minute.

United headed north with a crucial point in the bag. And after last season's sorry run against the big guns, ending the league campaign unbeaten against Arsenal, Liverpool, Newcastle and Chelsea can be considered a job well done.

Premiership table
At the end of 16/04/03

	P	PTS
1 Manchester United	34	71
2 Arsenal	33	68
3 Newcastle United	33	61
4 Chelsea	33	60
5 Everton	33	56
6 Liverpool	33	55
7 Blackburn Rovers	33	52
8 Tottenham Hotspur	33	47
9 Middlesbrough	33	46
10 Charlton Athletic	33	46
11 Southampton	32	45
12 Manchester City	33	42
13 Leeds United	33	38
14 Aston Villa	33	38
15 Fulham	33	38
16 Birmingham City	33	38
17 Bolton Wanderers	33	35
18 West Ham United	33	32
19 West Bromwich Albion	33	21
20 Sunderland	33	19

Sir Alex Ferguson

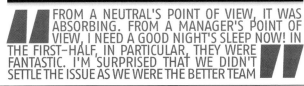

FROM A NEUTRAL'S POINT OF VIEW, IT WAS ABSORBING. FROM A MANAGER'S POINT OF VIEW, I NEED A GOOD NIGHT'S SLEEP NOW! IN THE FIRST-HALF, IN PARTICULAR, THEY WERE FANTASTIC. I'M SURPRISED THAT WE DIDN'T SETTLE THE ISSUE AS WE WERE THE BETTER TEAM

Manchester United 3
Van Nistelrooy 20, Scholes 41, 61

Blackburn Rovers 1
Berg 25

Phil Neville hitches a ride on scorer Ruud

Sharp-shooter Scholes gets the better of Short

On this very weekend 10 years ago, Blackburn Rovers defeated Aston Villa 3-0 at Ewood Park to inflict a grievous dent in the Midlanders' hopes of winning the first FA Premier League title. A few days later Villa capitulated again, at home to Oldham Athletic, and the championship was on its way to Old Trafford for the first time in more than a quarter of a century.

Fortunately, history wasn't about to repeat and extend a helping hand to Arsenal, United's running mates in this season's title race. Elsewhere on this particular day the Gunners were quietly helping themselves to three points against Steve McClaren's Middlesbrough at the Riverside.

The previous Wednesday's head-on clash between United and Arsenal in north London had provided little indication as to which way the pendulum will make its final swing at the season's close. So for both clubs the mission was simple – win all their remaining fixtures while expanding their goal differences.

This was United's fourth meeting with Rovers this season, and in keeping with earlier encounters, there was little to choose between the teams overall. Graeme Souness has assembled an exciting side which gave a solid and, at times, polished performance against a determined United, but they had no answer to the Reds' twin striking terrors. Ruud van Nistelrooy put United ahead after 20 minutes, with his 38th of the season to date.

Former United defender Henning Berg levelled the scores with a looping far-post header five minutes later, but Paul Scholes restored the lead shortly before the break after Phil Neville had opened up the visitors' defence with a charge down the left wing.

Moments after the break, Rovers were presented with a great opportunity to draw level when Ricardo, on for his Premiership debut in place of the injured Fabien Barthez, felled Andy Cole. David Dunn accepted the spot-kick responsibility, but was outfoxed by the Spaniard, whose dive to his left proved correct.

United eventually put the game beyond Rovers' reach in the 61st minute, when Scholes tapped in his second after some sterling approach play by Giggs and van Nistelrooy.

Sir Alex Ferguson

" I AM HAPPY WITH THE RESULT BUT I WAS DISAPPOINTED WE DIDN'T SCORE MORE GOALS. WE HAD SOME GREAT OPPORTUNITIES, ALTHOUGH THEIR GOALKEEPER MADE TWO OR THREE MAGNIFICENT SAVES AND WE HAD ONE ATTEMPT BLOCKED ON THE LINE. THEY HAD A REAL GO AT US "

**Saturday
19 April 2003
Old Trafford**
Attendance: **67,626**
Referee: **Andy D'Urso**

Manchester United: Barthez (Ricardo 46); Brown, Ferdinand, Silvestre, P Neville; Beckham, Scholes, Butt (Keane 55), Fortune, Giggs (Solskjaer 83); van Nistelrooy
Subs not used: G Neville, Forlan

Blackburn Rovers: Friedel; Neill, Berg (Taylor 64), Short, Gresko; Dunn, Flitcroft, Tugay, Duff (Suker 66); Cole, Yorke
Sub not used: Kelly, Grabbi, Todd

Possession	
47%	**53%**
Shots on target	
12	**2**
Shots off target	
6	**7**
Corners	
7	**3**
Offsides	
2	**3**
Fouls	
14	**12**

Man of the match
PAUL SCHOLES

There were numerous outstanding displays from players on both sides in this match, but United's pocket dynamo gets the nod because he decorated his performance with two vital strikes – the second of which saw him break the 100-goal barrier for the Reds. A true matchwinner.

Premiership results
Weekend beginning 18/04/03

Aston Villa	2-1	Chelsea
Bolton Wanderers	1-0	West Ham United
Charlton Athletic	0-2	Birmingham City
Everton	1-2	Liverpool
Fulham	2-1	Newcastle United
Middlesbrough	0-2	Arsenal
Southampton	3-2	Leeds United
Sunderland	1-2	West Bromwich Albion
Tottenham Hotspur	0-2	Manchester City

Premiership table
Top 10 at the end of 21/04/03

	P	PTS
1 Manchester United	35	74
2 Arsenal	34	71
3 Chelsea	35	63
4 Newcastle United	35	62
5 Liverpool	35	61
6 Everton	35	56
7 Blackburn Rovers	35	53
8 Tottenham Hotspur	35	50
9 Southampton	34	48
10 Manchester City	35	48

Ruud keeps his eye firmly on the ball

Tottenham Hotspur 0

Manchester United 2

Scholes 67, van Nistelrooy 90

Almost there: Ruud's face says it all

Saturday
27 April 2003
White Hart Lane
Attendance: **36,073**
Referee: **Jeff Winter**

When United completed the league leg of the Treble four years ago against Tottenham, the Spurs fans had banners saying "Let Them Win." And if the mood in the stands was the same this time, the sentiment failed to filter to goalkeeper Kasey Keller, who made it his day's mission to hand the impetus back to rivals Arsenal with a string of saves. But good things come to those who wait, and United's relentless attacks were rewarded with late goals from two Reds in unstoppable form.

With Roy Carroll in goal in place of Fabien Barthez and Paul Scholes and David Beckham restored to the side, United charged at the Spurs goal with just 15 seconds gone, only for Ruud van Nistelrooy to be thwarted by Keller – not for the last time. In fact, van Nistelrooy could have broken his 40-goal mark for the season on at least five first-half occasions.

At the other end of the park Carroll was rarely threatened, save for a brave block at the feet of Robbie Keane. Keane's namesake and former international captain worked tirelessly in the centre of the pitch, driving his team-mates on and launching a few well-timed verbal rockets whenever concentration and work-rate dropped below what he considered acceptable standards. It did the trick... despite the best efforts of Keller.

The second half started where the first left off, with the Spurs keeper tipping a fierce Solskjaer drive over the bar. Teddy Sheringham had the travelling fans cheering when he almost turned into his own net, forcing a rueful grin from the former Red.

With 18 goals in the last five league games, it seemed impossible that such continuous pressure would go unrewarded, and with 21 minutes remaining United made the breakthrough. Beckham supplied a pinpoint pass which was cleverly flicked by Scholes into the path of Ryan Giggs. Scholes continued into the box just in time to meet Giggs' perfect cross and open the scoring.

The win looked inevitable but these days no United victory is complete without a goal from van Nistelrooy, and the Dutchman duly delivered in the dying seconds – slotting home after a wonderful break from substitute Quinton Fortune.

Tottenham Hotspur: Keller; Carr, Taricco, King, Richards (Gardner 31); Davies, Poyet, Toda (Iversen 78), Etherington (Bunjevcevic 79); Sheringham, Keane
Subs not used: Sullivan, Acimovic

Manchester United: Carroll; Brown (G Neville 54), O'Shea, Ferdinand, Silvestre; Beckham, Keane, Scholes, Giggs; van Nistelrooy, Solskjaer (Fortune 72)
Subs not used: Blanc, Ricardo, Forlan

Possession
| 53% | 47% |

Shots on target
| 8 | 2 |

Shots off target
| 8 | 3 |

Corners
| 8 | 5 |

Offsides
| 1 | 3 |

Fouls
| 12 | 11 |

Man of the match
ROY KEANE
To coin a phrase, reports of Keano's demise have been greatly exaggerated. United's inspirational captain was at his harrying, hustling best and made sure this latest hurdle was safely negotiated.

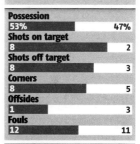

Premiership results
Weekend beginning 26/04/03
Birmingham City	3–0	Middlesbrough
Bolton Wanderers	2–2	Arsenal
Charlton Athletic	2–1	Southampton
Chelsea	1–1	Fulham
Everton	2–1	Aston Villa
Leeds United	2–3	Blackburn Rovers
Manchester City	0–1	West Ham United
Sunderland	0–1	Newcastle United
West Bromwich Albion	0–6	Liverpool

Premiership table
Top 10 at the end of 27/04/03
	P	PTS
1 Manchester United	36	77
2 Arsenal	35	72
3 Newcastle United	36	65
4 Chelsea	36	64
5 Liverpool	36	64
6 Everton	36	59
7 Blackburn Rovers	36	56
8 Tottenham Hotspur	36	50
9 Charlton Athletic	36	49
10 Southampton	35	48

Sir Alex Ferguson

PAUL SCHOLES WAS MARVELLOUS. IS THERE ANYONE BETTER AT GHOSTING INTO THE PENALTY BOX AND GETTING THOSE KIND OF CHANCES? I SAID AT HALF-TIME THAT PERSEVERANCE IS NECESSARY. RUUD'S GOAL KILLED THE GAME AND I COULD RELAX FOR AT LEAST THREE MINUTES

MAY

West Ham's bubble burst, Liverpool's Champions League place disappeared and United clinched an eighth Premiership title to kickstart the biggest party seen on Merseyside in years

As fans prepared for the title race to go down to the wire, old foes Leeds United recorded an improbable victory at Highbury on Sunday 4th May which confirmed United as champions for the 15th time – the eighth success in 11 years. The celebrations began immediately with few complaints that United had once again won the league without playing.

Elsewhere, issues remained unresolved until the final batch of games. With £500,000 in prize money per league position, Southampton's victory over Manchester City in the final game at Maine Road was worth £2million to the FA Cup finalists. Chelsea beat Liverpool for a more substantial prize – Champions League football. Liverpool reluctantly settled for the UEFA Cup, the competition neighbours Everton narrowly missed out on when United beat them prior to the trophy being presented at Goodison Park.

At the bottom end, Bolton stayed up and West Ham were relegated on a dramatic final day, the Hammers' impressive run of results under stand-in manager Trevor Brooking proving too little, too late.

For jubilant Reds lucky enough to get a ticket for Goodison and the chance to savour one of the most satisfying title triumphs imaginable, everything else was simply a side issue. Just when it seemed that half an hour of jumping about and singing "Champions" was enough, Ruud van Nistelrooy ran the width of the pitch and dodged a policeman before whipping his shirt off and throwing it, javelin style, into the throng of adoring United fans. A life affirming moment.

Barclaycard Premiership fixtures this month

Saturday 3rd	Charlton Athletic	Home
Sunday 11th	Everton	Away

In the Barclaycard Premiership this month

107,889
watched United play two games

United scored	United travelled
6 goals	**68** miles to and from games

	United fielded a total of
but conceded **2** goals	**16** players

FOCUS ON ROY KEANE

To win the Premiership, teams need a large dose of drive, courage, bottle and determination. During the most exciting title chase English football has seen in years, Manchester United had Roy Keane. The skipper performed heroically in the last quarter of the league season, particularly in the final three games against Spurs, Charlton and Everton. It's a credit to his leadership abilities that United made it look so easy in the end, when lesser teams could have crumbled under the pressure of playing catch-up all season. Keano being Keano, he was already looking forward to next season. "I know some of the lads are saying this one's the sweetest because we weren't playing particularly well at times, had a few injury problems and people were writing us off, but I always think the next one will be the sweetest…"

Manchester United 4
Beckham 11, van Nistelrooy 32, 37, 53

Charlton Athletic 1
Jensen 13

A familiar sight as Ruud laps up the applause

Beckham's joy at opening the scoring is apparent

Ole Gunnar Solskjaer had a great game

MATCH FACTS

Saturday
3 May 2003
Old Trafford
Attendance: **67,721**
Referee: **Mark Halsey**

Old Trafford waved goodbye to league action for another season as United edged ever closer to a record eighth Premiership title. Nothing less than a resounding victory was required against Charlton, and the Reds duly delivered in front of another record crowd. But, with the title not yet in the bag, the mood was one of anticipation mixed with satisfaction, rather than all-out jubilation.

David Beckham opened the scoring for United after just 11 minutes, sparking huge celebrations from the fans, not to mention the goalscorer. Mikael Silvestre whipped in a cross which was won in the box by Ruud van Nistelrooy. The ball fell to Beckham and Chris Powell's despairing lunge failed to stop it flying past Dean Kiely.

With the opening goal secured the full range of songs started pumping out of the stands, but just two minutes later Reds were momentarily silenced when Charlton levelled. Roy Keane slid a back pass to Roy Carroll but he sliced his clearance straight to Claus Jensen who lobbed the ball into the empty net.

It was almost 20 minutes before United regained the lead, but with Ruud van Nistelrooy in the form of his life, there was no doubt it was only a matter of time. The first goal of the latest hat-trick was a moment of poacher's genius and again, Silvestre and Beckham were involved. The England captain's corner was knocked down by Silvestre and van Nistelrooy swivelled acrobatically to fire a volley into the net. And if there was a feeling of surprise about the goal it wasn't that Ruud had scored again, more that it had come from a United corner, for the first time in the league this season. Just five minutes later, Ruud scored his second and put the result beyond any doubt. Again it started with a Silvestre cross, flicked on by Ole Solskjaer into the path of van Nistelrooy who controlled it perfectly and lifted it over Kiely.

This was no one man show, though. Ryan Giggs, Ole Gunnar Solskjaer and John O'Shea excelled once again and on any other Saturday Roy Keane would have walked home with the man-of-the-match award. But with Ruud netting his 43rd United goal of the season and scoring for the record-equalling ninth successive game, the champagne and another match ball was in the bag.

Manchester United: Carroll; O'Shea, Brown, Ferdinand, Silvestre; Beckham, Keane, Scholes (Veron 69), Giggs (Butt 77); van Nistelrooy, Solskjaer (Forlan 77)
Subs Not Used: Barthez, P Neville

Charlton Athletic: Kiely; Kishishev (Sankofa 73), Young, J Fortune, Powell; Lisbie (Johansson 84), Jensen, Parker, Konchesky; Bartlett, Euell (Bart-Williams 78)
Subs Not Used: Rachubka, Stuart
Booked: J Fortune

Possession	
54%	46%
Shots on target	
7	2
Shots off target	
8	2
Corners	
11	3
Offsides	
1	2
Fouls	
7	9

Man of the match
RUUD VAN NISTELROOY

The perfect response to the news that Thierry Henry had been named PFA and Football Writers' Player of the Year. Each goal in this latest hat-trick showcased a different quality – instinct, precision, power – but really, adjectives haven't been invented to describe the way van Nistelrooy has ended the season.

Premiership results
Weekend beginning 3/05/03

Aston Villa	1-0	Sunderland
Blackburn Rovers	1-1	West Bromwich Albion
Fulham	2-0	Everton
Liverpool	1-2	Manchester City
Middlesbrough	5-1	Tottenham Hotspur
Newcastle United	1-0	Birmingham City
Southampton	0-0	Bolton Wanderers
West Ham United	1-0	Chelsea
Arsenal	2-3	Leeds United

Premiership table
Top 10 at the end of 4/05/03

	P	PTS
1 Manchester United	37	80
2 Arsenal	36	72
3 Newcastle United	37	68
4 Chelsea	37	64
5 Liverpool	37	64
6 Everton	37	59
7 Blackburn Rovers	37	57
8 Manchester City	37	51
9 Tottenham Hotspur	37	50
10 Middlesbrough	37	49

Sir Alex Ferguson

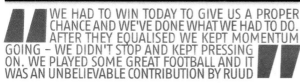

WE HAD TO WIN TODAY TO GIVE US A PROPER CHANCE AND WE'VE DONE WHAT WE HAD TO DO. AFTER THEY EQUALISED WE KEPT MOMENTUM GOING – WE DIDN'T STOP AND KEPT PRESSING ON. WE PLAYED SOME GREAT FOOTBALL AND IT WAS AN UNBELIEVABLE CONTRIBUTION BY RUUD

Everton 1
Campbell 8

Manchester United 2
Beckham 43, van Nistelrooy 79 (penalty)

While an afternoon of high drama was being played out all over the country, it was nothing more than party time for United on Merseyside. There was the small matter of an eighth Premiership trophy to be returned to its rightful owners after the game, but Roy Keane and the lads made sure the season ended on a high note – delivering United's 25th win of the league campaign.

Wayne Rooney's arrival on the scene has been nothing sort of breathtaking, but he must have stolen a glance at United's frontman and realised he has a long, long way to go before he's the finished article. When Ruud van Nistelrooy slotted home his penalty he became the first United player in history to score in 10 successive matches, and his 44 goals for the season gave him England's Golden Boot – beating Thierry Henry and James Beattie. The spot kick secured the win after David Beckham's outrageous free kick had cancelled out Kevin Campbell's early header.

Elsewhere, Paul Scholes was looking to add to his own record goal haul, but was thwarted by Toffees keeper Richard Wright on three occasions. Wes Brown's season ended early when his studs caught in the ground forcing him off before half-time. The

Altogether now: "We've got our trophy back..."

prognosis was a serious cruciate injury, another injury setback for the young defender. Laurent Blanc was given his chance to say goodbye after the break and must have been secretly looking forward to retirement when he was booked for a late lunge on Rooney, some 20 years his junior.

The day fell flat for Everton, however. Their defeat, coupled with Blackburn's win at Spurs, meant they had missed out on Europe, despite a Champions League place looking a distinct possibility earlier in the season. After waving goodbye to the home fans, a downcast but dignified David Moyes led his players in forming a guard of honour for the reinstated champions. After that, United players, staff and fans partied like it was 1999.

Sir Alex Ferguson

IT'S A GREAT DAY FOR MANCHESTER UNITED. DON'T BELIEVE ALL THE STORIES THAT'VE COME FROM SOUTH OF THE BIRMINGHAM DIVIDE – WE PROVED OURSELVES AS CHAMPIONS. I'M GLAD FOR THE PLAYERS AND I'M GLAD FOR THE FANS. I THINK WE'LL ENJOY OUR SUMMER BETTER THIS YEAR

The heart of United celebrate another Premiership crown

Sunday
11 May 2003
Goodison Park
Attendance: **40,168**
Referee: **Mike Riley**

Everton: Wright; Hibbert, Yobo, Stubbs, Unsworth; Watson, Carsley, Gravesen (N Chadwick 75), Naysmith (Pistone 83); Rooney, Campbell (Ferguson 40)
Subs not used: Simonsen, Gemmill
Booked: Hibbert, Stubbs, Gravesen, Rooney, Ferguson

Manchester United: Carroll; Brown (P Neville 40), Ferdinand, Silvestre, O'Shea (Blanc 45); Beckham, Keane, Scholes, Giggs, van Nistelrooy, Solskjaer (Fortune 78)
Subs not used: Veron, Butt
Booked: Ferdinand, P Neville, Blanc

Possession	
55%	**45%**
Shots on target	
10	**5**
Shots off target	
11	**7**
Corners	
6	**6**
Offsides	
1	**5**
Fouls	
16	**17**

Man of the match
ROY KEANE
Inspirational yet again. In the last few weeks of the season the captain made sure United galloped over the finishing line, with no let-up even when the title was won. Just think how he'll benefit from a long, relaxing and controversy-free summer...

Premiership results
Weekend beginning 11/05/03

Birmingham City	2-2	West Ham United	
Bolton Wanderers	2-1	Middlesbrough	
Charlton Athletic	0-1	Fulham	
Chelsea	2-1	Liverpool	
Leeds United	3-1	Aston Villa	
Manchester City	0-1	Southampton	
Sunderland	0-4	Arsenal	
Tottenham Hotspur	0-4	Blackburn Rovers	
West Bromwich Albion	2-2	Newcastle United	

Premiership table
Top 10 at the end of 11/05/03

	P	PTS
1 Manchester United	38	83
2 Arsenal	38	78
3 Newcastle United	38	69
4 Chelsea	38	67
5 Liverpool	38	64
6 Blackburn Rovers	38	60
7 Everton	38	59
8 Southampton	38	52
9 Manchester City	38	51
10 Tottenham Hotspur	38	50

Sir Alex and the first team celebrate at Carrington, a day after Leeds' victory over Arsenal guaranteed United another title

CHAMPIONS LEAGUE PHASE 1

United successfully negotiated the qualifying round and first phase of the continent's premier club tournament – which is more than can be said for old European foes Bayern Munich

United steered a path into the Champions League after disposing of Hungarians Zalaegerszeg, despite losing the first competitive game of the season. Both Milan clubs survived the qualifying rounds as did Barcelona, but Celtic weren't so fortunate. The Scottish champs went out to FC Basel on away goals, although their subsequent trip all the way to the UEFA Cup final made up for that disappointment.

The majority of the heavyweights strolled through the first group phase. Barcelona were the only team to achieve the maximum 18 points available, although United, Juventus, Valencia and Internazionale qualified with points to spare. Real Madrid, Arsenal and Milan topped tight groups, and were joined in the next phase by Newcastle United, Borussia Dortmund, Roma, Deportivo La Coruña, Ajax, Bayer Leverkusen, Lokomotiv Moscow and FC Basel. The Swiss club claimed the scalp of Liverpool along the way.

The major shock was the early exit of Bayern Munich. Germany's most celebrated club had an abject campaign, picking up just two points in a group containing Lens, Deportivo and Milan. Ottmar Hitzfeld's charges lost all four matches against their Spanish and Italian rivals and picked up a couple of draws against the French side Lens. Bayern legend Franz Beckenbauer was not happy. "All the teams of distinction are playing in the second group phase, except for us," he fumed. "It will hurt just to sit in front of the television." The Germans recovered and strolled to a record 18th *Bundesliga* title in April.

Champions League qualifier/ Phase 1

Weds 14th Aug	Zalaegerszeg	Away
Tues 27th Aug	Zalaegerszeg	Home
Weds 18th Sept	Maccabi Haifa	Home
Tues 24th Sept	Bayer 04 Leverkusen	Away
Tues 1st Oct	Olympiakos Piraeus	Home
Weds 23rd Oct	Olympiakos Piraeus	Away
Tues 29th Oct	Maccabi Haifa	Away
Weds 13th Nov	Bayer 04 Leverkusen	Home

In the UEFA Champions League Phase 1

361,060
watched United play eight games

United scored

21
goals

but conceded

10
goals

United travelled

11,208
miles to and from games

United fielded a total of

25
players

GOAL OF PHASE 1 JUAN SEBASTIAN VERON V OLYMPIAKOS, 1/10/02

Juan Sebastian Veron scored four goals in the UEFA Champions League this season, all of them coming in Phase 1. The first was a rocket against Maccabi Haifa at Old Trafford, then a sweet volley opened the scoring at home to Bayer Leverkusen and he grabbed a vital strike in Athens against Olympiakos. The pick of the bunch also came against the Greek side – this time in Manchester. With nearly half an hour gone and United 1–0 up thanks to a goal from Ryan Giggs, Seba combined with David Beckham. On collecting the return pass from his midfield partner, Veron stroked the ball with the outside of his boot over the dumbstruck goalkeeper Dimitrios Eleftheropoulos. A football genius from Argentina, the Stretford End decided. Right on both counts.

Zalaegerszeg 1
Koplarovics 90

Manchester United 0

MATCHFACTS

Wednesday 14 August 2002
Ferenc Puskas
Stadium
Attendance: **40,000**
Referee: **Wolfgang**
Stark (Germany)

Zalaegerszeg: Ilics; Szamosi, Budisa, Urbán, Babati; Faragó (Balogh 74), Egressy (Molnár 65), Csóka, Kenesei (Koplárovics 83); Ljubojevic, Vincze **Subs not used:** Turi, Sabo, Kral, Józsi
Booked: Ilics, Molnár

Manchester United: Carroll; Brown (P Neville 5), Blanc, O'Shea, Silvestre; Beckham, Veron, Keane, Giggs; Solskjaer (Forlan 80), van Nistelrooy
Subs not used: Butt, Stewart, Scholes, Tierney, Williams
Booked: Beckham, van Nistelrooy

Possession	
56%	44%
Shots on target	
5	3
Shots off target	
7	1
Corners	
8	5
Offsides	
9	3
Fouls	
14	20

United prepare to launch their latest European campaign

PUSKÁS FERENC STADION

Man of the match
OLE GUNNAR SOLSKJAER
The Norwegian hit the post after six minutes and was a constant threat to the ZTE defence. His movement, particularly in the first half when he regularly found space, was a factor in most of United's best moves. He also had a shot cleared off the line.

Sir Alex Ferguson

WE ONLY HAD OURSELVES TO BLAME BECAUS WE CONTROLLED THE GAME, ESPECIALLY IN THE SECOND HALF. WE ENJOYED COMPLETE DOMINATION, ONLY TO LOSE OUR CONCENTRATION AND LET THEM IN FOR A LATE WINNER. THE RESULT WAS A SHOCK FOR US

United's latest Champions League campaign got off to a shaky start with a defeat in the first leg of this qualifying tie at the hands of Hungarian champions Zalaegerszeg. And unlike the famous night in the Nou Camp in 1999, this time it was our turn to experience the cruel finality of a goal conceded in the dying seconds.

Normal time had already elapsed when substitute Béla Koplárovics stabbed home a low cross from Tamás Szamosi to give the home team a shock win. This wasn't supposed to happen. United were strong favourites and, despite losing Wes Brown with a broken ankle after five minutes, did much to justify that status in the early stages. In the fourth minute, Ole Gunnar Solskjaer controlled a lobbed pass from Ruud van Nistelrooy and beat the keeper, but his left-foot shot rebounded off the post.

After repelling United's early surges, ZTE began to mount some pressure of their own but their counter-attacks rarely produced a threat on goal. In the second half, United continued to dominate territorially, but the fitful attacks were too often sabotaged by an imprecise touch or wayward pass. True, those chances were not aided by a blustery wind and a playing surface scarred with divots but, these factors aside, this was a game the Reds could and should have won.

During the second half, van Nistelrooy had a goal disallowed, Roy Keane headed wide from a corner and David Beckham burst forward to drive a low shot into the body of former Charlton keeper Szasa Ilics.

Manchester United 5
van Nistelrooy 6, 76 (penalty), Beckham 15, Scholes 21, Solskjaer 84

Zalaegerszeg 0

Tuesday
27 August 2002
Old Trafford
Attendance: **66,814**
Referee: **Lucilio Cortez**
Batista (Portugal)

REVIEW
SHOOTING STAR

failure to overturn a 1-0 deficit from the first leg would have meant disaster for United, but Reds needn't have worried. A rampant performance made short work of Zalaegerszeg, who finally succumbed under the bright lights of Old Trafford.

Ruud van Nistelrooy got the party started after six minutes when he ran onto a Paul Scholes pass and slipped it past Szasa Ilics. David Beckham made it two on 15 minutes with one of his trademark free kicks and six minutes later it was 3-0, with Scholes slotting home from close range.

In 21 minutes of football, United not only brought themselves back into the game – they practically won it. This may have been Rio Ferdinand's full United debut but he couldn't have wished for a quieter match. It wasn't until the 43rd minute that ZTE tested Roy Carroll at all, as he kept hold of a Krisztian Kenesi free kick.

The night was spoiled somewhat just after the interval by the sight of Scholes being stretchered away in the wake of a crushing tackle that left him with a twisted ankle. Ole Gunnar Solskjaer ably replaced him, however, and helped maintain United's spell of relentless pressure from the previous half.

With 15 minutes to go, Ilics was red-carded for a dangerous challenge on Ruud in the box and the Dutchman converted the resultant penalty with customary decisiveness. Not long after Solskjaer had knocked in the fifth, Diego Forlan was denied his first competitive goal for the club when he headed in a Giggs cross which had been judged out of play.

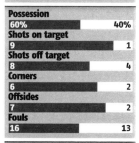

Manchester United: Carroll; P Neville, Ferdinand (O'Shea 68), Blanc, Silvestre; Beckham (Forlan 72), Keane, Veron, Scholes (Solskjaer 50); Giggs, van Nistelrooy
Subs not used: Williams, Chadwick, Stewart, Tierney

Zalaegerszeg: Ilics; Csoka, Urban, Budisa, Szamosi; Babati (Turi 75), Darko Ljubojevic (Farago 59), Molnar, Vincze (Balogh 64); Kenesei, Egressy
Subs not used: Sabo, Kral, Koplarovic, Joszi
Booked: Molnar **Sent Off:** Ilics

Possession	
60%	40%
Shots on target	
9	1
Shots off target	
8	4
Corners	
6	2
Offsides	
7	2
Fouls	
16	13

Man of the match
PAUL SCHOLES
For the 50 minutes he was on the field, Scholes was quite magical. The gentle touch to set up van Nistelrooy's first goal was sublime, and Scholes' mischievous creativity troubled the Zalaegerszeg defence all night.

Sir Alex Ferguson

> WE HIT THEM WITH THE PACE WE NEEDED, ESPECIALLY IN THE FIRST HALF, AND THEY JUST COULDN'T LIVE WITH US. THE SPEED OF OUR PASSING WAS AGAIN EXCEPTIONAL AND EVERYONE WORKED SO HARD THAT NOTHING WAS LEFT TO CHANCE. IT WAS OUR NIGHT

Phil Neville is first to congratulate David Beckham

Manchester United 5
Giggs 10, Solskjaer 35, Veron 46, van Nistelrooy 54, Forlan 89

Maccabi Haifa 2
Katan 8, Cohen 89

David Beckham
congratulates
Diego Forlan

Ruud netted
United's
fourth

Diego heads
for goal

MATCH FACTS

Wednesday
18 September 2002
Old Trafford
Attendance: **63,439**
Referee: **Paul**
Allaerts (Belgium)

United's Champions League adventure got off to a flyer with seven goals, two debuts and a long-awaited goal from a certain Uruguayan 22-year-old. United fans went home happy but it was all so different seven minutes into the match, when the unthinkable happened: Maccabi Haifa took a shock lead.

The Champions League debutants should have been overawed by the occasion but Haifa had obviously mislaid the script. They broke out of defence and, three touches later, United were 1-0 down. It was the the third match in a row that the Reds had gone behind. The architect of the goal was Walid Badir (who scored at Old Trafford for Wimbledon exactly three years previously) and it was neatly executed by Yaniv Katan, who sent the 3,000 travelling supporters into delirium.

Two minutes later the Reds equalised and 60,000 United fans breathed a collective sigh of relief. Phil Neville floated a ball into the box and Ryan Giggs rose to glance a header into the net. United took the lead on the half-hour when Ruud van Nistelrooy fed Ole Gunnar Solskjaer, who netted with the neatest of touches. It wasn't going all United's way, however, and Haifa twice went close before the half-time whistle.

If the first half was a struggle the second half was a stroll, and it took just 22 seconds for United to extend their lead. Sir Alex had hardly taken his place in the dug-out when Haifa gave away possession to Giggs. United broke and the ball ended up with Seba Veron, who thundered a fierce shot into the net. Less than 10 minutes later the Argentinian pinged a 40-yard pass into the Haifa box, which was expertly finished by Ruud for his second goal in open play this season.

On 55 minutes, Giggs made way for Diego Forlan and somehow we knew tonight would be the night Diego would break his duck. There were plenty of chances but the goal didn't come until the 89th minute, when he converted a spot kick awarded after David Beckham was felled inside the box. There were second-half debuts for keeper Ricardo and 19-year-old Danny Pugh, as well as a late goal for Haifa's Cohen, but the night belonged to you know who.

Sir Alex Ferguson

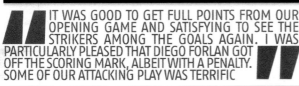

IT WAS GOOD TO GET FULL POINTS FROM OUR OPENING GAME AND SATISFYING TO SEE THE STRIKERS AMONG THE GOALS AGAIN. I WAS PARTICULARLY PLEASED THAT DIEGO FORLAN GOT OFF THE SCORING MARK, ALBEIT WITH A PENALTY. SOME OF OUR ATTACKING PLAY WAS TERRIFIC

Manchester United: Barthez (Ricardo 67); O'Shea, Blanc, Ferdinand, Silvestre; Beckham, Veron, P Neville, Giggs (Forlan 56); van Nistelrooy (Pugh 75), Solskjaer
Subs not used: G Neville, May, Chadwick, Stewart

Maccabi Haifa: Awat; Harazi (Cohen 74), Benado, Ejifor, Keissi, Almoshnino (Zano 56); Badir, Paralija, Rosso; Zandberg (Israilevich), Katan
Subs not used: Al Madon, Levy, Gabrin, Nagar **Booked:** Rosso

Possession	
60%	40%

Shots on target	
15	5

Shots off target	
7	5

Corners	
12	2

Offsides	
2	4

Fouls	
7	11

Man of the match
DIEGO FORLAN
Has Old Trafford ever wanted a goal from one player so badly? This was the night Diego's luck changed to reward the consistent workrate that has endeared the Uruguayan to United fans. The goal eventually came from a penalty but the smile that lit up Manchester said it all.

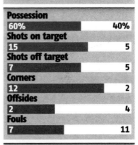

UEFA Champions League Phase 1 results 17/18 September 2002

Group A Arsenal	2-0	Dortmund
Auxerre	0-0	PSV
Group B FC Basel	2-0	Spartak
Valencia	2-0	Liverpool
Group C Genk	0-0	AEK Athens
Roma	0-3	Real Madrid
Group D Ajax	2-1	Lyon
Rosenborg	2-2	Internazionale
Group E Dynamo Kiev	2-0	Newcastle
Feyenoord	1-1	Juventus
Group F Olympiakos	6-2	Leverkusen
Group G Bayern Munich	2-3	Deportivo
AC Milan	2-1	Lens
Group H Barcelona	3-2	Club Brugge
Lokomotiv Moscow	0-2	Galatasaray

Phase 1 Group F table

At the end of 18/09/02	P	PTS
1 Olympiakos	1	3
2 Manchester United	1	3
3 Maccabi Haifa	1	0
4 Bayer Leverkusen	1	0

Bayer 04 Leverkusen 1
Berbatov 52

Manchester United 2
Van Nistelrooy 31, 44

Ruud grabs the crucial second goal for United

This will be remembered as the night United won in Germany for the first time in 37 years, but it was more of a struggle than it should have been given the scintillating first-half performance. United dominated with Ruud van Nistelrooy grabbing his fourth and fifth European goals of the season, but in the end the Reds in blue were happy to hold onto the win.

Bayer Leverkusen started as a shadow of the side that put United out at the semi-final stage last year and they looked even more depleted early on when Oliver Neuville, United's scourge last season, trudged off injured. United were looking dangerous and they opened the scoring on 31 minutes with a brilliant attacking move. Seba Veron picked up the ball wide on the left and delivered a looping cross that fooled the Leverkusen defence but reached van Nistelrooy, who expertly finished through the keeper's legs.

United had a scare 10 minutes later when Rio Ferdinand was booked after getting involved with Leverkusen's Thomas Brdaric on the edge of the box, but it didn't take long for United to extend the lead with the most sublime goal of the season so far. Phil Neville, again impressing in midfield, won the ball and found Ryan Giggs

Tuesday
24 September 2002
BayArena
Attendance: **22,500**
Referee: **Jan Wegereef (Holland)**

Bayer 04 Leverkusen: Jurić; Živković, Ramelow, Lucio; Balitsch (Franca 81), Babic, Ojigwe (Simak 64); Schneider, Basturk; Brdaric; Neuville (Berbatov 22)
Subs not used: Bierofka, Vranjes, Kleine

Manchester United: Barthez; O'Shea (G Neville 46), Ferdinand, Blanc, Silvestre; Beckham, Veron (Solskjaer 88), P Neville, Butt; Giggs; van Nistelrooy (Forlan 46)
Subs not used: Ricardo, May, Stewart, Pugh
Booked: Butt, Ferdinand

Possession	
47%	53%

Shots on target	
2	3

Shots off target	
3	9

Corners	
0	7

Offsides	
2	2

Fouls	
18	9

Man of the match
RUUD VAN NISTELROOY

The Dutch striker put last year's Champions League finalists to the sword almost single-handedly with a devastating first half performance before going off with a tight hamstring, as a precautionary measure. One thing is for certain, this is a competition that brings out the best in van Nistelrooy.

Diego Forlan takes the fight to Leverkusen

who slid a perfect ball to Nicky Butt in the box. Butt could have shot but instead passed to van Nistelrooy who finished sweetly to round off an effervescent first-half display from the Reds.

The second half opened with Gary Neville replacing Veron and van Nistelrooy making way for Diego Forlan, but after five minutes substitute Dimitar Berbatov pulled one back for the home side and United began to look rattled. The Germans were roused by the goal and went close on numerous occasions, none more so than when Berbatov hit the inside of the post with a glancing header. Leverkusen had by far the better of the second half but United showed enough resilience to claim three vital points and the first-ever win by a British side in the BayArena.

Sir Alex Ferguson

I HAVE TO PAY TRIBUTE TO VAN NISTELROOY'S TWO GOALS AND THE EXCELLENT BUILD-UPS WHICH PUT HIM IN. IT WAS GOOD TO SEE US GETTING BACK IN THE HABIT OF SCORING IN OUR AWAY GAMES IN EUROPE. WE WERE ON THE BACK FOOT AT TIMES, BUT OUR CONCENTRATION WAS GOOD

UEFA Champions League Phase 1 results 24/25 September 2002

Group A	Borussia Dortmund	2–1	Auxerre
	PSV Eindhoven	0–4	Arsenal
Group B	Liverpool	1–1	FC Basel
	Spartak Moscow	0–3	Liverpool
Group C	AEK Athens	0–0	Roma
	Real Madrid	6–0	Genk
Group D	Internazionale	1–0	Ajax
	Lyon	5–0	Rosenborg
Group E	Juventus	5–0	Dynamo
	Newcastle United	0–1	Feyenoord
Group F	Maccabi Haifa	3–0	Olympiakos
Group G	Deportivo La Coruña	0–4	AC Milan
	Lens	0–0	Bayern Munich
Group H	Club Brugge	0–0	Lokomotiv
	Galatasaray	0–2	Barcelona

Phase 1 Group F table

At the end of 25/09/02	P	PTS
1 Manchester United	2	6
2 Olympiakos	2	3
3 Maccabi Haifa	2	3
4 Bayer 04 Leverkusen	2	0

Manchester United 4

Giggs 19, 67, Veron 26, Solskjaer 77

Olympiakos Piraeus FC 0

Seba Veron was a
constant headache
for Olympiakos

REVIEW

Tuesday
1 October 2002
Old Trafford
Attendance: **66,902**
Referee: **Gilles Veissiere (France)**

STANDING TALL

According to Sir Alex, the first 26 minutes of this match contained United's best football of the season so far. For the first time in two months, United reminded the fans what this team is capable of. Movement, pace, penetration, finishing and discipline were all on display as the Reds relentlessly steam-rollered a bewildered visiting Olympiakos.

Upon arriving in Manchester, the Greek side must have fancied their chances after annihilating Bayer Leverkusen 6-2 in their second game of the phase, but from the first whistle it was clear there was only going to be one winner.

United – ordered by the ref to play in their blue third strip to prevent a clash with the Greeks' away kit – looked dangerous from the off and were rarely out of the Olympiakos half in the opening stages of the match.

In the 19th minute the pressure bore fruit, and it was a classic move. Neville passed down the right to Beckham to Solskjaer, who picked out Scholes, who then cut the ball back for Giggs. The Welsh winger got the luck of the bounce when his first touch came off the defender, but he instinctively struck the rebound into the net.

Though there was much to be admired in Giggs' finish, in the 26th minute the Welshman was well and truly upstaged by Juan Veron. After playing a one-two with Beckham that left Olympiakos flat-footed, the Argentinian lifted an exquisite chip over the keeper with the outside of his right foot from 18 yards.

Things got even worse for the Greeks when just before half-time Ze Elias, who had gone close with a dipping shot, was sent off for scything down Seba and leaving him grounded.

The second half was less about flair and more about discipline, although it didn't stop United from netting two more goals. Giggs got his second 20 minutes after the break when his cross was deflected in by a hapless Olympiakos defender, and Solskjaer put his name on the score sheet on 77 minutes to round off events.

With an unfit van Nistelrooy watching from the directors' box, a goal fest was the last thing United fans would have expected but it was no fluke and, encouragingly, the goals came from everywhere.

Manchester United: Barthez; G Neville, Ferdinand, Blanc (O'Shea 67), Silvestre; Beckham, Butt, Veron, Giggs (Fortune 67); Scholes (Forlan 78), Solskjaer
Subs not used: Ricardo, P Neville, May, Stewart
Booked: G Neville, Veron, Ferdinand

Olympiakos Piraeus: Eleftheropoulos; Amanatidis, Anatolakis, Antzas, Venetidis; Giannakopoulos (Dracena 46), Karembeu, Ze Elias, Djordjevic; Zetterberg, Oforiquaye (Alexandris 59) **Subs not used:** Patsatzoglou, Giannou, Giovanni, Kostoulas, Niniadis **Booked:** Karembeu, Anatolakis, Kostoulas, Niniadis **Sent off:** Ze Elias

Possession	
62%	38%

Shots on target	
9	2

Shots off target	
3	4

Corners	
4	0

Offsides	
3	4

Fouls	
16	12

Man of the match
GARY NEVILLE

In his first start since April 2002, Gary immediately showed what a difference he makes to United. Assured in possession and disciplined in his marking, his mere presence gave the team a lift. David Beckham certainly looked happy to have his best pal back in the team after a long lay-off.

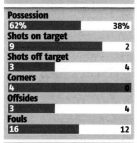

UEFA Champions League Phase 1 results 1/2 October 2002

Group A		
Auxerre	0-1	Arsenal
PSV Eindhoven	1-4	Dortmund
Group B Liverpool	5-0	Spartak
Valencia	6-2	FC Basel
Group C AEK Athens	3-3	Real Madrid
Genk	0-1	Roma
Group D Internazionale	1-2	Lyon
Rosenborg	0-0	Ajax
Group E Feyenoord	0-0	Dynamo
Juventus	2-0	Newcastle Utd
Group F Maccabi Haifa	0-2	Leverkusen
Group G Bayern Munich	1-2	AC Milan
Deportivo La Coruña	3-1	Bayern Munich
Group H Galatasaray	0-0	Club Brugge
Lokomotiv Moscow	1-3	Barcelona

Phase 1 Group F table
At the end of 2/1/2002

	P	PTS
1 Manchester United	3	9
2 Olympiakos	3	3
3 Bayer 04 Leverkusen	3	3
4 Maccabi Haifa	3	3

Sir Alex Ferguson

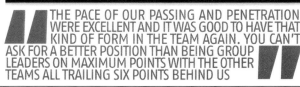

THE PACE OF OUR PASSING AND PENETRATION WERE EXCELLENT AND IT WAS GOOD TO HAVE THAT KIND OF FORM IN THE TEAM AGAIN. YOU CAN'T ASK FOR A BETTER POSITION THAN BEING GROUP LEADERS ON MAXIMUM POINTS WITH THE OTHER TEAMS ALL TRAILING SIX POINTS BEHIND US

Olympiakos Piraeus 2
Choutos 69, Djordjevic 73

Manchester United 3
Blanc 20, Veron 58, Scholes 83

Seba strikes to put United in front

Mikael Silvestre rides a strong challenge

"We never make it easy for ourselves," a relieved Sir Alex said after the final whistle – and after watching the Reds survive a nailbiting second-half wobble, the United fans who made the trip to Athens would certainly have concurred with his assessment.

On a humid night in Athens, Olympiakos, beset by all kinds of internal strife, seemed to bring their off-pitch woes with them onto the field. The opening stages saw them in complete disarray. In contrast, despite an arduous four-hour flight and 90-minute trek to the local training ground, United looked bright and eager.

After just five minutes the Reds almost grabbed the lead when a Laurent Blanc header was pushed wide, and then moments later Paul Scholes unleashed a ferocious strike from outside the box. With United enjoying almost total domination, and the Greek keeper Dimitrio Eleftheropoulos looking less than secure, a goal seemed inevitable.

The breakthrough eventually came after 20 minutes when, somehow standing alone in the centre of the penalty area, Blanc picked his spot and headed home from a David Beckham corner.

Just minutes after the restart Diego Forlan saw his shot saved, but it wasn't until the 58th minute that United added a second. Juan Sebastian Veron collected the ball in midfield, played a one-two with Ryan Giggs, then fired a low drive into the net from outside the box.

Confident that the Reds were in command, and mindful of the need to keep his players fresh for the challenges ahead, Sir Alex made a double substitution, replacing Giggs and Beckham with Quinton Fortune and Luke Chadwick. It was a decision, he later admitted, that almost backfired.

Seven minutes later Lampros Choutos capped a mazy run with a goal for Olympiakos, and within five minutes Predrag Djordjevic levelled the scores with a drilled shot into the left-hand corner. Though momentarily rocked, United steadily recovered composure and seven minutes from time Paul Scholes claimed the three points for the Reds with a long-range drive that somehow evaded the grasp of the eccentric Eleftheropoulos.

Sir Alex Ferguson

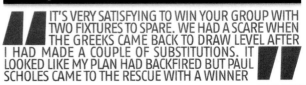

IT'S VERY SATISFYING TO WIN YOUR GROUP WITH TWO FIXTURES TO SPARE. WE HAD A SCARE WHEN THE GREEKS CAME BACK TO DRAW LEVEL AFTER I HAD MADE A COUPLE OF SUBSTITUTIONS. IT LOOKED LIKE MY PLAN HAD BACKFIRED BUT PAUL SCHOLES CAME TO THE RESCUE WITH A WINNER

Wednesday
23 October 2002
Rizoupoli
Attendance: **13,220**
Referee: **Pierluigi**
Collina (Italy)

Olympiakos Piraeus: Eleftheropoulos;
Patsatzoglou, Venetidis, Antzas, Anatolakis;
Karembeu, Zetterberg (Oforiquaye 70),
Dracena, Giannakopoulos (Mavrogenidis 87);
Giovanni (Choutos 45), Djordjevic
Subs not used: Katergianakis, Amanatidis,
Kostoulas, Niniadis **Booked:** Anatolakis, Venetidis

Manchester United: Barthez;
G Neville, Blanc, O'Shea, Silvestre;
P Neville, Veron (Richardson 87), Beckham
(Chadwick 62), Scholes, Giggs (Fortune 62), Forlan
Subs not used: Ricardo, May, Solskjaer, Roche
Booked: G Neville

United line up on
a humid night
in Athens

Possession
57%	43%

Shots on target
6	3

Shots off target
6	9

Corners
8	0

Offsides
0	2

Fouls
13	13

Man of the match
PAUL SCHOLES
Tireless and tenacious, the
England midfielder could have
scored a hat trick. As Scholes
unleashed a series of
sweetly-struck shots from
outside the 18-yard box, it was
hard to believe this was a player
returning from knee surgery, and
he fully deserved his winner,
despite help from the keeper.

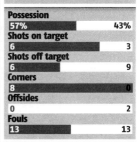

UEFA Champions League Phase 1
results 22/23 September 2002

Group A	Arsenal	1-2	Auxerre
	Borussia Dortmund	1-1	PSV
Group B	FC Basel	2-2	Valencia
	Spartak Moscow	1-3	Liverpool
Group C	Real Madrid	2-2	AEK Athens
	Roma	0-0	Genk
Group D	Ajax	1-1	Rosenborg
	Lyon	3-3	Internazionale
Group E	Dynamo Kiev	2-0	Feyenoord
	Newcastle Utd	1-0	Juventus
Group F	Bayer Leverkusen	2-1	Maccabi Haifa
Group G	Lens	3-1	Deportivo
	AC Milan	2-1	Bayern Munich
Group H	Barcelona	1-0	Lokomotiv
	Club Brugge	3-1	Galatasaray

Phase 1 Group F table
At the end of 23/10/02

	P	PTS
1 Manchester United	4	12
2 Bayer 04 Leverkusen	4	6
3 Olympiakos	4	3
4 Maccabi Haifa	4	3

Argentinian joy,
Greek tragedy

Maccabi Haifa 3
Katan 40, Zutauttas 56, Ayegbini 77 (penalty)

Manchester United 0

With qualification guaranteed thanks to a maximum 12 points out of 12, the result of this game was never going to be of dramatic importance. Reds travelling to Cyprus (instead of troubled Israel) relished the prospect of a few days in the sun and for some of United's young players, the trip contained even more enticing possibilities – an early introduction to club football's most prestigious tournament. Kieran Richardson started for the first time and Mads Timm and Daniel Nardiello made European debuts.

Yet United's first 11 boasted 10 internationals: Gary Neville, the tournament's most experienced player, Rio Ferdinand, the world's costliest defender and Ole Gunnar Solskjaer, a Champions League final goalscorer. This gave Bayer Leverkusen and Olympiakos, both requiring all three points to qualify, no room for complaint.

The game started brightly with Paul Scholes trying a long-range strike early on, but Ricardo was the first keeper called into action when he was forced to block a Haifa counter-attack. United twice came close to taking the lead, once through Solskjaer and then when the busy Diego Forlan found Richardson in space, but the 18-year-old snatched at his shot and it was deflected wide.

Rio forces the Maccabi keeper into action

Tuesday
29 October 2002
GSP Stadium
Attendance: **22,000**
Referee: **Lopez Nieto**
(Spain)

Then, with five minutes until half time and against the run of play, Maccabi took the lead. Yaniv Katan, the man who shocked Old Trafford with his opening strike in the home tie, danced past John O'Shea and rattled an unstoppable shot past Ricardo. Ten minutes after the break and it was a case of déjà vu when Raimondas Zutauttas hammered home from all of 35 yards.

Ricardo's night of heartbreak became complete when he hauled down Zutauttas in the box. Yakubu Ayegbeni, who scored a hat-trick against Olympiakos earlier in the group, converted the penalty. For the travelling Reds it was a night to forget – United's heaviest European defeat in eight years – but a valuable introduction to the Champions League for Richardson, Nardiello and Timm.

Maccabi Haifa: Awat; Zutautas (Zandberg 81), Harazi, Benado, Badir; Keissi, Pralija, Rosso, Zano; Ayegbeni (Almoshnino 84), Katan
Subs not used: Almadon, Sivilia, Cohen, Israilevic, Gabarin

Manchester United: Ricardo; G Neville, O'Shea, Ferdinand, Silvestre; P Neville, Scholes, Fortune, Richardson (Nardiello 62); Solskjaer, Forlan (Timm 79) **Subs not used:** Carroll, May, Pugh, Roche, Lynch
Booked: O'Shea, Silvestre, Ricardo

Sir Alex Ferguson

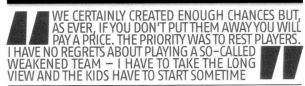

WE CERTAINLY CREATED ENOUGH CHANCES BUT, AS EVER, IF YOU DON'T PUT THEM AWAY YOU WILL PAY A PRICE. THE PRIORITY WAS TO REST PLAYERS. I HAVE NO REGRETS ABOUT PLAYING A SO-CALLED WEAKENED TEAM – I HAVE TO TAKE THE LONG VIEW AND THE KIDS HAVE TO START SOMETIME

Possession		
60%		40%
Shots on target		
4		5
Shots off target		
13		5
Corners		
11		1
Offsides		
1		3
Fouls		
12		16

Man of the match
PAUL SCHOLES
Some of the younger players brought in by Sir Alex made a bright start to the game, but it was the experienced head of Paul Scholes that kept the team going and pressing for a consolation right to the end – even in the face of those three demoralising Maccabi Haifa goals.

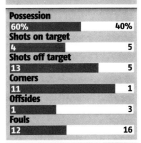

UEFA Champions League Phase 1 results 29/30 October 2002

Group A	Borussia Dortmund	2–1	Arsenal
	PSV Eindhoven	3–0	Auxerre
Group B	Liverpool	0–1	Valencia
	Spartak Moscow	0–2	FC Basel
Group C	AEK Athens	1–1	Genk
	Real Madrid	0–1	Roma
Group D	Internazionale	3–0	Rosenborg
	Lyon	0–2	Ajax
Group E	Juventus	2–0	Feyenoord
	Newcastle Utd	2–1	Dynamo
Group F	Bayer Leverkusen	2–0	Olympiakos
Group G	Deportivo La Coruña	2–1	Bayern Munich
	Lens	2–1	AC Milan
Group H	Club Brugge	0–1	Barcelona
	Galatasaray	1–2	Lokomotiv

Phase 1 Group F table
At the end of 30/10/02

	P	PTS
1 Manchester United	5	12
2 Bayer 04 Leverkusen	5	9
3 Maccabi Haifa	5	6
4 Olympiakos	5	3

Kieran Richardson gets stuck into his European debut

Manchester United 2
Veron 42, van Nistelrooy 69

Bayer 04 Leverkusen 0

Mikael Silvestre in determined mood

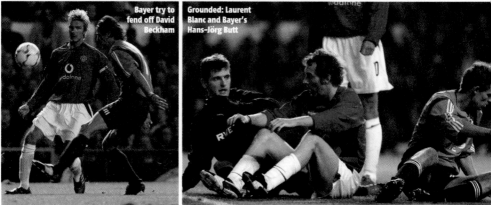

Bayer try to fend off David Beckham

Grounded: Laurent Blanc and Bayer's Hans-Jörg Butt

Responding to adversity is not a talent United players have been called upon to demonstrate in recent times. Under Sir Alex Ferguson the trophies have arrived thick and fast, and the dedication and application of the squad has tended to ensure that winning has become a habit to be maintained rather than aspired to. But, following a number of disappointments in the weeks prior to this match, not least a bitter derby defeat at Maine Road, the boss challenged his team to prove that their poor displays were isolated aberrations and not the early symptoms of a more acute malaise.

Sir Alex needn't have worried. United won with room to spare, in the process clinching top spot in the group and with it a place in the last 16 for the eighth consecutive year. In truth, the Reds probably should have won more convincingly – Ruud van Nistelrooy, who sealed the points with the second goal of the game in the 69th minute, might have had a hat-trick inside the opening half hour.

Yet despite United's early dominance, it was the visitors who spurned the best chance to open the scoring. Jan Simak blasted a 16th-minute penalty over the bar after Ricardo, preferred to Fabien Barthez in goal, had upended Thomas Brdaric.

United finally took the lead three minutes from half-time. The move began with David Beckham and, via a neat lay-off from van Nistelrooy, concluded when Seba Veron volleyed an unstoppable shot past Hans-Jörg Butt's right hand from the edge of the penalty area. It was a strike made all the more memorable by the Argentinian's first touch – an audacious and premeditated dink that lifted the ball to a height at which he could wield his right boot with optimum destruction.

Though not excessively celebrated – this was a night for business not festivity – the goal was clearly a boon to Veron's confidence. In the second half he ran the show, and was unlucky not score again when Butt stopped his close-range header in the closing stages. With the Reds already through to the next phase, this was not one of Old Trafford's most gripping occasions, but after one or two prior upsets, victory was both welcome and essential.

Wednesday
13 November 2002
Old Trafford
Attendance: **66,185**
Referee: **Vladimir Hrinak (Slovakia)**

REVIEW
NEVILLE WORSHIP

Manchester United: Ricardo; O'Shea, Blanc (G Neville 77), Ferdinand, Silvestre; Beckham (Solskjaer 82), Veron, Fortune, Giggs (Chadwick 81), Scholes; van Nistelrooy
Subs not used: Carroll, P Neville, Forlan, Nardiello **Booked:** Ricardo

Bayer 04 Leverkusen: Butt; Sebescen, Ramelow, Kleine, Zivkovic; Balitsch (Preuss 81); Babic, Simak, Bierofka (Dogan 77); Berbatov (Franca 62), Brdaric
Subs not used: Juric, Dzaka, Bozic, El Kasmi
Booked: Kleine, Simak, Sebescen

Possession	
52%	**48%**

Shots on target	
9	3

Shots off target	
6	10

Corners	
7	5

Offsides	
4	1

Fouls	
12	13

Man of the match
JOHN O'SHEA
Underlining his versatility once more, O'Shea played out of position at right back and put in a supremely confident display. He impressed with his positional sense, flawless technique and intelligent distribution – yet again.

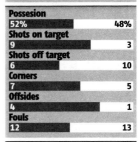

UEFA Champions League Phase 1 results 12/13 November 2002

Group A	Arsenal	0-0	PSV
	Auxerre	1-0	Dortmund
Group B	FC Basel	3-3	Liverpool
	Valencia	3-0	Spartak
Group C	Genk	1-1	Madrid
	Roma	1-1	AEK Athens
Group D	Ajax	1-2	Internazionale
	Rosenborg	1-1	Lyon
Group E	Dynamo Kiev	1-2	Juventus
	Feyenoord	2-3	Newcastle Utd
Group F	Olympiakos	3-3	Maccabi Haifa
Group G	Bayern Munich	3-3	Lens
	AC Milan	1-2	Deportivo
Group H	Barcelona	3-1	Galatasaray
	Lokomotiv Moscow	2-0	Club Brugge

Phase 1 Group F table
At the end of 13/11/02

	P	PTS
1 Manchester United	6	15
2 Bayer 04 Leverkusen	6	9
3 Maccabi Haifa	6	7
4 Olympiakos	6	4

Sir Alex Ferguson

OUR FIRST PHASE RECORD WAS GOOD. APART FROM MACCABI HAIFA, WE WON ALL OUR GAMES AND CAME OUT WITH A GOOD SCORING RATE. THE PLAYERS HAD NO DIFFICULTY RAISING THEIR GAME AGAINST BAYER LEVERKUSEN TO SUPPLY THE PROPER RESPONSE TO OUR DERBY DEFEAT

CHAMPIONS LEAGUE PHASE 2

United were the only English team to make it through Phase 2, while three of the four Italian sides marched on. Holders Real Madrid flirted with danger before reaching the last eight

'The group of death' is a phrase often employed in Champions League matters, and never more so than in this season's Phase 2. Manchester United were faced with Juventus, Deportivo La Coruña and FC Basel, while Newcastle were matching themselves against the best, taking on Inter, Barcelona and last year's finalists Bayer Leverkusen. Arsenal had to get past Valencia, Ajax and Roma if they were to progress.

The Highbury side got off to a flier, beating Roma 3-1 in the *Stadio Olimpico*, but that was as good as it got for Arsène Wenger's men. An away defeat to Valencia followed a series of four draws and another European campaign ended in disappointment for the Gunners.

The Geordies had a far more thrilling ride. Sir Bobby Robson saw the Magpies lose their first two games to Inter and Barcelona. They rallied by beating Leverkusen home and away and enjoyed an epic encounter in the San Siro where they were desperately unlucky not to win. The run ended in heartbreak as Barcelona won the final game 2-0 at St James Park.

The evergreen Sir Bobby thrived on the experience. "We liked it so much, we need it next year, we want it next year," he opined. Third place in the Premiership means they'll have another chance in 2003/04.

United, Barça, Valencia and Milan won their respective groups, the latter pipping Real Madrid who suffered a scare in their final game against Lokomotiv. The holders were a whisker away from elimination, but their 1-0 win was just enough. And what a difference that could have made in the long run...

Champions League Phase 2 fixtures

Tues 26th Nov	FC Basel	Away
Weds 11th Dec	Deportivo	Home
Weds 19th Feb	Juventus	Home
Tues 25th Feb	Juventus	Away
Weds 12th Mar	FC Basel	Home
Tues 18th Mar	Deportivo	Away

In the UEFA Champions League Phase 2

314,199
watched United play six games

United scored
11
goals

but conceded
5
goals

United travelled
5,590
miles to and from games

United fielded a total of
28
players

GOAL OF PHASE 2 RUUD VAN NISTELROOY V FC BASEL, 26/11/02

All season long Ruud van Nistelrooy has been conducting his own personal goal of the season competition... and let's face it, there have been plenty of them to choose from. One of the highlights was the second of his brace against Swiss champions FC Basel, and his timing couldn't have been better. Basel had enjoyed a one-goal lead for an hour in the first match of Phase 2, until van Nistelrooy equalised with a close-range header. A minute later and the Reds were in front thanks to one of the goals of the tournament. Van Nistelrooy won the ball in the left of the box, darted towards the byline and just when it seemed he'd taken it too far, the Dutchman looked up, curled a shot off the far post and into the net. The Swiss were shattered by the double strike and Solskjaer added a third five minutes later.

FC Basel 1
Gimenez 1

Manchester United 3
Van Nistelrooy 62, 63, Solskjaer 68

Ruud rounds the Basel defence on his route to goal

Solskjaer rounds off the scoring

The teams enter the impressive St Jakob Park

Tuesday
26 November 2002
St Jakob Park
Attendance: **29,501**
Referee: **Valentin Ivanov (Russia)**

Seconds out, phase two. Manchester United, or primarily Ruud van Nistelrooy, secured a thrilling victory against an opposition in the habit of giving British teams a bloody nose. United were made to fight for the three points, but one moment of footballing genius left the Swiss team on the ropes.

Given the home side's barnstorming performances against Liverpool and Celtic, it wasn't a major shock when Basel took the lead, but the speed of the goal couldn't have failed to take United by surprise. Less than a minute – or if you want Swiss-watch accuracy, 31 seconds – had passed when Barthez found the ball nestling in the back of his net. In fact, nine United players hadn't even touched the ball when Gimenez scored the sixth-fastest goal in Champions League history.

United were understandably stung by the goal and the setback gave the Reds an aggressive edge, with Scholes booked for one of a quartet of feisty challenges.

The brothers Yakin were causing United's defence all sorts of problems and after half an hour Sir Alex effected a tactical switch, moving O'Shea to left back and Silvestre to centre half alongside Brown. United kept the deficit down to one at the interval... and 15 minutes into the second half van Nistelrooy weighed up Basel's superiority and decided enough was enough.

The equaliser came from Ruud's head, courtesy of Solskjaer. Ole, operating on the right wing in the absence of Beckham, swung in an inch-perfect cross of which the striker took full advantage. It was the Dutchman's fourth goal in as many days, but 60 seconds later that goal was eclipsed by a slice of brilliance.

Picking up the ball on the left side of the box, Ruud swivelled past a couple of defenders before hitting the byline and curling a seemingly impossible shot off the post and into the net. Stunned by the quality of the one-two, the home side collapsed and it was no surprise when Basel's faulty defence allowed Solskjaer to sprint through and grab a third. With 20 minutes left, Ruud was replaced by Diego Forlan. As he left the field the travelling Reds gave him a reception fit for a hero. It was fully merited.

FC Basel: Zubi; Haas, M Yakin, Zwyssig, Atouba; Ergic (Barberis 85), Cantaluppi, Chipperfield (Tum 73), H Yakin; Gimenez, Rossi (Duruz 85) **Subs not used:** Rapo, Quennoz, Huggel, Varela **Booked:** Zwyssig, Atouba

Manchester United: Barthez; P Neville, O'Shea, Brown, Silvestre; Veron, Scholes, Fortune, Solskjaer (Chadwick 90); Giggs; van Nistelrooy (Forlan 73) **Subs not used:** Ricardo, Stewart, Pugh, Richardson **Booked:** Scholes, Fortune, Veron

Possession	
52%	48%

Shots on target	
5	5

Shots off target	
4	7

Corners	
5	9

Offsides	
4	6

Fouls	
13	9

Man of the match
RUUD VAN NISTELROOY
This double brought his Euro total to 18 in 20 games. And the worrying news for defences all over the continent is that he's just getting started. Ruud's second goal was dazzling in its execution and will live long in the memory of all who witnessed it.

UEFA Champions League Phase 2 results 26/27 November 2002

Group A	Bayer Leverkusen	1-2	Barcelona
	Newcastle United	1-4	Internazionale
Group B	Roma	1-3	Arsenal
	Valencia	1-1	Ajax
Group C	Lokomotiv Moscow	1-2	Dortmund
	AC Milan	1-0	Real Madrid
Group D	Deportivo La Coruña	2-2	Juventus

Phase 2 Group D table
At the end of 26/11/02

	P	PTS
1 Manchester United	1	3
2 Deportivo La Coruña	1	1
3 Juventus	1	1
4 FC Basel	1	0

Sir Alex Ferguson

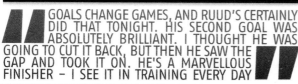

" GOALS CHANGE GAMES, AND RUUD'S CERTAINLY DID THAT TONIGHT. HIS SECOND GOAL WAS ABSOLUTELY BRILLIANT. I THOUGHT HE WAS GOING TO CUT IT BACK, BUT THEN HE SAW THE GAP AND TOOK IT ON. HE'S A MARVELLOUS FINISHER – I SEE IT IN TRAINING EVERY DAY "

Manchester United 2
Van Nistelrooy 7, 54

Deportivo La Coruña 0

Ruud van Nistelrooy confirmed his status as one of the top strikers in world football by scoring a brace to help the Reds sweep aside Deportivo in the quest for European glory.

The Dutch striker was United's catalyst with a strike in each half which not only won the match but also made him United's highest-ever scorer in the European Cup with 20 goals in 21 appearances. He also had two goals disallowed in a performance that gave United the perfect follow-up to the victory in Basel.

From the first whistle, the Spanish side's goal came under siege, with van Nistelrooy having a shot saved by Juanmi after three minutes. But the Dutchman was not to be denied and when Paul Scholes sent in a tempting cross, he headed the ball into the right-hand corner after just seven minutes. Scholes almost doubled United's lead but shot wide from eight yards, and soon after van Nistelrooy headed the ball the wrong side of a post. On 26 minutes, he hit the target with another header – only to be harshly penalised for a foul on Juanmi.

Deportivo looked lacklustre, a pale shadow of last season's visitors, and even the introduction of Diego Tristan failed to shake

Ruud van Nistelrooy in full flight

Wednesday
11 December 2002
Old Trafford
Attendance: **67,014**
Referee: **Terje Hauge**
(Norway)

UNITED REVIEW

RICARDO

them from their lethargy. After having a penalty appeal turned down seconds after coming on, he too succumbed to mediocrity.

In the 52nd minute, van Nistelrooy netted again, only for it to be disallowed for offside. But Deportivo's respite was short lived, as van Nistelrooy scored United's second two minutes later.

Scholes' shot from the right was parried by Juanmi, who was then beaten to the rebound by Solskjaer. When the ball fell to van Nistelrooy just six yards out, the outcome was inevitable.

Fabien Barthez made a couple of late saves from Roy Makaay, although by this stage United were dictating the tempo of the game with such imperious authority that Deportivo were fortunate not to find themselves on the end of a more severe hiding.

Sir Alex Ferguson

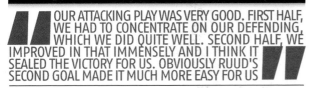

OUR ATTACKING PLAY WAS VERY GOOD. FIRST HALF, WE HAD TO CONCENTRATE ON OUR DEFENDING, WHICH WE DID QUITE WELL. SECOND HALF, WE IMPROVED IN THAT IMMENSELY AND I THINK IT SEALED THE VICTORY FOR US. OBVIOUSLY RUUD'S SECOND GOAL MADE IT MUCH MORE EASY FOR US

Manchester United: Barthez; G Neville, Brown, Silvestre, O'Shea (Beckham 80); Solskjaer, P Neville (Forlan 80), Veron, Giggs; Scholes, van Nistelrooy (Richardson 88) **Subs not used:** Ricardo, Chadwick, Stewart, Pugh **Booked:** Veron, Solskjaer

Deportivo La Coruña: Juanmi; Capdevila, Cesar, Romero, Scaloni; Mauro Silva, Sergio, Amavisca (Tristan 45), Valeron (Acuna 65); Victor (Luque 75), Makaay **Subs not used:** Mallo, Manuel Pablo, Donato, Hector **Booked:** Capdevila

Possession

48%	52%

Shots on target

11	4

Shots off target

6	6

Corners

5	6

Offsides

5	4

Fouls

17	7

Man of the match
RUUD VAN NISTELROOY

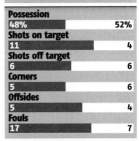

Another devastating display from the deadly Dutchman, whose two typically predatory strikes took his latest goal tally in the Champions League to a reality-defying 29 in 30 matches (including eight for his former club PSV Eindhoven).

UEFA Champions League Phase 2 results 10/11 December 2002

Group A	Barcelona	3-1	Newcastle Utd
	Internazionale	3-2	Leverkusen
Group B	Ajax	2-1	Roma
	Arsenal	0-0	Valencia
Group C	Borussia Dortmund	0-1	AC Milan
	Real Madrid	2-2	Lokomotiv
Group D	Juventus	4-0	FC Basel

Ole looks on in delight as Ryan Giggs celebrates

Phase 2 Group D table

At the end of 11/12/02

	P	PTS
1 Manchester United	2	6
2 Juventus	2	4
3 Deportivo La Coruña	2	1
4 FC Basel	2	0

Manchester United 2
Brown 4, van Nistelrooy 85

Juventus 1
Nedved 90

Wes Brown can't
conceal his joy at
netting the opener

Wednesday
19 February 2003
Old Trafford
Attendance: **66,703**
Referee: **Kim Milton Nielsen (Denmark)**

In more than 100 appearances for the Reds, Wes Brown has camouflaged his instinct for scoring goals so successfully that when, four minutes into this fixture, he finally broke his duck, 66,000 jaws almost dropped off their hinges.

The Longsight lad certainly picked an opportune moment to perfect his Joe Jordan impression; following recent setbacks against Manchester City in the league and Arsenal in the FA Cup, an early goal against the Italian champions and leaders of *Serie A* was the ideal antidote.

But Juve quickly served notice that, despite missing key players because of a flu bug that had decimated their squad, they had not come to Old Trafford to play dead. In fact seven of Juve's team had been struck down with flu, and star man Alessandro del Piero was out with a thigh injury – prompting rumours that coach Marcello Lippi had requested the game be postponed, which was later denied. For the rest of the first half Lippi's makeshift team dominated and, though they lacked a cutting edge, Edgar Davids and Pavel Nedved were causing disquiet on the United bench – especially when Nedved hit the post on 20 minutes.

After the break, United, inspired by David Beckham, finally established a foothold. Davids and Nedved increasingly found themselves turned towards their own goal, where Ruud van Nistelrooy and Paul Scholes were beginning to pose a threat. On the hour the Dutchman seemed certain to extend United's lead. One-on-one with Juve keeper Antonio Chimenti, he was upended in the box, but the referee gave nothing and Scholes could only slam the rebound against a post.

Thanks to van Nistelrooy's ninth Champions League goal of the season, a subtle one-touch finish over the head of Chimenti following a Beckham chip in the 85th minute, Sir Alex Ferguson could afford to be philosophical on the final whistle. But if Juventus, who grabbed a last-minute consolation goal through Nedved's shot-cum-cross, had denied United victory, Signor Chimenti's actions would certainly have been the subject of a more colourful post-match debate.

Manchester United: Barthez; G Neville, Ferdinand, Brown, Silvestre (O'Shea 52); Beckham, Keane, Butt, Giggs (Forlan 90); Scholes (Solskjaer 80), van Nistelrooy **Subs not used:** Ricardo, P Neville, Pugh, Fletcher **Booked:** Scholes, Keane

Juventus: Chimenti; Pessotto, Montero, Ferrara, Zenoni; Nedved, Davids, Tacchinardi, Camoranesi; Trezeguet (Olivera 65), Zalayeta **Subs not used:** Bonnefoi, Fresi, Paro, Gastaldello **Booked:** Davids, Tacchinardi

Possession	
47%	53%

Shots on target	
2	3

Shots off target	
3	8

Corners	
3	7

Offsides	
4	1

Fouls	
9	16

Man of the match
DAVID BECKHAM

Instrumental in the win, it was Beckham's precise corner which Wes Brown headed home in the fourth minute, and it was the England skipper who released Ruud to strike United's second with just five minutes left.

UEFA Champions League Phase 2 results 18/19 February 2003

Group A	Barcelona	3–0	Internazionale
	Bayer Leverkusen	1–3	Newcastle Utd
Group B	Arsenal	1–1	Ajax
	Roma	0–1	Valencia
Group C	AC Milan	1–0	Lokomotiv
	Real Madrid	2–1	Dortmund
Group D	FC Basel	1–0	Deportivo

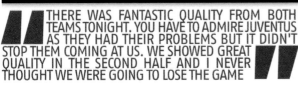

THERE WAS FANTASTIC QUALITY FROM BOTH TEAMS TONIGHT. YOU HAVE TO ADMIRE JUVENTUS AS THEY HAD THEIR PROBLEMS BUT IT DIDN'T STOP THEM COMING AT US. WE SHOWED GREAT QUALITY IN THE SECOND HALF AND I NEVER THOUGHT WE WERE GOING TO LOSE THE GAME

Phase 2 Group D table

At the end of 19/2/03	P	PTS
1 Manchester United	3	9
2 Juventus	3	4
3 FC Basel	3	3
4 Deportivo La Coruña	3	1

Juventus 0

Manchester United 3

Giggs 51, 41, van Nistelrooy 63

Goal-den Giggs: Ryan was the scourge of Juve

There have been more dramatic European nights, even a few more important ones, but for slow-burning soak-it-up satisfaction this was as good as it gets. Despite being restored to nigh-on-full strength, Juventus were blown away by a United performance that, save a couple of early defensive lapses, approximated perfection.

At the back, Roy Keane and Rio Ferdinand were supreme – their shackling of Trezeguet and Di Vaio resulting in the latter's withdrawal. In midfield Phil Neville and Nicky Butt were immense, and it was their industry that allowed Seba Veron to demonstrate the vast dimensions of his genius.

Leading the line, Ole Solskjaer worked his socks off, as did the two full backs Gary Neville and John O'Shea. Ruud van Nistelrooy, a second-half substitute, played his part too, notching his customary goal to make it 3-0 on 63 minutes. Yet even on this, a night of collective excellence, it was the individual brilliance of one man that will live longest in the memory.

Ryan Giggs was only on the field for 41 minutes, coming on for the injured Diego Forlan early in the first half and hobbling off himself in the second, but it was long enough for the Welshman

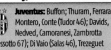

Tuesday
25 February 2003
Stadio de Alpi
Attendance: **59,111**
Referee: **Markus Merk**
(Germany)

☆☆ **Juventus:** Buffon; Thuram, Ferrara, Montero, Conte (Tudor 46); Davids, Nedved, Camoranesi, Zambrotta (Pessotto 67); Di Vaio (Salas 46), Trezeguet **Subs not used:** Chimenti, Iuliano, Birindelli, Zalayeta **Booked:** Nedved

Manchester United: Barthez; G Neville, Ferdinand, Keane, O'Shea (Pugh 60); Beckham, Butt, P Neville, Veron; Solskjaer, Forlan (Giggs 8, van Nistelrooy 48) **Subs not used:** Ricardo, Fletcher, Roche, Richardson **Booked:** P Neville

Possession
45%	55%

Shots on target
6	2

Shots off target
3	12

Corners
2	7

Offsides
4	5

Fouls
16	16

Man of the match
RYAN GIGGS

A remarkable night for Ryan Giggs. During a magical first half the Welshman's golden boots dazzled the meanest defence in Italy and his double sent United through to the final stages of the Champions League. And all after coming on as a substitute...

Juventus try to shackle Nicky Butt and Ole Gunnar Solskjaer

to make the game's most telling contributions. After 15 minutes he put United ahead, calmly side-footing a Veron cross past Gianluigi Buffon into the far corner.

"Feared by the Blues, loved by the Reds" sang the travelling hordes of United fans. It was music to Giggs' ears. His legs seemed to benefit too – that familiar zip and a swagger, oddly absent in recent weeks, was back. Big style. His second goal, four minutes before half time, was drop-dead gorgeous. Picking up the ball on the half-way line, Giggs ran diagonally towards goal with the ball seemingly stapled to his boot, accelerated past two defenders, drew Buffon and reversed a right-footed shot into the far corner. Coming soon to a compilation video near you...

UEFA Champions League Phase 2 results 25/26 February 2003

Group A	Internazionale	0-0	Barcelona
	Newcastle United	3-1	Leverkusen
Group B	Ajax	0-0	Arsenal
	Valencia	0-3	Roma
Group C	Dortmund	1-1	Real Madrid
	Lokomotiv Moscow	0-1	AC Milan
Group D	Deportivo La Coruña	1-0	FC Basel

Sir Alex Ferguson

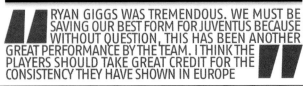

RYAN GIGGS WAS TREMENDOUS. WE MUST BE SAVING OUR BEST FORM FOR JUVENTUS BECAUSE WITHOUT QUESTION, THIS HAS BEEN ANOTHER GREAT PERFORMANCE BY THE TEAM. I THINK THE PLAYERS SHOULD TAKE GREAT CREDIT FOR THE CONSISTENCY THEY HAVE SHOWN IN EUROPE

Phase 2 Group D table
At the end of 25/2/03

	P	PTS
1 Manchester United	4	12
2 Juventus	4	4
3 Deportivo La Coruña	4	4
4 FC Basel	4	3

Manchester United 1
G Neville 53

FC Basel 1
Giménez 14

Gary Neville makes his mark

Kieran Richardson enjoys another start

As promised, Sir Alex appointed a new cast for this fixture and, while the changes were not as wholesale as some had predicted given that United had already qualified for the quarter-finals, the new-look Reds took time learning their lines. The first half made for uneasy viewing. While United stuttered, Basel bristled – especially in midfield, where Scott Chipperfield, Hakan Yakin and Sébastien Barberis enjoyed disturbingly long periods of possession, their rat-tat-tat interchanges carving frenzied triangles on the Old Trafford turf like an abstract oil on canvas.

The visitors took just 14 minutes to make the breakthrough. A deflected pass down the inside-right channel was pulled back from the touchline to Haas, who curled a right-footed cross towards Christian Giménez. The Argentine, seizing on a rare error of judgement by Rio Ferdinand, who found himself sucked under the ball, controlled with his chest then lashed a half-volley into the top corner. Roy Carroll barely had time to twitch.

Though visibly stung, the Reds failed to muster an immediate response; 33 minutes had elapsed before Forlan drove a free kick into the arms of Pascal Zuberbühler. It was United's first meaningful effort on target.

Heeding the boss's instructions to up the tempo, United started the second half in more dynamic fashion. Giggs, on for Kieran Richardson, restored some thrust to United's attack, while on the right debutant Darren Fletcher began to exude the carefree aura of someone enjoying the best night out of his life.

Eight minutes into the half, United drew level. Prior to this match, Gary Neville had made 76 appearances in the Champions League and his left-footed strike from the edge of the box – though generously deflected by Thimothée Atouba – was a fitting reward for his efforts. In search of a winner, Sir Alex pitched David Beckham and Paul Scholes into the mix, but despite some late pressure, the visitors stood firm.

In truth, a winner would probably have flattered the Reds. It would also have diluted the contribution of Gary Neville, Old Trafford's latest – and unlikeliest – striking sensation.

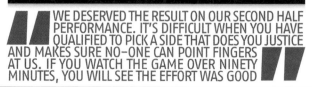

Sir Alex Ferguson

WE DESERVED THE RESULT ON OUR SECOND HALF PERFORMANCE. IT'S DIFFICULT WHEN YOU HAVE QUALIFIED TO PICK A SIDE THAT DOES YOU JUSTICE AND MAKES SURE NO-ONE CAN POINT FINGERS AT US. IF YOU WATCH THE GAME OVER NINETY MINUTES, YOU WILL SEE THE EFFORT WAS GOOD

Diego Forlan is closely followed by FC Basel's Atouba

**Wednesday
12 March 2003
Old Trafford**
Attendance: **66,870**
Referee: **Claus Bo–
Larsen (Denmark)**

Manchester United: Carroll; G Neville, Blanc (Scholes 73), Ferdinand, O'Shea; Fletcher (Beckham 73), P Neville, Butt, Richardson (Giggs 45); Solskjaer, Forlan
Subs Not Used: Ricardo, van Nistelrooy, Pugh, Webber **Booked:** P Neville

FC Basel: Zuberbühler; Atouba, Murat Yakin, Zwyssig, Haas; Chipperfield, Cantaluppi, Barberis, Hakan Yakin; Giménez (Tum 77), Rossi (Huggel 62) **Subs Not Used:** Rapo, Quennoz, Varela, Duruz, Degen **Booked:** Cantaluppi

Possession	
53%	47%
Shots on target	
3	2
Shots off target	
5	10
Corners	
1	3
Offsides	
5	4
Fouls	
18	4

Man of the match
GARY NEVILLE

His goal may have grabbed the headlines, but this was a performance worthy of wider acclaim. When he wasn't sending volleys towards the Basel goal, Gary was crunching into tackles and making vital covering interceptions. Bravo.

UEFA Champions League Phase 2 results 11/12 March 2003

Group A	Barcelona	2–0	Leverkusen
	Internazionale	2–2	Newcastle Utd
Group B	Ajax	1–1	Valencia
	Arsenal	1–1	Roma
Group C	Borussia Dortmund	3–0	Lokomotiv
	Real Madrid	3–1	AC Milan
Group D	Juventus	3–2	Deportivo

Phase 2 Group D table
At the end of 12/3/03

	P	PTS
1 Manchester United	5	13
2 Juventus	5	7
3 Deportivo La Coruña	5	4
4 FC Basel	5	4

Deportivo La Coruña 2
Victor 32, Lynch o.g. 47

Manchester United 0

United's youngsters prepare to taste the Champions League

Darren Fletcher: made a big impression

Danny Webber showed some neat touches

Tuesday
18 March 2003
Estadio Riazor
Attendance: **25,000**
Referee: **Vladimir Hrinak (Slovakia)**

The Estadio Riazor in La Coruña may be a long way from Moss Lane, Altrincham, but for the youngsters in an experimental United side charged with seeing out Group D, this was an unexpected seat at the Champions League table. Boasting nine internationals in their starting 11, the eliminated Deportivo were always the stronger side but it was a valuable lesson for United's latest flock of fledglings.

The opening exchanges were tame – hardly surprising given the unimportance of the outcome. Acuña was first to head for goal, his long-distance strike licking the paintwork of United's post, before Luque saw his shot tipped round the other post.

United's first chance followed when Darren Fletcher was given time on the right to cross for Diego Forlan, whose shot blazed over the bar. The home crowd were lifted out of their reverie when Valerón and Laurent Blanc tussled in the box and tumbled to the Spanish turf, but the referee blanked the Riazor's whistles.

Depor took the lead on the half-hour mark and, given the young legs on show, it was unfortunate that Blanc was the one forced to give chase to Luque. The lightning-quick Spaniard outstripped the Frenchman for pace and squared to Victor, who was given the simplest of tasks to open the scoring.

Sir Alex made one change at half-time, replacing Lee Roche with Michael Stewart, but it was debutant Mark Lynch who could have been forgiven for wishing he'd been hooked. Valerón fired over a vicious cross that bounced in off Lynch's head under pressure from Luque. It was an unfortunate moment in a hard-working performance from the 21-year-old Mancunian.

United heads refused to drop though, and the Reds had chances to draw level. Fletcher flicked onto Ryan Giggs, who cut the ball back, but his strike was blocked on the line. A few minutes later, Fletcher returned the compliment – setting up Giggs to turn and shoot against the woodwork. With 20 minutes left, Forlan and Giggs made way for Danny Webber and Kieran Richardson but, though both showed neat touches, neither could force the goal United's second-half display merited.

Deportivo La Coruña: Mallo; Pablo, Andrade (Djorovic 64), César, Capdevila; Victor (Héctor 78), Duscher, Acuña, Fran (Scaloni 52); Valerón, Luque
Subs not used: Juanmi, Romero, Tristan, Sergio
Booked: Acuña

Manchester United: Ricardo; Roche (Stewart 46), Blanc, O'Shea; Pugh, Fletcher, P Neville, Butt, Lynch; Forlan (Richardson 72), Giggs (Webber 72)
Subs not used: Carroll, May, Davis, Nardiello
Booked: P Neville

Possession	
39%	61%

Shots on target	
2	4

Shots off target	
8	10

Corners	
1	7

Offsides	
4	5

Fouls	
16	7

Man of the match
JOHN O'SHEA
United's defence was given a torrid time but O'Shea stood tall throughout. It's a testament to the strides the Irishman has taken this season that he was considered one of the experienced old heads here.

UEFA Champions League Phase 2 results 18/19 March 2003

Group A	Bayer 04 Leverkusen	0–2	Internazionale
	Newcastle United	0–2	Barcelona
Group B	Roma	1–1	Ajax
	Valencia	2–1	Arsenal
Group C	Lokomotiv	0–1	Real Madrid
	Milan	0–1	Dortmund
Group D	FC Basel	2–1	Juventus

Sir Alex Ferguson

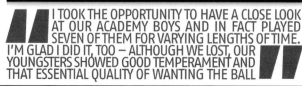

I TOOK THE OPPORTUNITY TO HAVE A CLOSE LOOK AT OUR ACADEMY BOYS AND IN FACT PLAYED SEVEN OF THEM FOR VARYING LENGTHS OF TIME. I'M GLAD I DID IT, TOO – ALTHOUGH WE LOST, OUR YOUNGSTERS SHOWED GOOD TEMPERAMENT AND THAT ESSENTIAL QUALITY OF WANTING THE BALL

Phase 2 Group D table

At the end of 18/03/03	P	PTS
1 Manchester United	6	13
2 Juventus	6	7
3 FC Basel	6	7
4 Deportivo La Coruña	6	7

CHAMPIONS LEAGUE FINAL STAGES

The world looked on in awe as United and Real Madrid contested what was dubbed 'El Derby De Europa' by the Spanish press, and the Milan giants enjoyed their own titanic struggle

It was no real surprise when United were handed a trip to Madrid in the Champions League quarter-final draw; somehow it just seemed predestined. And incredibly, given the hype and hysteria leading up to the ties, the dramatic matches in the *Bernabéu* and Old Trafford lived up to their billing and then some, but more of that later.

Elsewhere in the quarter-finals, Milan beat Ajax 3-2 in a riveting second leg at the San Siro after a goal-less draw in Amsterdam, while their city rivals Inter despatched Valencia on away goals.

The other quarter-final between Juventus and Barcelona was an epic tussle. The European giants shared a 1-1 draw in the first leg in Turin, with Javier Saviola's late strike cancelling out Paolo Montero's opener for the home side.

The second leg at the *Nou Camp* also ended 1-1 at full-time. Pavel Nedved gave the visitors a second-half lead but Xavi Hernández levelled. Although Juventus ended the match with 10 men after the dismissal of Edgar Davids, the Italian side stole the glory when substitute Marcelo Zalayeta netted the winner in extra time.

In the semi-finals, AC Milan eventually overcame Inter in the second leg courtesy of an away goal from Andrei Shevchenko. The first leg finished goal-less.

Milan would face Juventus in the first all-Italian Champions League final, after Real Madrid unexpectedly capitulated to the newly-crowned *Serie A* champions 3-1 in the second leg – squandering their 2-1 advantage from the *Bernabéu* (printing schedules mean we are unable to cover the final).

Champions League quarter-final fixtures

| Tues 8th April | Real Madrid | Away |
| Weds 23rd April | Real Madrid | Home |

In the UEFA Champions League quarter final

141,708
watched United play two games

United scored
5
goals

but conceded
6
goals

United travelled
2,140
miles to and from games

United fielded a total of
17
players

GOAL OF THE QUARTER-FINAL DAVID BECKHAM V REAL MADRID 23/04/03
Transfer speculation reached fever pitch before United's quarter-final first leg with Real Madrid, and threatened to overshadow the match. United's No.7 was a somewhat peripheral figure in the match at the *Bernabéu* and was given a place on the bench for the Old Trafford leg, Ole Solskjaer continuing his fine form on the right side of midfield. With 20 minutes to go and United needing goals, Beckham replaced a tiring Seba Veron and was given the chance he was desperate for. It took him just eight minutes to make his mark on the game. The free kick on the edge of the Real box was pure Beckham territory and he didn't disappoint, curling an unstoppable shot past Iker Casillas. With five minutes to go Beckham bundled in another goal which made United fans think, "Maybe, just maybe…"

Real Madrid 3
Figo 12, Raul 28, 49

Manchester United 1
Van Nistelrooy 52

For the 4,000 travelling Reds crammed into the highest corner of the Bernabéu, disappointment at this result was tempered by the knowledge that they had witnessed arguably one of the best football sides of all time performing at the peak of their powers. Real Madrid's first-half display had pundits breathlessly comparing them to Pelé's Brazil in 1970 and even Di Stefano's 1960 Madrid side. But for all Real's fantasy football, United gave a battling second-half display and grabbed that away goal.

United started brightly and came close twice in the first 10 minutes, much to the bemusement of the fanatical *Ultra Sur* behind Iker Casillas' goal. Real's prodigious keeper scrambled away a shot from Paul Scholes and then watched in horror as Ruud van Nistelrooy's overhead kick flew inches over the bar.

Unfortunately for United, this acted as a red rag to the proverbial bull as Madrid's matadors went to work. The Whites took the lead on 12 minutes when Luis Figo exchanged a series of passes with Zinedine Zidane on the edge of the box before curling an improbable shot into the corner of the net. Moments later the home side looked for a penalty when Wes Brown blocked Ronaldo,

Ruud fires United's lifeline past Iker Casillas

Tuesday 8 April 2003
Estadio Santiago Bernabéu
Attendance: **75,000**
Referee: **Anders Frisk (Sweden)**

but referee Anders Frisk turned a blind eye. Near the half-hour mark and with Real turning on the style, Raúl took control. Fed by Zidane, the golden boy of Madrid rolled Rio Ferdinand and placed his shot past Fabien Barthez.

Madrid went three up four minutes after the break, and this time Figo turned provider. United's tormentor passed to Raúl, who struck his 43rd Champions League goal. Three-nil down and almost out, United struck back through our own European hitman. Giggs's shot was parried by Casillas into the path of van Nistelrooy, who headed home to give the Reds a lifeline. He almost grabbed a second as the home side faltered, but to expect more drama from this incredible match would have been greedy.

Real Madrid: Casillas; Salgado, Hierro, Helguera, Carlos; Zidane, Figo, Conceiçao, Makelele; Raúl, Ronaldo (Guti 83) **Subs not used:** César, McManaman, Morientes, Portillo, Solari, Pavon

Manchester United: Barthez; G Neville (Solskjaer 86), Ferdinand, Brown, Silvestre (O'Shea 57); Beckham, Butt, Keane, Giggs, Scholes; van Nistelrooy **Subs not used:** Ricardo, Blanc, Forlan, Fortune, Fletcher **Booked:** Scholes, van Nistelrooy, G Neville, Keane

Sir Alex Ferguson

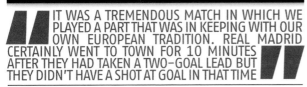

IT WAS A TREMENDOUS MATCH IN WHICH WE PLAYED A PART THAT WAS IN KEEPING WITH OUR OWN EUROPEAN TRADITION. REAL MADRID CERTAINLY WENT TO TOWN FOR 10 MINUTES AFTER THEY HAD TAKEN A TWO-GOAL LEAD BUT THEY DIDN'T HAVE A SHOT AT GOAL IN THAT TIME

Possession	
47%	53%

Shots on target	
7	7

Shots off target	
6	10

Corners	
4	4

Offsides	
2	1

Fouls	
20	12

Man of the match
RUUD VAN NISTELROOY
In the end the important thing was the record-breaking goal, but van Nistelrooy's never-say-die attitude and constant running gave United hope. With so much world-class talent on show, Ruud proved he can mix it with the best of them.

UEFA Champions League Quarter-final 1st leg results

Tuesday 8 April 2003
Amsterdam ArenA
Attendance 50,967

Ajax	0-0	AC Milan

Wednesday 9 April 2003
San Siro
Attendance 52,500

Internazionale	1-0	Valencia
Vieri 14		

Wednesday 9 April 2003
Stadio delle Alpi
Attendance 48,500

Juventus	1-1	Barcelona
Montero 16		Saviola 77

David Beckham pressures Real

Manchester United 4
Van Nistelrooy 43, Helguera (o.g.) 52, Beckham 71, 85

Real Madrid 3
Ronaldo 12, 50, 59

Wes Brown and Roberto Carlos tussle

Ruud nets his 12th Champions League goal of the season

CASILLAS
1

Three words: what a game! Yes, United lost the tie overall and with it the chance of staging a truly historic final home match of the season. But this was a night to savour: if this game had been a movie, the bookies would be refusing to take bets on next year's Oscar for Best Picture – it was thriller, drama and tragedy rolled into one. United's pre-match brief had been tough but simple: a 2-0 win, or victory by three clear goals. If it looked an improbable dream it seemed an impossible one when Ronaldo – all pace, power and poise – smashed a 12th-minute opener past Fabien Barthez. Four goals needed.

Yet United came so close. Fuelled by a highly-charged crowd, the game ebbed and flowed in joyous rhythm and, on 43 minutes, hope sprang. Giggs and Solskjaer linked up down the right, allowing Ruud van Nistelrooy to slot home from close range. It was his 12th strike in this year's competition, making him the highest scorer in a Champions League campaign.

The Red wave continued after the break, but commitment to attack saw United undone again, Ronaldo tapping in a Roberto Carlos cross on 50 minutes.

No matter. Before the crowd caught its breath, Juan Veron's scuffed cross-shot was bundled into his own net by Helguera. Real restored the advantage on 59 minutes – Ronaldo completing his hat-trick with a stunning run and 25-yard strike.

The introduction of David Beckham was rewarded with two more goals for the Reds – a glorious free-kick in the 71st minute and a toe-poke from van Nistelrooy's deflected shot in the 85th.

Despite a frantic finale, during which Beckham again went close with a free kick, the Reds couldn't force the two goals that would have clinched overall victory and revived hopes of a third European Cup win.

But the spectacle will live long in the memory – not just for United's resolve, but for Ronaldo's contribution. The standing ovation given by the whole of the ground on his substitution showed that the Theatre of Dreams, despite United's broken ambition, is a stage where all heroes are cherished.

Sir Alex Ferguson

YOU CAN'T LEGISLATE FOR SOMEONE SCORING LIKE THAT AND I THOUGHT RONALDO WAS FANTASTIC. WE PUT UP A TREMENDOUS FIGHT AND WERE DESPERATE TO GET TO THE FINAL. I SAID BEFORE THE GAME WE HAD TO STOP THEM SCORING AND IT'S BEEN PROVED WE SIMPLY COULD NOT DO THAT

**Wednesday
23 April 2003**
Old Trafford
Attendance: **66,708**
Referee: **Pierluigi
Collina (Italy)**

COMETH
THE HOUR

Ole Gunnar
Solskjaer
slides in

Manchester United: Barthez;
Brown, Silvestre (P Neville 78),
Ferdinand, O'Shea; Butt, Giggs,
Veron (Beckham 63), Keane (Fortune 81);
van Nistelrooy, Solskjaer
Subs not used: Ricardo, Blanc, Forlan,
Fletcher

Real Madrid: Casillas; Salgado,
Hierro, Helguera; Carlos; Zidane,
McManaman (Portillo 68), Figo,
Makelele; Ronaldo (Solari 62), Guti
Subs not used: César, Morientes, Conceiçao,
Cambiasso, Pavon

Possession	
46%	54%
Shots on target	
13	4
Shots off target	
8	5
Corners	
3	1
Offsides	
0	5
Fouls	
19	18

Man of the match
RUUD VAN NISTELROOY

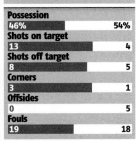

Ruud's credentials
were boosted further
still by another towering
display of verve and power.
His unerring ability to be in
the right place at the right
time got United back into the
game – a Real menace. A
fitting finale to his record-
breaking Euro campaign.

UEFA Champions League
Quarter-final
2nd leg results

Tuesday 22 April 2003
Nou Camp
Attendance 98,000

Barcelona	1–2	Juventus
Xavi 66		Nedved 53
(aet) agg 2–3		Zalayeta 114

Tuesday 22 April 2003
Mestalla
Attendance 48,000

Valencia	2–1	Internazionale
Aimar 6, Baraja 51		Vieri 4
(agg 2–2)		

Wednesday 23 April 2003
San Siro
Attendance 76,079

AC Milan	3–2	Ajax
Inzaghi 30, Shevchenko 64		Litmanen 63
Tomasson 90		Pienaar 78
(agg 3–2)		

FA CUP

A trio of home ties awaited United in the FA Cup this year, where Arsenal gained revenge for their Old Trafford league defeat and four First Division teams made it into the last eight

The media dusted down their clichés for another year as big gun met small fry for the latest taste of FA Cup romance. No less than seven Premiership sides fell at the first hurdle including Everton, who were humbled by Third Division Shrewsbury Town (managed by former Goodison hero Kevin Radcliffe). No such drama for United, who put four past Pompey.

The fourth round served up the ultimate David and Goliath tie. And while United were hitting West Ham for six at Old Trafford, Arsenal brushed aside non-League Farnborough. The shock of the round was Liverpool's replay defeat by Crystal Palace.

United's quest for the FA Cup fizzled out at Old Trafford in a bad-tempered fifth round clash with Arsenal, but the result was overshadowed by post-match events in the home dressing room. Wolves, Sheffield United, Burnley and Watford were the First Division shock troops in the last eight.

Sheffield United dumped Leeds out at the quarter final stage, repeating their earlier Worthington Cup feat. There was another local derby when Arsenal beat Chelsea after a replay, with Thierry Henry struck by objects thrown from the crowd in both matches.

In the first semi-final at Old Trafford, Arsenal controversially beat Sheffield United 1-0, while Southampton brushed past Watford in the other tie at Villa Park – setting up their first Cup final appearance since they beat United in 1976. But it wasn't to be Saints' day in Cardiff. The Gunners went 1-0 up in the first half and narrowly held on to their lead to retain the Cup.

FA Cup fixtures 2002/03

Sat 4th Jan	Portsmouth (R3)	Home
Sun 26th Jan	West Ham (R4)	Home
Sat 15th Feb	Arsenal (R5)	Home

In the FA Cup this year

201,612
watched United play three games

United scored

10
goals

but conceded

3
goals

United travelled

0
miles to and from games

United fielded a total of

20
players

GOAL OF THE FA CUP PHIL NEVILLE V WEST HAM, 4/02/03

United dug the shooting boots out for January's FA Cup matches, knocking 10 goals past Portsmouth and West Ham at Old Trafford (four of them from the feet of Ruud van Nistelrooy). Choosing the best goal out of this lot is no easy task but Phil Neville's goal against the Hammers (the fourth in a 6–0 rout) was arguably the pick of the bunch. A minute after van Nistelrooy had put United three ahead, the Reds broke through West Ham's brittle defence once again, with Diego Forlan playing a sublime one–two with Phil Neville. United's Mr Versatile, operating at left back once again, found himself in the box and chipped David James for his first ever FA Cup goal. An honourable mention must also go to David Beckham's inch–perfect free kick in the game against Portsmouth – another one for the scrapbook.

Manchester United 4
Van Nistelrooy 4, 81 (both pens), Beckham 17, Scholes 90

Portsmouth 1
Stone 38

Dutch master: Ruud was spot on again

Put it there: Ryan Giggs congratulates Paul Scholes

Ruud salutes the fans after his second spot kick

MATCHFACTS

**Saturday
4 January 2003
Old Trafford**
Attendance: **67,222**
Referee: **Mike Riley**

A trademark David Beckham free kick was the highlight of United's FA Cup opener and ensured there would be no romance for First Division leaders Portsmouth. Harry Redknapp's south coast side were roared on by 9,000 travelling fans clearly hoping for an upset but in truth, they didn't have much to cheer.

Sir Alex made seven changes to the side that defeated Sunderland in the previous game, with Roy Carroll deputising for Fabien Barthez and Kieran Richardson making his first home start. Elsewhere, Laurent Blanc, Ruud van Nistelrooy, the Neville brothers and Ryan Giggs all returned to action.

But it was business as usual for the Reds. Faced by a blistering opening salvo, the visitors could have been forgiven for thinking they'd turned up at the wrong Old Trafford, with a cricket score looking likely.

Pompey fell a goal behind on four minutes, Linvoy Primus felling Ryan Giggs in the box after good work by van Nistelrooy. The Dutchman coolly dispatched the penalty to Shaka Hislop's right, and saw two more efforts go wide in the opening 10 minutes.

Beckham extended United's advantage on 17 minutes with a vintage 30-yard free kick which left Hislop clawing air. He nearly repeated the feat on the half-hour mark, striking the angle of post and bar from a similar distance. But, unexpectedly, Steve Stone gave Pompey hope, thumping home from close range seven minutes from the interval.

Michael Stewart got his first taste of home action, replacing Roy Keane at half-time. The break gave Pompey the chance to regroup, and they re-emerged in more confident mood, despite losing veteran playmaker Paul Merson to an ankle injury.

Enjoying plenty of possession, if no real cutting edge, Portsmouth had a genuine chance of an equaliser on 65 minutes. United's back line was sliced open, allowing Nigel Quashie a clear run on goal from 40 yards but, perhaps unnerved by the opportunity, he spooned his shot high over the bar.

The miss was the turning point for Pompey and their players were clearly deflated. Soon afterwards, Rio Ferdinand had a header cleared off the line, but it was van Nistelrooy who secured victory.

After being brought down by Hayden Foxe on 81 minutes, the Dutchman coolly converted his second spot-kick of the match. A Svetoslav Todorov strike was ruled offside as Pompey battled gamely on, but in the final minute a long clearance found substitute Paul Scholes, who calmly lifted the ball over Hislop from 12 yards to make it 4-1.

Manchester United: Carroll; G Neville, Ferdinand, Blanc, Silvestre; (Brown 82), Beckham, Keane (Stewart 45), P Neville, Richardson (Scholes 59); van Nistelrooy, Giggs
Subs not used: Ricardo, Forlan

Portsmouth: Hislop; Primus, Foxe, Tavlaridis; Harper, Stone (Burton 89), Diabate (Pericard 45), Quashie, Taylor; Merson (O'Neil 45), Todorov
Subs not used: Kawaguchi, Crowe
Booked: Diabate, Tavlaridis

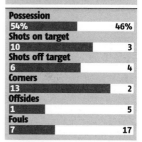

Possession	
54%	46%
Shots on target	
10	3
Shots off target	
6	4
Corners	
13	2
Offsides	
1	5
Fouls	
7	17

Man of the match
DAVID BECKHAM
One free kick straight out of the top drawer and another against the woodwork that would have eclipsed it for genius. Consistently inventive and enthusiastic, Beckham's willingness to run for the cause was a key difference between the sides.

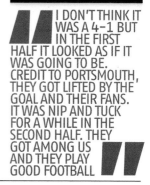

Sir Alex Ferguson

I DON'T THINK IT WAS A 4-1 BUT IN THE FIRST HALF IT LOOKED AS IF IT WAS GOING TO BE. CREDIT TO PORTSMOUTH, THEY GOT LIFTED BY THE GOAL AND THEIR FANS. IT WAS NIP AND TUCK FOR A WHILE IN THE SECOND HALF. THEY GOT AMONG US AND THEY PLAY GOOD FOOTBALL

Manchester United 6

Giggs 8, 29, van Nistelrooy 49, 58, P Neville 50, Solskjaer 69

West Ham United 0

Ruud-imentary: two FA Cup ties and four goals

This was not a day West Ham manager Glenn Roeder will want to remember. Despite threatening to rack up the sort of scoreline the BBC's old vidiprinter used to have to spell out in brackets, United demolished the hapless Hammers without ever hitting top gear.

The draw had conjured up memories of 28 January 2001, when West Ham dumped United out of the Cup thanks to Paolo di Canio's impudence. Well, if they say revenge is a dish best served cold, United didn't even bother defrosting, swaggering into the fifth round in Harlem Globetrotters fashion.

The writing was on the wall after eight minutes when Ryan Giggs, a subject of recent criticism, sent a message to the naysayers with a rare home goal. Ian Pearce stopped Paul Scholes extending his impressive scoring run to seven consecutive games with a goal-line clearance, only to see the ball fall at the feet of Giggs, who steadied himself and placed a shot past David James.

The biggest shock was that United only added one more in this half, when Giggs scored again with the aid of a deflection off the shoulder of Gary Breen. To say it wasn't Breen's day would be something of an understatement.

Sunday
26 January 2003
Old Trafford
Attendance: **67,181**
Referee: **Steve Bennett**

Manchester United: Barthez; G Neville, O'Shea, Ferdinand, P Neville; Beckham (Solskjaer 63), Veron (Butt 51), Keane, Giggs; Scholes (Forlan 45), van Nistelrooy
Subs not used: Carroll, Brown
Booked: Veron

West Ham United: James; Lomas, Breen (Dailly 80), Pearce, Minto; Bowyer, Cisse (Garcia 80), Carrick, Sinclair (Johnson 80); Defoe, Cole
Subs not used: van der Gouw, Hutchison
Booked: Minto, Defoe

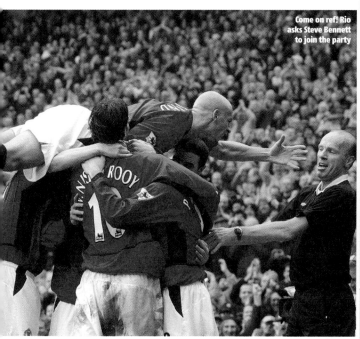

Come on ref! Rio asks Steve Bennett to join the party

Possession	
59%	41%
Shots on target	
8	7
Shots off target	
5	2
Corners	
7	3
Offsides	
2	4
Fouls	
5	10

Man of the match
RUUD VAN NISTELROOY
Take your pick from any number of men in red, but the Dutchman's invigorating display and well-taken brace topped the lot. Ruud will come up against meaner defences but his was football with a smile on its face.

The best move of the match was not to result in a goal, however. Ten minutes before the break, United played keep-ball with a wonderful spell of 27 passes and the move ended with Scholes crashing a shot off the post. Any hopes of continuing his scoring run ended when he stayed in the dressing room at half-time feeling unwell, to be replaced by Diego Forlan.

The second-half goal spree started with a peach from Ruud van Nistelrooy. The deadly Dutchman's soft-shoe shuffle on the edge of the box created just enough space to fire home with five minutes of the half gone. Phil Neville got in on the act with one of those sublime goals he likes to surprise us with every now and again, thanks to some clever link-up play with Forlan, and Ruud helped himself once more after 58 minutes when he made the most of a cute ball from David Beckham.

Ten minutes later, Ole Gunnar Solskjaer grabbed his predictable piece of the action when he rattled home with ease. With 20 minutes still on the clock, United decided that the punchdrunk visitors had taken enough punishment and eased off. It was, in truth, a noble act of kindness.

Sir Alex Ferguson

I THOUGHT SOME OF OUR PASSING WAS VERY GOOD AND THERE WERE PERIODS IN THE FIRST HALF WHEN SOME OF THE MOVES WERE TERRIFIC. WE COULD HAVE GOT EVEN MORE. SOME OF THE GOALS WERE VERY GOOD AND THERE IS A LOT OF CONFIDENCE IN THE TEAM

Manchester United 0

Arsenal 2
Edu 34, Wiltord 52

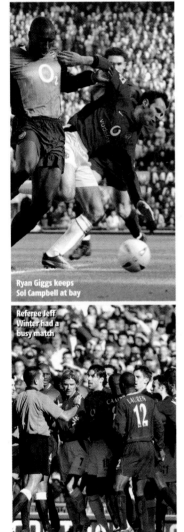

Ryan Giggs keeps Sol Campbell at bay

Referee Jeff Winter had a busy match

Fortress Old Trafford was breached for the first time in over 20 games as United fell to Arsenal in a bad-tempered FA Cup tie played in the early afternoon sunshine. From the first peep of Jeff Winter's whistle, this match exploded into action, with three names going into the book in the first seven minutes.

Tackles were flying in all over the pitch, and Winter turned down two strong penalty shouts by United in the opening exchanges. First Ole Gunnar Solskjaer and then Ruud van Nistelrooy were both bundled over in the box. Ruud was booked for clattering Martin Keown and their battle – recalling the feud between the two players during United's 2-0 league win over Arsenal in December – continued all afternoon.

After two mass confrontations sparked by strong challenges from Sol Campbell and Paul Scholes, the beleaguered ref pulled the two captains together and told them in no uncertain terms that things had to cool down or else.

Amid the mayhem a football match almost broke out. Solskjaer had a clear chance to open the scoring when his shot beat David Seaman, only to see his effort come off the post, but then came the moment that had the Stretford End aghast.

A long ball from David Beckham was missed by Keown and as Seaman rushed out to clear the danger, Ryan Giggs pounced on the ball with a deft touch and bypassed both the keeper and Campbell. Faced with an empty net, he lifted his shot over the bar – going for power instead of rolling the ball in.

Moments later, Arsenal took advantage of the miss by taking the lead. The visitors were handed a dubious free kick just outside the area after Roy Keane was judged to have halted the progress of Patrick Vieira, and Edu's subsequent strike cannoned off the United wall and into the net, with Fabien Barthez stranded.

The Gunners put the game out of reach seven minutes into the second half when a clever square ball from Edu gave Sylvain Wiltord the space to dance past Wes Brown and finish past Barthez. United continued to create opportunities but struggled to make them count. Solskjaer hit the side netting and Giggs, replaced by Diego Forlan on 71 minutes, should have done better from an inviting Beckham cross.

With the game petering out, Wes Brown stopped Wiltord putting the seal on an Arsenal victory with a last-gasp tackle when the French striker was put clean through by substitute Thierry Henry, but it didn't alter the outcome as Arsenal cleared a path to a potential third FA Cup Final in a row.

**Saturday
15 February 2003
Old Trafford**
Attendance: **67,209**
Referee: **Jeff Winter**

Manchester United: Barthez;
G Neville, Ferdinand, Brown,
Silvestre; Beckham (Butt 83),
Scholes, Keane, Giggs (Forlan 71);
van Nistelrooy, Solskjaer
Subs not used: Ricardo, P Neville, O'Shea
Booked: Scholes, Keane, van Nistelrooy

Arsenal: Seaman; Lauren,
Keown, Campbell, Cole; Parlour,
Vieira, Edu, Pires (van Bronckhorst
84); Jeffers (Henry 73), Wiltord (Toure 90)
Subs not used: Warmuz, Cygan
Booked: Vieira

Possession	
47%	53%

Shots on target	
0	3

Shots off target	
8	2

Corners	
2	5

Offsides	
2	1

Fouls	
14	14

**Man of the match
WES BROWN**

With Arsenal gaining the
upper hand in the midfield
battle the United defence
was always under pressure,
but Brown was a match for
the threat of Wiltord and
Jeffers. Wes's magnificent
tackle on a goal-bound
Wiltord surely kept the
scoreline pegged to 2-0.

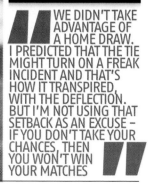

Sir Alex Ferguson

WE DIDN'T TAKE
ADVANTAGE OF
A HOME DRAW.
I PREDICTED THAT THE TIE
MIGHT TURN ON A FREAK
INCIDENT AND THAT'S
HOW IT TRANSPIRED,
WITH THE DEFLECTION.
BUT I'M NOT USING THAT
SETBACK AS AN EXCUSE –
IF YOU DON'T TAKE YOUR
CHANCES, THEN
YOU WON'T WIN
YOUR MATCHES

Ashley Cole under
pressure from
David Beckham

WORTHINGTON CUP

The much-derided League Cup format received an unlikely boost thanks to Sir Alex's selection policy as the showpiece final the sponsors were desperate for came to fruition

Eyebrows were raised when the United team for the third round tie against Leicester City included Beckham, Ferdinand, Solskjaer and the Nevilles but not everyone was taking the tournament as seriously as United. A makeshift Arsenal side lost at home to Sunderland in the Third Round, while Tottenham, Manchester City, West Ham, Middlesbrough, Leeds and Newcastle United were also early casualties.

The fourth round saw United beat Burnley and elsewhere Liverpool sneaked into the last eight, winning on penalties at home to Ipswich. Sunderland were knocked out by this season's dark horses Sheffield United, while Wigan put paid to Fulham's challenge, their third Premiership scalp of the tournament. And in the tie of the round, Chelsea crushed Everton 4-1 at Stamford Bridge.

Villa Park hosted a remarkable quarter-final clash when Aston Villa played Liverpool in mid-December. The 7.45pm kick off kick was delayed for 80 minutes due to a ticketing fiasco, but it was worth waiting for, as Danny Murphy snatched a last-minute winner to give Liverpool a 4-3 win. Officials breathed a sigh of relief, as the game would have finished the other side of midnight had it went to extra time and penalties. At Old Trafford, a late winner from Forlan gave United a win against Chelsea.

With United easing past Blackburn in the semi final, the showpiece final the sponsors were desperate for came alive when Liverpool edged through against Sheffield United. The final is covered on page 164/165.

Worthington Cup fixtures 2002/03

Tues 5th Nov	Leicester City (R3)	Home
Tues 3rd Dec	Burnley (R4)	Away
Tues 17th Dec	Chelsea (R5)	Home
Tues 7th Jan	Blackburn (semi-1st leg)	Home
Weds 22nd Jan	Blackburn (semi-2nd leg)	Away
Sun 2nd March	Liverpool (final)	Cardiff

In the Worthington Cup this year

294,155
watched United play six games

United scored

9
goals

but conceded

4
goals

United travelled

523
miles to and from games

United fielded a total of

24
players

GOAL OF THE WORTHINGTON CUP DIEGO FORLAN V CHELSEA 17/12/02

It was a League Cup clash of the titans when high-flying Chelsea visited Old Trafford for the quarter finals. Only one point separated the teams in the league and the Premiership match at Stamford Bridge in August had been a humdinger, so hopes were high of another sparkling occasion. As it turned out, the match was a tight affair with both teams enjoying spells of possession without particularly troubling Barthez or Cudicini. The game looked to be edging towards extra-time when Diego Forlan grabbed his seventh goal of the season. With ten minutes to go, Beckham capitalised on a rare error from the evergreen Gianfranco Zola and found Forlan in an advanced position. The Uruguayan charged towards Cudicini and slotted through the Italian's legs to book United's place in the semi-final.

Manchester United 2
Beckham 80 (penalty), Richardson 90
Leicester City 0

MATCHFACTS

Tuesday
5 November 2003
Old Trafford
Attendance: **47,848**
Referee: **Chris Foy**

Manchester United: Carroll;
G Neville, Ferdinand, May, O'Shea;
Forlan, Beckham, P Neville
(Scholes 59), Fortune (Veron 65); Solskjaer,
Nardiello (Richardson 74)
Subs not used: Barthez, Pugh
Booked: Beckham, P Neville

Leicester City: Walker; Sinclair,
Heath, Elliott (Summerbee 51),
Rogers (Stevenson 81); Impey,
Izzet, Davidson, Stewart; Dickov (Benjamin),
Scowcroft **Subs not used:** Reeves, Oakes
Booked: Heath, Impey, Sinclair

Possession	
56%	44%
Shots on target	
5	2
Shots off target	
6	5
Corners	
5	6
Offsides	
0	1
Fouls	
11	16

Man of the match
DAVID BECKHAM

The United skipper gave
a performance of dazzling
creativity, energy and
passion – which goes to
prove that whoever the
opposition, David can
always be relied upon
to put in a full shift and
dispense more than his
fair share of inspiration.

Sir Alex Ferguson

THE PENALTY
WAS A BIT SOFT.
YOU DON'T
ALWAYS GET THOSE. WE
FIELDED A STRONG SIDE.
I SHALL CONTINUE TO
SELECT TEAMS CAPABLE
OF WINNING EVERY
MATCH, TEMPERED WITH
ONE OR TWO PLAYERS
WHO DON'T GET
REGULAR
GAMES IN THE
PREMIERSHIP

Kieran Richardson
grabs his first
United goal

David Beckham
celebrates the
opener

Attempting to second-guess Sir Alex Ferguson's team selection is
an exercise fraught with difficulty. Frankly, men have had more joy
forecasting variations in the Manchester weather. Against
Leicester City the gaffer sprang yet another surprise, selecting a
first XI studded with established internationals. Youth team
hotshot Daniel Nardiello was the only fresh face in the starting
line-up, although Kieran Richardson and Danny Pugh provided
youthful back-up on the bench.

Leicester boss Micky Adams must have cursed his luck when
the teams were announced, but the Foxes more than held their
own in the first half, matching United's commitment in midfield
and restricting chances to a minimum. Diego Forlan, buoyant
following his winner against Southampton in the league three
days earlier, went close with a diving header and Ole Gunnar
Solskjaer also tested Ian Walker with a stinging left-footed drive.

United upped the tempo after the interval but were unable to
force the breakthrough. With 60 minutes gone Sir Alex sent for the
cavalry, bringing on Paul Scholes and Seba Veron for Phil Neville
and Quinton Fortune. The substitutions gave United fresh
impetus, but the Reds were forced to wait until 10 minutes from
time to open the scoring – David Beckham firing home a penalty
after Andrew Impey had been penalised for a push on Solskjaer.

The goal was just reward for the skipper who, operating in
central midfield, was the architect of all United's incisive forays.
Indeed, it was Beckham who also inspired United's second goal,
fizzing in a typically searching cross from which substitute Kieran
Richardson, making his home debut for the Reds, applied the
finishing touch with a diving header from close range.

Burnley 0

Manchester United 2

Forlan 35, Solskjaer 65

Tuesday
3 December 2002
Turf Moor
Attendance: **22,034**
Referee: **Neale Barry**

Burnley: Beresford; West, Davis, Gnohere (A Moore 73), Branch; Weller, Cook (Grant 57), Briscoe (Papadopoulos 67), Little; Blake, Taylor
Subs not used: I Moore, McGregor

Manchester United: Carroll; P Neville, Brown, May, Silvestre; Pugh, Chadwick, Stewart (Scholes 58), O'Shea; van Nistelrooy (Solskjaer 46), Forlan (Giggs 76)
Subs not used: Ricardo, Roche
Booked: Brown

United eased into the quarter-finals of the Worthington Cup with a hard-fought victory against battling Burnley thanks to goals from Diego Forlan and Ole Gunnar Solskjaer. Sir Alex opted for an intriguing mix of youth and experience in his team selection and there was no shortage of strength at the back, including captain for the night David May and Wes Brown. Michael Stewart, Danny Pugh and Luke Chadwick were eager to impress in midfield alongside the versatile John O'Shea, while up front, the big guns were in town.

The match started brightly for Burnley with Robbie Blake and Gareth Taylor conspiring to threaten Roy Carroll's goal twice early on. The Clarets looked in the mood to cause an upset, but were to rue their first-half misses.

The United faithful aired new anthems celebrating the recent league win away at Liverpool and it was the hero of Anfield who gave the Reds the lead. O'Shea beat the Burnley offside trap with a precision pass for Forlan and the on-fire Uruguayan made no mistake. Burnley could have equalised with a header from Taylor but Carroll made an instinctive one-handed save.

Ole replaced Ruud van Nistelrooy at the break and Stewart soon made way for Paul Scholes. Again Burnley started brightly, but United could have scored again when Pugh had two gilt-edged chances to mark his first full start with a goal, shooting first high and then wide.

No matter, because Solskjaer made no mistake with a scorching strike to make it 2-0. Burnley huffed and puffed to try and salvage something from the match, but when Paul Weller shot wildly over with 10 minutes left, the Clarets knew their hopes of staying in the tournament were going underground.

Possession	
53%	47%

Shots on target	
10	8

Shots off target	
7	10

Corners	
4	8

Offsides	
2	3

Fouls	
11	13

Man of the match
WES BROWN

Burnley belied their First Division status with a smart passing game, but they couldn't break down a United defence superbly marshalled by Wes Brown. With competition tough for a regular place in central defence, Wes staked his claim with an impressive performance.

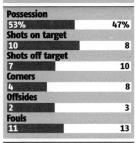

Ole Gunnar Solskjaer smashes home United's second

Sir Alex Ferguson

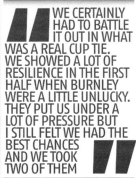

WE CERTAINLY HAD TO BATTLE IT OUT IN WHAT WAS A REAL CUP TIE. WE SHOWED A LOT OF RESILIENCE IN THE FIRST HALF WHEN BURNLEY WERE A LITTLE UNLUCKY. THEY PUT US UNDER A LOT OF PRESSURE BUT I STILL FELT WE HAD THE BEST CHANCES AND WE TOOK TWO OF THEM

Manchester United 1
Forlan 80

Chelsea 0

Diego Forlan
was once again
United's hero

Tuesday
17 December 2002
Old Trafford
Attendance: **57,985**
Referee: **Steve Bennett**

Eight wins and five clean sheets on the bounce. The statistics told their own tale although, if he wanted to seek comfort in defeat, Chelsea manager Claudio Ranieri could take solace from the fact that his side asked more questions of United than either Liverpool or Arsenal could muster in the weeks before this match.

Indeed, one could argue that defeat was hard on the Londoners. With the game seemingly destined for extra time, it was the Reds who summoned the requisite resources to land the killer blow, their sense of self-belief clearly heightened by a run of good form.

In an evenly-contested first half, both teams created chances. With Gianfranco Zola and Jimmy Floyd Hasselbaink combining intelligently up front for Chelsea, Wes Brown and Mikael Silvestre had to be on their toes to prevent the visitors capitalising on the break, but it was United who were playing the more progressive football.

Paul Scholes was again prominent. Playing in a withdrawn role to support Diego Forlan, his tricky footwork routinely bewildered his markers and his sudden changes of direction around the box confused Chelsea's defenders. Scholes was unlucky not to get on the scoresheet himself, flashing two venomous shots narrowly wide.

United's best chance of the half fell to Ryan Giggs, however. Picked out by Seba Veron, whose pass travelled such a distance it gave the illusion of having emanated from the car park behind the West Stand, the Welshman lifted the ball over the advancing Carlo Cudicini but his lob was cleared off the line by the retreating Mario Melchiot.

But it wasn't all United. Fabien Barthez made a terrific save from Hasselbaink just after the game started, and had to react quickly to block the Dutchman's firm header from a Graeme Le Saux corner.

In the second half, Chelsea enjoyed more possession and seemed certain to take the lead when, on 65 minutes, an unmarked Frank Lampard unleashed a goalbound shot from 10 yards out. But somehow Gary Neville, launching himself full length, made up enough ground to block the shot and the ball was cleared. It was to be the pivotal moment of the match.

Fifteen minutes later, Forlan, released by a deft pass from David Beckham following a mistake by the otherwise impeccable Zola, nutmegged Cudicini to clinch a 1-0 victory and propel United towards the semi-final of this competition for the first time in nine years. It was the Uruguayan's seventh goal in nine starts.

Manchester United: Barthez; G Neville, Brown, Silvestre, O'Shea; Beckham, Veron, P Neville, Giggs; Forlan, Scholes
Subs Not Used: Carroll, Blanc, Stewart, Nardiello, Richardson
Booked: P Neville

Chelsea: Cudicini; Melchiot, Gallas, Terry, Le Saux; De Lucas (Zenden 66), Lampard, Morris, Stanic; Hasselbaink (Gudjohnsen 78), Zola
Subs Not Used: de Goey, Ferrer, Desailly
Booked: Terry, Stanic

Possession

51%	49%

Shots on target

2	4

Shots off target

6	7

Corners

4	9

Offsides

8	4

Fouls

8	14

Man of the match
MIKAEL SILVESTRE

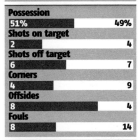

His performance in shackling the twin threats of Hasselbaink and Zola contributed hugely to United's success and secured the Reds' fifth clean sheet in a row. Usually a left-back for United and France, Silvestre also excels as a centre-half.

Sir Alex Ferguson

THEY HAD THEIR MOMENTS BUT OVERALL WE DEFENDED BRILLIANTLY. WES BROWN AND MIKAEL SILVESTRE WERE FANTASTIC AND HAVE WORKED UP A GREAT PARTNERSHIP. WE WERE ALSO A THREAT GOING FORWARD – SOME OF OUR FOOTBALL WAS BEAUTIFUL TO WATCH

Manchester United 1
Scholes 58

Blackburn Rovers 1
Thompson 61

Far post predator
Paul Scholes put
United in front

United were clear favourites to win this semi-final home tie, but Graeme Souness' Blackburn proved stubborn opposition, gaining a deserved score draw that placed Sir Alex Ferguson's record of having never lost in the last four of a domestic competition in peril.

The Reds carried the fight to Rovers from the off, but were unable to find a way past the in-form Brad Friedel. United's best chance of the first period came within seconds of the interval. Put through by a cute pass from Paul Scholes, Ruud van Nistelrooy bore down on goal, and with only the big American to beat the crowd were already rising to acknowledge the opening score of the game. But it wasn't to be – Friedel leapt to his left to block the Dutchman's shot.

After the break Blackburn grew in confidence and, with Dwight Yorke and Andy Cole dovetailing in familiar fashion up front, began to pose a greater threat. Yet it was United who continued to fashion the clearer openings. On 56 minutes, following a tenacious run and cross from David Beckham, the Reds again looked certain to take the lead, only for van Nistelrooy

Tuesday
7 January 2003
Old Trafford
Attendance: **62,740**
Referee: **Uriah Rennie**

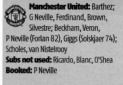

Manchester United: Barthez;
G Neville, Ferdinand, Brown,
Silvestre; Beckham, Veron,
P Neville (Forlan 82), Giggs (Solskjaer 74);
Scholes, van Nistelrooy
Subs not used: Ricardo, Blanc, O'Shea
Booked: P Neville

Blackburn Rovers: Friedel;
Neill, Taylor, Todd, McEveley;
Thompson (Jansen 66), Tugay,
Flitcroft, Dunn (Gillespie 19); Cole, Yorke
Subs not used: Kelly, Ostenstad, Johansson
Booked: McEveley, Neill

Possession	
54%	46%

Shots on target	
4	3

Shots off target	
6	3

Corners	
13	4

Offsides	
1	9

Fouls	
17	12

Man of the match
PAUL SCHOLES

On a pitch containing more bobbles than an overly-laundered cardigan, Scholes' ability to cushion heavy passes effortlessly was awe-inspiring, enhancing his reputation as one of the most technically gifted footballers on Earth.

Gary Neville clears his lines

to scoop over from six yards. No one could quite believe it, least of all the Dutchman who, incredulous at his own inaccuracy, smothered his head in his hands.

The breakthrough finally came just before the hour when Paul Scholes, making a nuisance of himself at the far post, bundled home a deflected right wing cross from David Beckham that had been spilled by Friedel. But Rovers drew level three minutes later, David Thompson placing a firm diving header past Fabien Barthez after a jinking run and centre from ex-Red Keith Gillespie.

Boosted by their goal, the visitors began to enjoy increasing periods of possession in midfield, but, as the final whistle drew closer, United steeled themselves for a late rally. Ole Gunnar Solskjaer and Diego Forlan entered the fray as substitutes and, with Scholes and Beckham at their mischievous best, the Rovers defence began to show signs of wear and tear.

Victory was nearly snatched at the death, but Solskjaer's last-minute shot was miraculously cleared off the line by teenage full back James McEveley, leaving the Reds facing a tricky excursion to Ewood Park for the away leg.

Sir Alex Ferguson

> BLACKBURN WERE THE BETTER TEAM, PARTICULARLY IN THE SECOND HALF. OVERALL, IT WAS A STRANGE GAME. THE FIRST HALF WAS LUKEWARM AND LACKED THE PASSION OF A SEMI-FINAL. I'M SURE THE SECOND LEG WILL BE DIFFERENT. WE WILL HAVE TO PLAY BETTER

Blackburn Rovers 1
Cole 12

Manchester United 3
Scholes 30, 42, van Nistelrooy 77 (pen)

United's heroes savour the moment

Chairman Martin Edwards leads the applause

Sir Alex: 'Our fans created a great atmosphere'

Wednesday
22 January 2003
Ewood Park
Attendance: **29,048**
Referee: **Jeff Winter**

United booked their place in a Cardiff final for the first time by brushing past Blackburn to set up a Worthington Cup showdown with old rivals Liverpool. The tie was evenly poised after the first leg, but Sir Alex clearly wasn't in the mood to lose his first domestic semi-final, despite seeing his troops go behind early on with a goal from Andy Cole.

It was created by the ever-alert Tugay, who picked up a loose ball, dinked it over the defence and into the path of Cole, who lobbed Fabien Barthez to give Rovers first blood. Five minutes later the United old boy had a clear opportunity to double his tally when he took on Wes Brown, twisting and turning before shooting weakly. It was a missed chance Rovers and the Ewood Park faithful would come to rue.

The half-hour mark saw United back on level terms with yet another strike from man of the moment Paul Scholes. Making the most of the Reds' first-half pressure, David Beckham rifled a ball into the box which Scholes drove sweetly home at the second time of asking.

Twelve minutes later, the Reds took control of the tie with a goal that was pure, undiluted United. Roy Keane broke up a Blackburn attack in his own box and slid the ball to Beckham, who quickly found Gary Neville.

The right back went on a sprint and just when he looked to have ran out of juice, found another burst of speed which took him past 17-year-old James McEveley and into the area. Scholes, having lost his marker, waited for Neville's clever cut-back and stroked the ball home to complete the move in style.

Five minutes into the second half the match developed an edge when Beckham tumbled in the Rovers box under pressure from David Thompson. Referee Jeff Winter waved play on but there was no question when Ruud van Nistelrooy was felled in the box by Brad Friedel with 15 minutes to go.

The move was started by another long ball from Keane that sent Ruud on a one-on-one chase with sub Keith Gillespie, who found himself in an unlikely position as the last line of defence.

Passing the flailing Irishman, it was left to Friedel to try and stop Ruud's progress, which he did, albeit illegally. Blackburn's stopper was shown clemency by Winter, however, who sheepishly flashed a yellow card when it should have been red. Ruud duly dispatched the penalty for his first Worthington Cup goal. With 10 minutes to go United's night was complete when Nicky Butt came on to signal his return to fitness.

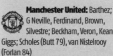

Blackburn Rovers: Friedel; Neill, Todd, Taylor, McEveley; Thompson, Flitcroft, Tugay, Duff (Gillespie 34); Cole, Yorke
Subs not used: Short, Jansen, Ostenstad, Robinson
Booked: Friedel, Thompson

Manchester United: Barthez; G Neville, Ferdinand, Brown, Silvestre; Beckham, Veron, Keane, Giggs; Scholes (Butt 79), van Nistelrooy (Forlan 84)
Subs not used: P Neville, O'Shea, Ricardo

Possession	
55%	45%

Shots on target	
10	4

Shots off target	
3	3

Corners	
6	6

Offsides	
2	3

Fouls	
15	11

Man of the match
PAUL SCHOLES

Proving more predatory than some strange shark/ piranha hybrid, United's midfield genius stretched his scoring run to seven goals in six games. Paul's two strikes against Rovers capped a great all-round performance – he also dictated much of the Reds' attacking play.

Sir Alex Ferguson

BLACKBURN JUST COULDN'T CONTROL PAUL SCHOLES, PARTICULARLY IN THE FIRST HALF, AND HE WON THE MATCH FOR US. I'M ALSO PLEASED FOR THE FANS – THEY CREATED A REAL CUP TIE ATMOSPHERE AND THE PLAYERS WOULD BE THE FIRST TO SAY HOW MUCH IT HELPED THEM

Liverpool 2
Gerrard 39, Owen 86

Manchester United 0

Mikael Silvestre heads off Diouf

United had to settle for second best in a fiercely-competed final in which great rivals Liverpool overcame a run of indifferent form with another win in Cardiff's magnificent Millennium Stadium.

Perhaps the most important factor in the Worthington Cup making its way to Merseyside was Anfield goalkeeper Jerzy Dudek, whose match-winning performance was packed with irony – it was the Pole's errors against United earlier this season that led to his axing from Gérard Houllier's side.

In Cardiff, however, Dudek – re-instated after first-choice keeper Chris Kirkland succumbed to injury – went from blunder to wonder. And he wasn't the only Liverpool player to find an extra gear when it was most needed.

In a first half of resolute defending and swift counter-attacking, it was always going to take something out of the ordinary to break the deadlock – and Steven Gerrard supplied it. Receiving possession 30 yards out from John Arne Riise, Gerrard drove the ball home into the top corner past a helpless Fabien Barthez courtesy of a wicked deflection from David Beckham.

United were enjoying a fair share of the possession but for all their increased vigour after falling behind, could never make it count in the final third. Seba Veron decided to go the Gerrard route just before half-time but saw his effort blocked by Dudek, and Stephane Henchoz somehow managed to deflect Paul Scholes' follow-up strike over the bar.

David Beckham is blocked by Riise

United needed to take the game to their opponents after the interval and Sir Alex looked to a substitution to make the required impact. Ole Gunnar Solskjaer replaced Wes Brown, Ryan Giggs moved to left back and United began to find gaps in the Anfield side's back-line.

Dudek, however, proved an immovable object, saving Ruud van Nistelrooy's smart turn and shot then denying the same player when the Dutchman was in acres of space.

Dietmar Hamann's felling of Scholes in the box looked a decent penalty shout as the pressure mounted, but as the clock ran down, Hamann exploited a mix-up between Mikael Silvestre and Rio Ferdinand to put Michael Owen clear.

One-on-one, there are few better strikers in the game and he netted with ease to provide a mountain too steep for United to climb. The delirious Liverpool fans almost raised the closed roof on this spectacular arena as referee Paul Durkin's final whistle signified the end of the match, while United will have to wait another year to taste success in the Millennium Stadium.

Sunday
2 March 2003
Millennium Stadium
Attendance: **74,500**
Referee: **Paul Durkin**

Liverpool: Dudek; Carragher, Henchoz, Hyypia, Riise; Hamann, Diouf (Biscan 90), Gerrard, Murphy; Heskey (Baros 60 (Smicer 88)), Owen
Subs not used: Arpexhad, Traore
Booked: Henchoz

Manchester United: Barthez; G Neville, Ferdinand, Brown (Solskjaer 73), Silvestre; Beckham, Veron, Keane, Giggs; Scholes, van Nistelrooy
Subs not used: Carroll, P Neville, Butt, O'Shea

Possession	
51%	**49%**
Shots on target	
9	7
Shots off target	
3	1
Corners	
4	3
Offsides	
2	0
Fouls	
19	11

Man of the match
FABIEN BARTHEZ

The man in the gloves kept his team in the game with a point-blank save from Gerrard in the second half and couldn't be blamed for either goal. Again, Fabien's faultless distribution injected some urgency into United's play when it was required.

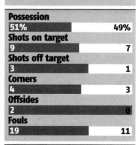

Sir Alex Ferguson

ON SUCH BIG OCCASIONS, YOU NEED A BREAK AND WE DIDN'T GET ONE. HOWEVER, YOU MAKE YOUR OWN LUCK IN THIS GAME AND THERE IS NO DENYING THAT WE DID NOT CASH IN ON THE CHANCES WE HAD, WHILE COMING UP AGAINST A GOALKEEPER IN INSPIRED FORM

Roy Keane leads out United for their first Cardiff final

Manchester United 2
Van Nistelrooy (2)

Boca Juniors 0

Saturday 10 August 2002 Old Trafford
Old Trafford's curtain-raiser for the season
was a glamour clash with Argentinian
visitors Boca Juniors, all in aid of UNICEF.
Note the use of the word "clash" as opposed
to "friendly", as this was no bounce game.
UNICEF ambassador and one-time 007 Roger
Moore watched a full-bloodied match which
saw Rio Ferdinand limp off after 28 minutes
into his first home game for United, while
Boca's Carlos Tevez was sent off for elbowing
Paul Scholes. Both United goals came from
Ruud van Nistelrooy – who else? – the first
after 17 minutes when he curled a cross-shot
into the bottom corner, and the second five
minutes before half-time following good
work from Solskjaer. Ole also had a goal
disallowed and 56,724 fans clearly enjoyed the
return of football to M16, despite Rio's injury.

Parma 0

Manchester United 3
Giggs, Veron, Solskjaer

Sunday 4 August 2002 AmsterdamArenA
United completed their involvement in the
Amsterdam tournament with an impressive
win over Parma. With Scholes, van Nistelrooy,
Blanc and Barthez absent and Keane sitting
out the first half, David Beckham and Seba
Veron took the initiative and excelled against
the young Italian side.

Veron capped his performance with a
brilliant individual goal, a perfectly-weighted
chip over a flailing keeper. Not to be outdone,
Beckham set up United's two other goals,
finished off by Giggs and Solskjaer.

The tournament's bizarre points system
meant United failed to qualify for the latter
stages but ended up in third place behind
Ajax and Barcelona.

Ajax 2
Sikora, Ibrahimovic

Manchester United 1
Scholes

Friday 2 August 2002 AmsterdamArenA

United travelled to Amsterdam to take part in Ajax's prestigious pre-season tournament and were unlucky enough to meet the home side on the first night – naturally eager to put on a good show for their fans. Sir Alex delighted the travelling Reds by fielding a strong side, only missing injured Gary Neville and recuperating Ole Gunnar Solskjaer. Ruud van Nistelrooy almost opened the scoring just before the half hour mark but moments later new signing Victor Sikora gave the home side the lead following a blocked free kick.

Sir Alex changed things after the break with Danny Pugh and Wes Brown replacing van Nistelrooy and Rio Ferdinand. With 68 minutes gone, Ibrahimovic extended the home side's lead; 10 minutes later Paul Scholes netted a consolation for the Reds.

Aarhus XI 0

Manchester United 5
Van Nistelrooy (2), Giggs, Solskjaer, Forlan

6/07/02 Idraetspark, Denmark
"Not the greatest performance," said Sir Alex after the match, but a convincing win all the same. Ruud van Nistelrooy continued his pre-season form with a double against the Danish side, with Ryan Giggs, Ole Gunnar Solskjaer and Diego Forlan also on the scoresheet.

Valerenga 1
Kah

Manchester United 2
Solskjaer, Keane

30/07/02 Ulevaal Stadium, Norway
Ole Gunnar Solskjaer was named United captain on his return home and he marked the occasion with a first-half penalty in front of a capacity crowd in Norway. Pa-Modou Kah equalised with a stunning strike but Keane struck the winner with six minutes remaining.

Chesterfield 0

Manchester United 5
Blanc, van Nistelrooy, Forlan, Keane, Richardson

27/07/02 Saltergate, England
United played two friendlies against lower-league opposition on the same day, and Second Division Chesterfield came off the worst. Laurent Blanc opened the scoring after 19 minutes, and van Nistelrooy, Forlan, Keane and Richardson later got in on the act.

Bournemouth 2
Caceres, Fletcher

Manchester United 3
Veron, Muirhead, Stewart

27/07/02 Dean Court, England
The media descended on the south coast to see Rio Ferdinand make his first appearance in a United shirt, in a benefit for John Duncan – one of Rio's first managers. The home side took the lead and gave it a go, but Premiership class shone through in the end.

Shelbourne 0

Manchester United 5
Van Nistelrooy (3), Yorke, Forlan

20/07/02 Tonka Park, Ireland
Roy Keane returned to Ireland for his first match since his controversial World Cup exit, and received a hero's welcome in Dublin. The 8,000 crowd saw a hat-trick from Ruud van Nistelrooy and the last goal in a United shirt from Dwight Yorke before his departure for Blackburn.

SEASON STATISTICS

AUGUST		RESULT	STARTING LINE-UP								
Wed 14 Zalaegerszeg	Away	0-1	CARROLL	BROWN	BLANC	O'SHEA	SILVESTRE	BECKHAM*	VERON	KEANE	GIGGS
Sat 17 West Bromwich Albion	Home	1-0	CARROLL	NEVILLE P	BLANC	O'SHEA	SILVESTRE	BECKHAM	VERON	KEANE*	GIGGS
Fri 23 Chelsea	Away	2-2	CARROLL	NEVILLE P*	BLANC	O'SHEA	SILVESTRE	**BECKHAM**	BUTT	KEANE	**GIGGS**
Tue 27 Zalaegerszeg 8.10pm	Home	5-0	CARROLL	NEVILLE P*	BLANC	FERDINAND	SILVESTRE	**BECKHAM**	VERON	KEANE	GIGGS
Sat 31 Sunderland	Away	1-1	CARROLL	NEVILLE P*	BLANC	FERDINAND	SILVESTRE	BECKHAM*	VERON	KEANE*	**GIGGS**
SEPTEMBER											
Tue 3 Middlesbrough	Home	1-0	BARTHEZ	NEVILLE P*	BLANC	FERDINAND	SILVESTRE	BECKHAM	VERON*	BUTT	GIGGS
Wed 11 Bolton Wanderers	Home	0-1	BARTHEZ	NEVILLE P*	BLANC	FERDINAND	SILVESTRE	BECKHAM	VERON	BUTT	GIGGS
Sat 14 Leeds United 12pm	Away	0-1	BARTHEZ	O'SHEA	BLANC	FERDINAND	SILVESTRE	BECKHAM	NEVILLE P	BUTT	GIGGS
Wed 18 Maccabi Haifa	Home	5-2	BARTHEZ	O'SHEA	BLANC	FERDINAND	SILVESTRE	BECKHAM	**VERON**	NEVILLE P	**GIGGS**
Sat 21 Tottenham Hotspur	Home	1-0	BARTHEZ	NEVILLE P	FERDINAND	O'SHEA	SILVESTRE	BECKHAM	BUTT	VERON	GIGGS
Tue 24 Bayer 04 Leverkusen	Away	2-1	BARTHEZ	O'SHEA	FERDINAND*	BLANC	SILVESTRE	BECKHAM	VERON	NEVILLE P	BUTT*
Sat 28 Charlton Athletic	Away	3-1	BARTHEZ	O'SHEA	FERDINAND	BLANC	NEVILLE P*	BECKHAM*	BUTT	FORLAN*	GIGGS
OCTOBER											
Tue 1 Olympiakos Piraeus FC	Home	4-0x	BARTHEZ	NEVILLE G*	FERDINAND*	BLANC	SILVESTRE	BECKHAM	**VERON**	BUTT	GIGGS
Mon 7 Everton	Home	3-0	BARTHEZ	NEVILLE G	O'SHEA	BLANC	SILVESTRE	BECKHAM	VERON	BUTT	GIGGS
Sat 19 Fulham	Away	1-1	BARTHEZ*	NEVILLE G	BLANC*	O'SHEA	SILVESTRE	BECKHAM	VERON	NEVILLE P	GIGGS
Wed 23 Olympiakos Piraeus FC	Away	3-2	BARTHEZ	NEVILLE G	**BLANC**	O'SHEA	SILVESTRE	BECKHAM	**VERON**	NEVILLE P	GIGGS
Sat 26 Aston Villa	Home	1-1	BARTHEZ	O'SHEA	SILVESTRE	BLANC	FERDINAND	NEVILLE P	BECKHAM*	VERON	SCHOLES
Tue 29 Maccabi Haifa	Away	0-3	RICARDO*	NEVILLE G	SILVESTRE*	FERDINAND	O'SHEA*	NEVILLE P	SCHOLES	FORTUNE	RICHARDSON
NOVEMBER											
Sat 2 Southampton	Home	2-1	BARTHEZ	NEVILLE G	BLANC	FERDINAND	O'SHEA	BECKHAM	VERON	**NEVILLE P**	SCHOLES
Tues 5 Leicester City (WC3)	Home	2-0	CARROLL	NEVILLE G	MAY	FERDINAND	O'SHEA	BECKHAM.	FORTUNE	NEVILLE P*	NARDIELLO
Sat 9 Manchester City 12.15pm	Away	1-3	BARTHEZ	NEVILLE G	BLANC	FERDINAND	SILVESTRE	VERON	NEVILLE P*	SCHOLES	GIGGS
Wed 13 Bayer 04 Leverkusen	Home	2-0	RICARDO	O'SHEA	BLANC	FERDINAND	SILVESTRE	BECKHAM	**VERON**	SCHOLES	GIGGS
Sun 17 West Ham United 4.05pm	Away	1-1	BARTHEZ	BROWN	BLANC	O'SHEA	SILVESTRE	SCHOLES	VERON	SOLSKJAER	FORTUNE
Sat 23 Newcastle United 12.15pm	Home	5-3	BARTHEZ	O'SHEA	BROWN	BLANC	SILVESTRE	**SOLSKJAER**	**SCHOLES**	FORTUNE	GIGGS
Tue 26 FC Basel	Away	3-1	BARTHEZ	O'SHEA	SILVESTRE	BROWN	NEVILLE P	FORTUNE*	SCHOLES*	VERON*	GIGGS
DECEMBER											
Sun 1 Liverpool 12.15pm	Away	2-1	BARTHEZ	O'SHEA	BROWN*	NEVILLE G	SILVESTRE	SOLSKJAER	SCHOLES	FORTUNE	GIGGS
Tues 3 Burnley (WC4)	Away	2-0	CARROLL	NEVILLE P	MAY	BROWN*	SILVESTRE	CHADWICK	STEWART	O'SHEA	PUGH
Sat 7 Arsenal 12.15pm	Home	2-0	BARTHEZ	NEVILLE G	BROWN	SILVESTRE	O'SHEA	SOLSKJAER	VERON*	NEVILLE P*	GIGGS
Wed 11 RC Deportivo La Coruña	Home	2-0	BARTHEZ	NEVILLE G	BROWN	SILVESTRE	O'SHEA	SOLSKJAER	VERON*	NEVILLE P*	GIGGS
Sat 14 West Ham United 12.15pm	Home	3-0x	BARTHEZ	NEVILLE G	BROWN	SILVESTRE	O'SHEA	**SOLSKJAER**	**VERON**	NEVILLE P*	GIGGS
Tue 17 Chelsea (WC5)	Home	1-0	BARTHEZ	NEVILLE G	BROWN	SILVESTRE	O'SHEA	BECKHAM	VERON	NEVILLE P*	GIGGS
Sun 22 Blackburn Rovers 2pm	Away	0-1	BARTHEZ	NEVILLE G*	BROWN	SILVESTRE	O'SHEA	SOLSKJAER	NEVILLE P	SCHOLES	GIGGS
Thu 26 Middlesbrough 4pm	Away	1-3	BARTHEZ	NEVILLE G	BLANC	BROWN	SILVESTRE	KEANE	**GIGGS**	VERON	SCHOLES*
Sat 28 Birmingham City	Home	2-0	BARTHEZ	BROWN*	FERDINAND	SILVESTRE	O'SHEA	**BECKHAM**	KEANE	VERON	SCHOLES
JANUARY											
Wed 1 Sunderland 2pm	Home	2-1	BARTHEZ	BROWN	FERDINAND	SILVESTRE	O'SHEA	**BECKHAM**	KEANE	VERON	**SCHOLES**
Sat 4 Portsmouth (FAC3) 12.30pm	Home	4-1	CARROLL	NEVILLE G	FERDINAND	BLANC	SILVESTRE	**BECKHAM**	KEANE	NEVILLE P	RICHARDSON
Tue 7 Blackburn (semi-1st leg)	Home	1-1	BARTHEZ	NEVILLE G	FERDINAND	BROWN	SILVESTRE	BECKHAM	VERON	NEVILLE P*	GIGGS
Sat 11 West Bromwich Albion	Away	3-1	BARTHEZ	NEVILLE G	FERDINAND	BROWN	SILVESTRE	NEVILLE P	BECKHAM	KEANE	**SCHOLES**
Sat 18 Chelsea 12.30pm	Home	2-1	BARTHEZ	NEVILLE G	FERDINAND	BROWN	SILVESTRE	NEVILLE P	BECKHAM	KEANE	**SCHOLES**
Wed 22 Blackburn (semi-2nd leg)	Away	3-1	BARTHEZ	NEVILLE G	FERDINAND	BROWN	SILVESTRE	BECKHAM	VERON	KEANE	GIGGS
Sun 26 West Ham United (FAC4) 1pm	Home	6-0	BARTHEZ	NEVILLE G	FERDINAND	O'SHEA	**NEVILLE P**	BECKHAM	VERON	KEANE	**GIGGS 2**
FEBRUARY											
Sat 1 Southampton	Away	2-0	BARTHEZ	NEVILLE G	FERDINAND	O'SHEA	SILVESTRE	BECKHAM	VERON	KEANE	**GIGGS**
Tue 4 Birmingham City	Away	1-0	CARROLL	NEVILLE G	FERDINAND	BROWN	SILVESTRE	BECKHAM	VERON	KEANE*	GIGGS
Sun 9 Manchester City 12.30pm	Home	1-1	CARROLL	NEVILLE G	FERDINAND	BROWN	SILVESTRE	BECKHAM	VERON	KEANE	GIGGS
Sat 15 Arsenal (FAC5) 12.15pm	Home	0-2	BARTHEZ	NEVILLE G	FERDINAND	BROWN	SILVESTRE	BECKHAM	SCHOLES*	KEANE*	GIGGS
Wed 19 Juventus FC	Home	2-1	BARTHEZ	NEVILLE G	FERDINAND	**BROWN**	SILVESTRE	BECKHAM	KEANE*	BUTT	GIGGS
Sat 22 Bolton Wanderers 12pm	Home	1-1	BARTHEZ	NEVILLE G	BROWN	FERDINAND	O'SHEA	BECKHAM	KEANE*	VERON	GIGGS
Tue 25 Juventus FC	Away	3-0	BARTHEZ	NEVILLE G	KEANE	FERDINAND	O'SHEA	NEVILLE P*	BECKHAM	BUTT	VERON
MARCH											
Sun 2 Liverpool (WC final) 2pm	Away	0-2	BARTHEZ	NEVILLE G	BROWN	FERDINAND	SILVESTRE	BECKHAM	KEANE	VERON	GIGGS
Wed 5 Leeds Utd	Home	2-1x	BARTHEZ	O'SHEA	FERDINAND	KEANE	**SILVESTRE**	BECKHAM	BUTT	VERON	FORTUNE
Wed 12 FC Basel	Home	1-1	CARROLL	**NEVILLE G**	BLANC		FLETCHER	NEVILLE P*	BUTT*		RICHARDSON
Sat 15 Aston Villa 12.30pm	Away	1-0	BARTHEZ	NEVILLE G	FERDINAND	SILVESTRE	O'SHEA	**BECKHAM**	BUTT	SCHOLES*	GIGGS
Tue 18 RC Deportivo La Coruña	Away	0-2	RICARDO	LYNCH	ROCHE	BLANC	O'SHEA	PUGH	FLETCHER	NEVILLE P*	BUTT
Sat 22 Fulham 12.30pm	Home	3-0	BARTHEZ	NEVILLE G*	FERDINAND	BROWN	O'SHEA	BECKHAM	BUTT	SCHOLES	GIGGS
APRIL											
Sat 5 Liverpool 12.30pm	Home	4-0	BARTHEZ	NEVILLE G	FERDINAND	BROWN	SILVESTRE	NEVILLE P	KEANE	SCHOLES	**GIGGS**
Tue 8 Real Madrid (CL QF 1st Leg)	Away	1-3	BARTHEZ	NEVILLE G*	FERDINAND	BROWN	SILVESTRE	KEANE*	BUTT	BECKHAM	SCHOLES*
Sat 12 Newcastle United 12.30pm	Away	6-2	BARTHEZ	O'SHEA	FERDINAND	BROWN	SILVESTRE	KEANE	BUTT	**GIGGS**	**SCHOLES 3**
Wed 16 Arsenal	Away	2-2	BARTHEZ	BROWN	FERDINAND	SILVESTRE	O'SHEA	SOLSKJAER	BUTT*	KEANE*	**GIGGS**
Sat 19 Blackburn Rovers	Home	3-1	BARTHEZ	NEVILLE P	BROWN	FERDINAND	SILVESTRE	BECKHAM	BUTT	**SCHOLES 2**	FORTUNE
Wed 23 Real Madrid (CL QF 2nd Leg)	Home	4-3x	BARTHEZ	BROWN	FERDINAND	SILVESTRE	O'SHEA	**VERON**	BUTT	KEANE	GIGGS
Sun 27 Tottenham Hotspur 4.05pm	Away	2-0	CARROLL	BROWN	FERDINAND	O'SHEA	SILVESTRE	BECKHAM	KEANE	**SCHOLES**	GIGGS
MAY											
Sat 3 Charlton Athletic 12.30pm	Home	4-1	CARROLL	BROWN	FERDINAND	SILVESTRE	O'SHEA	**BECKHAM**	KEANE	SCHOLES	GIGGS
Sun 11 Everton	Away	2-1	CARROLL	BROWN	FERDINAND*	SILVESTRE	O'SHEA	**BECKHAM**	KEANE	SCHOLES	GIGGS

■ Barclaycard Premiership ■ UEFA Champions League ■ Worthington Cup ■ FA Cup **BOLD NAME** GOAL • PENALTY x OWN-GOAL (15) SUBSTITUT[E]

		SUBSTITUTES	REFEREE	ATTENDANCE
SOLSKJAER	V NISTELROOY*	P NEVILLE (24) FORLAN (20) BUTT, STEWART, SCHOLES, TIERNEY, WILLIAMS	W STARK	40,000
BUTT	V NISTELROOY	SOLSKJAER (4) SCHOLES (3) FORLAN (27) WILLIAMS, TIERNEY	S BENNETT	67,645
SCHOLES	V NISTELROOY	SOLSKJAER (18) FORLAN (7) WILLIAMS, CHADWICK, STEWART, TIERNEY	G POLL	41,541
SCHOLES	V NISTELROOY 2	SOLSKJAER (18) O'SHEA (11) FORLAN (10) WILLIAMS, TIERNEY	C CORTEZ BATISTA	66,814
SOLSKJAER	V NISTELROOY	FORLAN (20) O'SHEA (27) STEWART, WILLIAMS, CHADWICK	U RENNIE	47,586
SCHOLES	V NISTELROOY .	O'SHEA (7) FORLAN (18) SOLSKJAER (10) RICARDO, PUGH	M RILEY	67,508
SOLSKJAER	V NISTELROOY	FORLAN (4) CHADWICK, STEWART, O'SHEA, RICARDO	G BARBER	67,623
SOLSKJAER*	V NISTELROOY	FORLAN (10) CHADWICK (8), RICARDO, PUGH, ROCHE	J WINTER	39,622
SOLSKJAER	V NISTELROOY	RICARDO (1) FORLAN.(11) PUGH (10) G NEVILLE, MAY, CHADWICK, STEWART	P ALLAERTS	63,439
SOLSKJAER	V NISTELROOY . *	NEVILLE G (4) FORLAN (20) PUGH (11) RICARDO, STEWART	R STYLES	67,611
GIGGS	V NISTELROOY 2	NEVILLE G (22) FORLAN (10) SOLSKJAER (4) RICARDO, MAY, STEWART, PUGH	J WEGEREEF	22,500
SCHOLES	SOLSKJAER	V NISTELROOY (21) NEVILLE G (8) RICARDO, MAY, STEWART	D GALLAGHER	26,630
SCHOLES	SOLSKJAER	O'SHEA (5) FORTUNE (11) FORLAN (18) RICARDO, NEVILLE P, MAY, STEWART	G VEISSIERE	66,902
SCHOLES 2	V NISTELROOY	SOLSKJAER (4) FORLAN (8) P NEVILLE (10) RICARDO, FORTUNE	M DEAN	67,629
SCHOLES	SOLSKJAER	FORLAN (27) FORTUNE (3) RICARDO, MAY, RICHARDSON	M DEAN	18,103
SCHOLES	FORLAN	RICARDO, MAY, CHADWICK (2) SOLSKJAER, FORTUNE (11) ROCHE, RICHARDSON (4)	P COLLINA	13,220
SOLSKJAER	FORLAN	FORTUNE (3) ROCHE, O'SHEA, RICHARDSON, RICARDO	G POLL	67,619
SOLSKJAER	FORLAN	NARDIELLO (42) TIMM (21) CARROLL, MAY, PUGH, ROCHE, LYNCH	L NIETO	22,000
SCHOLES	V NISTELROOY	RICARDO, SOLSKJAER (27) FORLAN (3) O'SHEA (10) FORTUNE	U RENNIE	67,691
SOLSKJAER	FORLAN	SCHOLES (3) VERON (25) RICHARDSON (40) BARTHEZ, PUGH	CJ FOY	47,848
SOLSKJAER*	V NISTELROOY	RICARDO, O'SHEA (2) FORLAN (4) MAY, FORTUNE	P DURKIN	34,649
FORTUNE	V NISTELROOY	CARROLL, NEVILLE G (5) NEVILLE P, CHADWICK (11), SOLSKJAER (7) FORLAN, NARDIELLO	H VLADIMIR	66,185
GIGGS	V NISTELROOY	RICARDO, NEVILLE P, RICHARDSON, FORLAN, DAVIS	M HALSEY	35,049
FORLAN	V NISTELROOY 3	VERON (21) ROCHE (5) RICHARDSON (10) RICARDO, CHADWICK	S DUNN	67,619
SOLSKJAER	V NISTELROOY 2*	CHADWICK (20) MAY (24) RICARDO, STEWART, FORLAN, PUGH, RICHARDSON	V IVANOV	29,501
FORLAN 2*	V NISTELROOY*	NEVILLE P (25) MAY (10) STEWART (21) RICARDO, CHADWICK	A WILEY	44,250
FORLAN	V NISTELROOY	SCHOLES (17) GIGGS (21) SOLSKJAER (10) RICARDO, ROCHE	N BARRY	22,034
SCHOLES	V NISTELROOY	RICARDO, MAY, CHADWICK, STEWART, FORLAN	D GALLAGHER	67,650
SCHOLES	V NISTELROOY 2	FORLAN (3) RICHARDSON (10) BECKHAM (22) RICARDO, CHADWICK, STEWART, PUGH	T HAUGE	67,014
SCHOLES	V NISTELROOY	BLANC (22) BECKHAM (20) FORLAN (18) RICARDO, RICHARDSON	R STYLES	67,555
FORLAN	SCHOLES	CARROLL, BLANC, STEWART, NARDIELLO, RICHARDSON	S BENNETT	57,985
FORLAN	V NISTELROOY	BLANC (3) KEANE (21) BECKHAM (11) RICARDO RICHARDSON	D ELLERAY	30,475
SOLSKJAER	V NISTELROOY	BECKHAM (22) FERDINAND (22) RICARDO, FORLAN, NEVILLE P	G BARBER	34,673
FORLAN	SOLSKJAER	NEVILLE P (20) RICHARDSON (18) GIGGS (16) RICARDO, NEVILLE G	M DEAN	67,640
FORLAN	SOLSKJAER*	CARROLL (1) GIGGS (22) NEVILLE G(4) NEVILLE P, RICHARDSON	G POLL	67,609
GIGGS	V NISTELROOY 2..	RICARDO, FORLAN, SCHOLES (42), STEWART (16), BROWN (3)	M RILEY	67,222
SCHOLES	V NISTELROOY	SOLSKJAER (11) FORLAN (3) RICARDO, BLANC, O'SHEA	U RENNIE	62,740
SOLSKJAER	V NISTELROOY	FORLAN (20) O'SHEA (16) RICARDO, BLANC, RICHARDSON	N BARRY	27,129
SOLSKJAER	V NISTELROOY*	GIGGS (3) FORLAN (10) VERON (27) CARROLL, O'SHEA	P DURKIN	67,606
SCHOLES 2	V NISTELROOY.	BUTT (18) FORLAN (10) RICARDO, NEVILLE P, O'SHEA	J WINTER	29,048
SCHOLES	V NISTELROOY 2	FORLAN (18) BUTT (4) SOLSKJAER (7) CARROLL, BROWN	S BENNETT	67,181
SOLSKJAER	V NISTELROOY	CARROLL (1) SCHOLES (7) FORLAN (10) NEVILLE P, BROWN	P DOWD	32,085
SCHOLES	V NISTELROOY	SOLSKJAER (10) RICARDO, BUTT, NEVILLE P, FORLAN	S DUNN	29,475
SCHOLES	V NISTELROOY	BUTT (4) SOLSKJAER (11) RICARDO, NEVILLE P, O'SHEA	A WILEY	67,646
SOLSKJAER	V NISTELROOY*	BUTT (7) FORLAN (11) RICARDO, NEVILLE P, O'SHEA	J WINTER	67,209
SCHOLES*	V NISTELROOY	O'SHEA (27) SOLSKJAER (18) FORLAN (11) RICARDO, NEVILLE P, PUGH, FLETCHER	K NIELSON	66,703
SOLSKJAER	V NISTELROOY	FORLAN (11) NEVILLE P (24) BUTT (4) RICARDO, FLETCHER	A D'URSO	27,409
FORLAN	SOLSKJAER	GIGGS 2 (21) V NISTELROOY (11) PUGH (22) RICARDO, FLETCHER, ROCHE, RICHARDSON	M MERK	59,111
SCHOLES	V NISTELROOY	SOLSKJAER (24) CARROLL, NEVILLE P, BUTT, O'SHEA	P DURKIN	74,500
SCHOLES	V NISTELROOY	GIGGS (25) NEVILLE G (10) NEVILLE P (4) CARROLL, FLETCHER	G POLL	67,626
SOLSKJAER	FORLAN	GIGGS (42) BECKHAM (31) SCHOLES (5) RICARDO, PUGH, WEBBER, VAN NISTELROOY	C BO-LARSEN	66,870
SOLSKJAER	V NISTELROOY	RICARDO, NEVILLE P, FLETCHER, FORLAN, BLANC	M DEAN	42,602
FORLAN	GIGGS	STEWART (34) WEBBER (11) RICHARDSON (21) CARROLL, MAY, DAVIS, NARDIELLO	V HRINAK	25,000
SOLSKJAER	V NISTELROOY. 3	RICARDO, BLANC, FORLAN, FORTUNE, FLETCHER	S BENNETT	67,706
SOLSKJAER	V NISTELROOY..	O'SHEA (27) BECKHAM (3) BUTT (18) RICARDO, FORLAN	M RILEY	67,639
GIGGS	V NISTELROOY*	O'SHEA (27) SOLSKJAER (2) RICARDO, BLANC, FORLAN, FORTUNE, FLETCHER	A FRISK	75,000
SOLSKJAER	V NISTELROOY	NEVILLE G (22) BLANC (24) FORLAN (11) RICARDO, NEVILLE P	S DUNN	52,164
SCHOLES	V NISTELROOY	NEVILLE G (22) RICARDO, NEVILLE P, BECKHAM, FORTUNE	M HALSEY	38,164
GIGGS	V NISTELROOY	RICARDO (1) KEANE (8) SOLSKJAER (11) NEVILLE G, ROCHE	A D'URSO	67,626
SOLSKJAER	V NISTELROOY	BECKHAM 2 (4) NEVILLE P (27) FORTUNE (16) RICARDO, BLANC, FORLAN, FLETCHER	P COLLINA	66,708
SOLSKJAER	V NISTELROOY	NEVILLE G (24) FORTUNE (20) RICARDO, BLANC, FORLAN	J WINTER	36,073
SOLSKJAER	V NISTELROOY. 3	VERON (18) BUTT (11) FORLAN (20) BARTHEZ, P NEVILLE	M HALSEY	67,721
SOLSKJAER	V NISTELROOY.	P NEVILLE* (24) BLANC* (22) FORTUNE (20) VERON, BUTT	M RILEY	40,168

PPEARANCE AND SQUAD NUMBER OF PLAYER REPLACED * AFTER EXTRA TIME * YELLOW CARD * RED CARD

SEASON STATISTICS

TOP TEN PASSERS 2002/03

100% ACCURACY

50%

0%

SCHOLES	SILVESTRE	BECKHAM	VERON	KEANE	FERDINAND	O'SHEA	G NEVILLE	GIGGS	P NEVILLE
1,629 PASSES	1,578 PASSES	1,531 PASSES	1,497 PASSES	1,422 PASSES	1,162 PASSES	1,135 PASSES	1,114 PASSES	1,102 PASSES	1,009 PASSES

Paul Scholes, United's pass master

Alan Smith is beaten by the Reds' top tackler

TOP TEN TACKLERS 2002/03

100% TACKLES WON

50%

0%

SILVESTRE	KEANE	SCHOLES	BECKHAM	O'SHEA	GIGGS	VERON	BROWN	P NEVILLE	G NEVILLE
106 TACKLE ATTEMPTS	84 TACKLE ATTEMPTS	77 TACKLE ATTEMPTS	76 TACKLE ATTEMPTS	74 TACKLE ATTEMPTS	70 TACKLE ATTEMPTS	68 TACKLE ATTEMPTS	66 TACKLE ATTEMPTS	66 TACKLE ATTEMPTS	60 TACKLE ATTEMPTS

UNITED DISCIPLINE 2002/03

	Fouls			Points
V NISTELROOY	58	3	0	67
P NEVILLE	38	7	0	59
SCHOLES	45	4	0	57
BECKHAM	40	5	0	55
SOLSKJAER	40	4	0	52
BROWN	37	3	0	46
SILVESTRE	39	2	0	45
KEANE	24	4	1	42
G NEVILLE	22	3	0	31
GIGGS	27	0	0	27
VERON	24	1	0	27
FERDINAND	18	3	0	27
BUTT	24	1	0	27
O'SHEA	23	0	0	23
BLANC	15	2	0	21
FORLAN	7	2	0	13
FORTUNE	7	1	0	10
BARTHEZ	0	1	0	3
RICARDO	1	0	0	1
ROCHE	1	0	0	1
CARROLL	0	0	0	0
PUGH	0	0	0	0
RICHARDSON	0	0	0	0
CHADWICK	0	0	0	0
MAY	0	0	0	0
STEWART	0	0	0	0

Foul = 1pt, Yellow = 3pts, Red = 6pts

UNITED PLAYER CAREER STATS

	LEAGUE		FA CUP		LEAGUE CUP		EUROPE		OTHERS		TOTAL	
	A	G	A	G	A	G	A	G	A	G	A	G
Fabien Barthez	92	0	4	0	4	0	37	0	2	0	139	0
David Beckham	237(28)	62	22(2)	6	10(2)	1	79(4)	15	8(2)	1	356(38)	85
Laurent Blanc	44(4)	1	3	0	0	0	24	3	0	0	71(4)	4
Wes Brown	73(9)	0	4(1)	0	6(1)	0	23(5)	1	0	0	107(16)	1
Nicky Butt	198(51)	20	20(4)	1	5(1)	0	54(12)	1	8	2	285(68)	24
Roy Carroll	14(3)	0	2	0	3	0	4	0	0	0	23(3)	0
Luke Chadwick	11(14)	2	1(2)	0	5	0	1(5)	0	0	0	18(21)	2
Jimmy Davis	0	0	0	0	1	0	0	0	0	0	1	0
Bojan Djordjic	0(1)	0	0	0	1	0	0	0	0	0	1(1)	0
Rio Ferdinand	27(1)	0	3	0	4	0	11	0	0	0	45(1)	0
Darren Fletcher	0	0	0	0	0	0	2	0	0	0	2	0
Diego Forlan	13(25)	6	0(2)	0	3(2)	2	6(12)	1	0	0	22(41)	9
Quinton Fortune	23(13)	5	0	0	3	0	7(9)	0	1(2)	2	34(24)	7
Ryan Giggs	341(41)	79	39(4)	9	21(5)	6	77(5)	19	10(1)	0	488(56)	113
Roy Keane	252(10)	29	36(1)	1	11(2)	0	70(1)	14	10	2	379(14)	46
Mark Lynch	0	0	0	0	0	0	1	0	0	0	1	0
David May	68(17)	6	6	0	9	1	13(2)	1	2(1)	0	98(20)	8
Daniel Nardiello	0	0	0	0	1(1)	0	0(1)	0	0	0	1(2)	0
Gary Neville	249(14)	3	28(2)	0	9(1)	0	77(5)	1	7(1)	0	370(23)	4
Phil Neville	169(44)	5	19(4)	1	12(1)	0	35(17)	1	6(2)	0	241(68)	7
Ruud van Nistelrooy	62(4)	48	3(2)	6	4	1	24(1)	24	1	1	94(7)	80
John O'Shea	30(11)	0	1	0	7	0	12(7)	0	0	0	50(18)	0
Danny Pugh	0(1)	0	0	0	1	0	1(2)	0	0	0	2(3)	0
Ricardo	0(1)	0	0	0	0	0	3(1)	0	0	0	3(2)	0
Kieran Richardson	0(2)	0	1	0	0(1)	1	2(3)	0	0	0	3(6)	1
Lee Roche	0(1)	0	0	0	1	0	1	0	0	0	2(1)	0
Paul Scholes	206(54)	68	12(8)	5	10(4)	8	62(11)	20	8	0	298(77)	101
Mikael Silvestre	120(10)	2	6	0	5	0	38(6)	1	5	0	174(16)	3
Ole Gunnar Solskjaer	135(65)	84	9(10)	6	7(3)	6	33(40)	18	5(3)	0	189(121)	114
Michael Stewart	5(2)	0	0(1)	0	2(2)	0	0(2)	0	0	0	7(7)	0
Mads Timm	0	0	0	0	0	0	0(1)	0	0	0	0(1)	0
Juan Sebastian Veron	45(6)	7	2	0	4(1)	0	24	4	0	0	75(7)	11
Danny Webber	0	0	0	0	1(1)	0	0(1)	0	0	0	1(2)	0

all:sports

HOW WE SCORE

HOW WE CONCEDE

WHEN WE SCORE

WHEN WE CONCEDE

WHERE WE SCORE AND CONCEDE

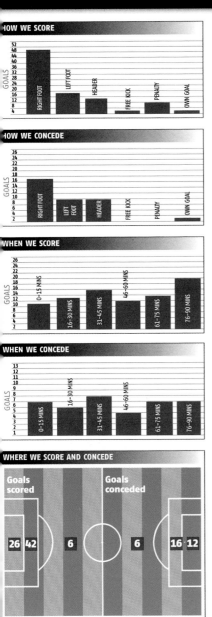

Goals scored: 26 42 6
Goals conceded: 6 16 12

FINAL PREMIERSHIP TABLE 2002/03

	P	W	D	L	F	A	GD	PTS
1 Manchester United	38	25	8	5	74	34	40	83
2 Arsenal	38	23	9	6	85	42	43	78
3 Newcastle United	38	21	6	11	63	48	15	69
4 Chelsea	38	19	10	9	68	38	30	67
5 Liverpool	38	18	10	10	61	41	20	64
6 Blackburn Rovers	38	16	12	10	52	43	9	60
7 Everton	38	17	8	13	48	49	-1	59
8 Southampton	38	13	13	12	43	46	-3	52
9 Manchester City	38	15	6	17	47	54	-7	51
10 Tottenham Hotspur	38	14	8	16	51	62	-11	50
11 Middlesbrough	38	13	10	15	48	44	4	49
12 Charlton Athletic	38	14	7	17	45	56	-11	49
13 Birmingham City	38	13	9	16	41	49	-8	48
14 Fulham	38	13	9	16	41	50	-9	48
15 Leeds United	38	14	5	19	58	57	+1	47
16 Aston Villa	38	12	9	17	42	47	-5	45
17 Bolton Wanderers	38	10	14	14	41	51	-10	44
18 West Ham United	38	10	12	16	42	59	-17	42
19 West Bromwich Albion	38	6	8	24	29	65	-36	26
20 Sunderland	38	4	7	27	21	65	-44	19

SEASON-BY-SEASON PERFORMANCE

1999/00: DEFEATS 3, DRAWS 7, WINS 28
2000/01: DEFEATS 6, DRAWS 8, WINS 24
2001/02: DEFEATS 9, DRAWS 5, WINS 24
2002/03: DEFEATS 5, DRAWS 8, WINS 25

GAMES AND GOALS 2002/03

	PREMIERSHIP		EUROPEAN		LEAGUE CUP		FA CUP		TOTAL	
	A	G	A	G	A	G	A	G	A	G
Fabien Barthez	30	0	10	0	4	0	2	0	46	0
David Beckham	27(4)	6	10(3)	3	5	1	3	1	45(7)	11
Laurent Blanc	15(4)	0	9	1	0	0	1	0	25(4)	1
Wes Brown	22	0	6	1	5	0	1(1)	0	34(1)	1
Nicky Butt	14(4)	0	8	0	0(1)	0	0(2)	0	22(7)	0
Roy Carroll	8(2)	0	3	0	2	0	1	0	14(2)	0
Luke Chadwick	0(1)	0	0(3)	0	1	0	0	0	1(4)	0
Rio Ferdinand	27(1)	0	11	0	4	0	3	0	45(1)	0
Darren Fletcher	0	0	2	0	0	0	0	0	2	0
Diego Forlan	7(18)	6	5(8)	1	3(2)	2	0(2)	0	15(30)	9
Quinton Fortune	5(4)	0	3(3)	0	1	0	0	0	9(7)	0
Ryan Giggs	32(4)	8	13(2)	4	4(1)	0	3	2	52(7)	14
Roy Keane	19(2)	0	6	0	2	0	3	0	30(2)	0
Mark Lynch	0	0	1	0	0	0	0	0	1	0
David May	0(1)	0	0(1)	0	2	0	0	0	2(2)	0
Daniel Nardiello	0	0	0(1)	0	1	0	0	0	1(1)	0
Gary Neville	19(7)	0	8(2)	1	5	0	3	0	35(9)	1
Phil Neville	19(6)	1	10(2)	0	4	0	2	1	35(8)	2
Ruud van Nistelrooy	33(1)	25	10(1)	14	4	1	3	4	50(2)	44
John O'Shea	26(6)	0	12(4)	0	3	0	1	0	42(10)	0
Danny Pugh	0(1)	0	1(2)	0	1	0	0	0	2(3)	0
Ricardo	0(1)	0	3(1)	0	0	0	0	0	3(2)	0
Kieran Richardson	0(2)	0	2(3)	0	0(1)	1	1	0	3(6)	1
Lee Roche	0(1)	0	1	0	0	0	0	0	1(1)	0
Paul Scholes	31(2)	14	9(1)	2	4(2)	3	2(1)	1	46(6)	20
Mikael Silvestre	34	1	13	0	5	0	2	0	54	1
Ole Gunnar Solskjaer	29(8)	9	9(5)	4	1(3)	1	1(1)	1	40(17)	15
Michael Stewart	0(1)	0	0(1)	0	1	0	0(1)	0	1(3)	0
Mads Timm	0	0	0(1)	0	0	0	0	0	0(1)	0
Juan Sebastian Veron	21(4)	2	11	4	4(1)	0	1	0	37(5)	6
Danny Webber	0	0	0(1)	0	0	0	0	0	0(1)	0

Appearances

1. Ole Gunnar Solskjaer 37
2. Ryan Giggs 36
=3. Ruud van Nistelrooy 34
=3. Mikael Silvestre 34
5. Paul Scholes 33

Shots

1. Ruud van Nistelrooy 100
2. Paul Scholes 70
3. Ole Gunnar Solskjaer 66
4. David Beckham 56
5. Ryan Giggs 49

Assists

1. Ryan Giggs 11
2. David Beckham 8
3. Mikael Silvestre 7
4. Ole Gunnar Solskjaer 6
=5. Gary Neville 4
=5. Ruud van Nistelrooy 4

Crosses

1. David Beckham 363
2. Ryan Giggs 200
3. Ole Gunnar Solskjaer 97
4. Mikael Silvestre 91
5. Gary Neville 77

Clearances

1. Rio Ferdinand 277
2. Mikael Silvestre 196
3. Wes Brown 148
4. John O'Shea 145
5. Laurent Blanc 103

Dribbles

1. Ryan Giggs 217
2. Ruud van Nistelrooy 136
3. David Beckham 125
4. Mikael Silvestre 122
5. Paul Scholes 112

TOP FIVES

opta
opta index

The definitive guide to who did what and how often they did it for United during season 2002/03

Fouls committed		Fouls won	
1	Ruud van Nistelrooy 58	1	Mikael Silvestre 54
2	Paul Scholes 45	2	Ruud van Nistelrooy 49
=3	David Beckham 40	3	David Beckham 48
=3	Ole Gunnar Solskjaer 40	4	Ole Gunnar Solskjaer 37
5	Mikael Silvestre 39	5	John O'Shea 35

NUMBER CRU

24

Diego Forlan finally scored his first Premiership goal for Manchester United on his 24th Premiership appearance

29

Ruud van Nistelrooy averaged a shot every 29 minutes

32% of Ruud van Nistelrooy's goals came from the penalty spot

45

The number of points Manchester United took from a possible 51 between December 28th and May 4th when the title was clinched. Arsenal took just 30 points from a possible 48 in the same period

68%

Manchester United won 68% of all Premiership games in which David Beckham played

33

was the total of points Manchester United won away from home — more than any other side. The team with the best away record has won the Premiership in all but one of the Premiership's 11 seasons

NCHING

50%

Thirteen of the 26 players to appear for Manchester United in the Premiership during 2002–03 came through the club's youth ranks

89%

Roy Keane completed a higher percentage of passes than any other regular Premiership player

47

David Beckham delivered more successful corners than any other player

31

Manchester United had 31 shots in the 2–1 victory against Sunderland at Old Trafford – the most shots by a team in a single game during the season

opta
opta index

100%

All of Ruud van Nistelrooy's goals came from inside the penalty area

11

The number of goals Manchester United scored in two games against Newcastle

Fabien Barthez

Magic moment: The save against Hamann at Anfield grabbed the headlines, but his penalty stop against Fulham at Loftus Road was just as crucial – complete with a routine guaranteed to freak out any potential penalty taker.

1 **Position:** Goalkeeper

Born: Lavelanet, France, 28 June 1971
Signed: from AS Monaco, May 2000
Previous clubs: Toulouse, Olympique Marseille, AS Monaco
Senior United debut: 13 August 2000 v Chelsea, Wembley, FA Charity Shield
United record: League: 92 games, 0 goals; FA Cup: 4 games, 0 goals; League Cup: 4 games, 0 goals; Europe: 37 games, 0 goals; Others: 2 games, 0 goals
Total: 139 games, 0 goals
International: 57 caps for France

Barthez's hopes of putting a miserable World Cup behind him were put on hold for a month as he missed the first five games of United's season with a hip injury. The French No.1 returned for the home win against Middlesbrough, but suffered when Bolton and Leeds chalked up shock victories in the next two games.

Blameless during those setbacks, Barthez steadied the ship and enjoyed a wonderful week in December when he broke Liverpool and Arsenal hearts in consecutive league matches with a string of world-class saves. One stop from Dietmar Hamann at Anfield was described by pundits as "the save of the season" and almost overshadowed Forlan's glory double during the same game – but not quite.

Barthez kept 14 clean sheets in 43 matches and was named Man of the Match by *United Review* in three games. That included a heroic display at Bolton which ensured United escaped the Reebok Stadium with a point. He lost his place to Roy Carroll for the last three games of the season.

Gary Neville

Magic moment: As he freely admits, a Gary Neville goal is an all-too-rare event but they're worth waiting for. This time, Gary's annual strike levelled the scores when Swiss battlers Basel came to town.

2 **Position:** Defender

Born: Bury, 18 February 1975
Signed: Trainee, 8 July 1991
Senior United debut: 16 September 1992 v Torpedo Moscow, home, UEFA Cup
United record: League: 249 (14) games, 3 goals; FA Cup: 28 (2) games, 0 goals; League Cup: 9 (1) games, 0 goals; Europe: 77 (5) games, 1 goal; Others: 7 (1) games, 0 goals
Total: 370 (23) games, 4 goals
International: 56 caps for England

The broken foot suffered in United's Champions League semi-final defeat to Bayer Leverusen in April 2002 kept Gary out of the summer's World Cup and the first six weeks of the season. He made three substitute appearances before returning to the first XI against Olympiakos in October (a month after celebrating his 10th year in the first team). In November, he suffered arguably the worst moment of his career, as an uncharacteristic error gifted Shaun Goater the first of a double in Maine Road's last-ever derby clash. Never one to hide, Neville recovered immediately and was a virtual ever-present at right back as Sir Alex shuffled his defensive deck.

If the derby was the low point of his season, the league double over Liverpool went a long way towards healing the pain. A booking in the *Bernabéu* meant he was suspended for the epic Real Madrid match at Old Trafford. Gary missed the last three games due to injury, but hobbled onto the pitch at Goodison to pick up his medal and join in the party.

Phil Neville

3 **Position:** Defender

Magic moment: Inspirational when Arsenal came to Old Trafford in December, nullifying the World Cup-winning threat of Vieira and Gilberto, and picking up the Man of the Match award as United won 2-0.

Born: Bury, 21 January, 1977
Signed: Trainee, 5 July 1993
Senior United debut: 28 January 1995 v Wrexham, home, FA Cup
United record: League: 169 (44) games, 5 goals; FA Cup: 19 (4) games, 1 goal; League Cup: 12 (1) games, 0 goals; Europe: 35 (17) games, 1 goal; Others: 6 (2) games, 0 goals
Total: 241 (68) games, 7 goals
International: 37 caps for England

Uncertain about his place in the first team at the start of the season, Neville the younger enjoyed an unbroken run of 11 starts during August and September, mostly filling in for injured brother Gary at right back. As the injuries started to bite in midfield, Phil was moved into the centre of the pitch for the Fulham away game in October – taking on the unlikely role of midfield enforcer in the absence of Keane and Butt. Neville was a revelation, and capped an excellent spell of form with the opening goal against Southampton in the league in November.

The visit of Arsenal was his crowning glory, though. United were still missing Keane, Butt and Beckham while the champions were at the peak of their game, but Phil Neville's performance outshone everyone on the park on a day described by Ruud van Nistelrooy as "the best performance I have ever played in". Neville added another goal in January, a sweet strike in the 6-0 FA Cup mauling of West Ham, and starred in the 3-0 win over Juventus in Turin. He passed the 300 appearances mark in January.

Juan Sebastian Veron

4 **Position:** Midfield

Magic moment: With Beckham on the bench for the visit of West Ham in December, Seba was elevated to chief free kick taker and the Argentinian made the most of the opportunity with a perfect 30-yard strike.

Born: Buenos Aires, Argentina, 9 March 1975
Signed: from SS Lazio, July 2001
Other clubs: Estudiantes de La Plata, Boca Juniors, Sampdoria, Parma, SS Lazio
Senior United debut: 19 August 2001 v Fulham, home, Premiership
United record: League: 45 (6) games, 7 goals; FA Cup: 2 games, 0 goals; League Cup: 4 (1) games, 0 goals; Europe: 24 games, 4 goals; Others: 0 games, 0 goals
Total: 75 (7) games, 11 goals
International: 51 caps for Argentina

Juan Veron was another player desperate to throw himself into the new season in order to forget a disappointing summer in Japan. With many of United's midfield engine room sidelined, Seba steered the Reds through the Champions League first phase, scoring in three straight European games. He also had his shooting boots on for the visit of Londoners Arsenal and West Ham in December, as the Argentinian started to show the sort of form that persuaded Sir Alex to shell out a record fee in 2001.

Some "experts" were of the opinion that Veron was the sort of player who would flourish in the rarefied atmosphere of the Champions League but could struggle in the Premiership's rough-and-tumble. On a freezing February night at St Andrew's (never the most hospitable of venues), Seba got stuck in against Birmingham City, inspiring United to a vital 1-0 win. The win in the Stadio delle Alpi was another highlight for the ex-*Serie A* star, but he was devastated at missing the Madrid first leg through injury. And did he enjoy picking up his first Premiership medal? You bet.

Laurent Blanc

Magic moment: Blanc's towering header, powered in from a Beckham corner, that gave the Reds a dream start during the Champions League group phase encounter with Olympiakos in Athens.

Born: Ales, France, 19 November 1965
Signed: from Internazionale in Sept 2001
Previous clubs: Montpellier, Napoli, Nimes, St Etienne, Auxerre, Barcelona, Marseille, Internazionale
Senior United debut: 8 September 2001 v Everton, home, Premiership
United record: League: 44 (4) games, 1 goal; FA Cup: 3 games, 0 goals; League Cup: 0 games, 0 goals; Europe: 24 games, 3 goals; Others: 0 games, 0 goals
Total: 71 (4) games, 4 goals
International: 96 caps for France

The arrival of Rio Ferdinand and return to fitness of Wes Brown meant Laurent Blanc had to content himself with a watching brief for the bulk of the 2002/03 season. But when called upon, the Frenchman performed with his customary panache. In the early season clash at Sunderland, Blanc was an oasis of calm at the back – making countless interceptions and headed clearances as the Reds battled to a 1-1 draw. His performance didn't attract headlines (Roy Keane's sending off dominated the next day's newsprint), but it did see him singled out for praise by the boss.

Following the turn of the year, Blanc's first-team appearances became tightly rationed; between 4 January and the end of the season he made just three starts – against Portsmouth in the third round of the FA Cup and in the Champions League fixtures at home to FC Basel and away to Deportivo. On the day Arsenal's defeat to Leeds clinched the title for the Reds – adding yet another medal to his collection – the 37-year-old announced his retirement, and he waved goodbye at Goodison Park.

Rio Ferdinand

Magic moment: On any other day, Diego Forlan's late winner at home to Southampton would have guaranteed the Man of the Match award, but the game's standout performance came from Rio.

Born: Peckham, 11 July 1978
Signed: from Leeds United, July 2002
Senior United debut: 27 August 2002 v Zalaegerszeg, home, Champions League qualifier
United record: League: 27 (1) games, 0 goals; FA Cup: 3 games, 0 goals; League Cup: 4 games, 0 goals; Europe: 11 games, 0 goals; Others: 0 games, 0 goals
Total: 45 (1) games, 0 goals
International: 31 caps for England

When invited to pinpoint his motivation for moving from Leeds United to Old Trafford in the summer of 2002, Rio Ferdinand's response was simple: to win trophies. That he should have that wish fulfilled in his first season is a testament to his good taste, talent and, perhaps above all, his strength of character. As United's record signing, Ferdinand was a target for every tabloid sniper in Fleet Street. Like forensic scientists at a crime scene, they scrutinised his every move – eager to condemn him as the biggest waste of money since the Millennium Dome. But Rio tucked his £30m price tag inside his jersey, proved his ability and, after a brief settling-in period, emerged as United's defensive mainstay.

Suddenly, the individual errors and collective disarray that had characterised much of the Reds' defending in season 2001/02 were gone. In their place was a vacuum-sealed back line that completed the season with the best goals against record in the Premiership. Rio wasn't alone in effecting this turnaround, but his part was often the most prominent.

David Beckham

7 Position: Midfield

Magic moment: Sunderland endured a season of misery but they put up a valiant fight at Old Trafford on the first day of 2003, only to lose two late goals, one from David Beckham, who was simply world class.

Born: Leytonstone, 2 May 1975
Signed: Trainee, 8 July 1991
Senior United debut: 23 September 1992 v Brighton and Hove Albion, away, FA Cup
United record: League: 237 (28) games, 62 goals; FA Cup: 22 (2) games, 6 goals; League Cup: 10 (2) games, 1 goal; Europe: 79 (4) games, 15 goals; Others: 8 (2) games, 1 goal
Total: 356 (38) games, 85 goals
International: 59 caps for England

Kidnap threats, a second son, broken ribs and a boot in the face from Sir Alex... 2002/03 was a season in which the British press had plentiful opportunity to indulge their obsession with David Beckham. Fortunately, it wasn't just the tabloids that got their money's worth, though.

Despite the media circus that seems to attend his every move off the field, United's No.7 still managed to maintain a degree of consistency on the pitch that few players are able to equal. His delivery, especially from wide areas, again proved to be a potent attacking weapon.

In total Beckham collected eight assists in the Premiership, among them a typically high-velocity cross for Paul Scholes to head home at Old Trafford against Chelsea and a sumptuous 40-yard ball that allowed Ruud van Nistelrooy to complete his hat-trick against Charlton in the season's penultimate match. He also notched eight goals from open play and three trademark free kicks – against Portsmouth, Real Madrid and, the icing on the championship cake, at Everton.

Nicky Butt

8 Position: Midfield

Magic moment: There were many heroes in Turin, but Nicky Butt worked tirelessly in the centre of midfield against the giants of Juventus – giving Veron, Giggs and Beckham the space to weave their magic.

Born: Manchester, 21 January 1975
Signed: Trainee, 8 July 1991
Senior United debut: 21 November 1992 v Oldham, home, Premiership
United record: League: 198 (51) games, 20 goals; FA Cup: 20 (4) games, 1 goal; League Cup: 5 (1) games, 0 goals; Europe: 54 (12) games, 1 goal; Others: 8 games, 2 goals
Total: 285 (68) games, 24 goals
International: 26 caps for England

Nicky Butt returned from Japan/Korea 2002 with the plaudits of some of football's most famous names ringing in his ears. Against the world's elite midfielders he had been outstanding – even attracting the admiration of Pelé, who proclaimed him the best player on show.

On the face of it this was great news for United, who looked forward to reaping the benefits of an invigorated and confidence-oozing Butt for the season ahead. Sadly, things didn't quite go to plan. Perhaps it was the physical demands placed upon him in the Far East, perhaps it was simply football's natural cycle of give and take but whatever the reason, Gorton's finest found his appearances severely restricted by injury.

Yet when he wasn't keeping the physios busy, Butt's influence was there for all to see. His best run in the first team – a series of five starts – came towards the end of the season and, tellingly, coincided with United's most impressive spell of the campaign, taking in wins over Newcastle and Real Madrid and the 2-2 draw with Arsenal at Highbury.

Ruud van Nistelrooy

10 **Position:** Forward

Magic moment: That slaloming run and finish from the half-way line against Fulham in March. Pace, power and composure – a 10-second masterclass in finishing performed in front of an adoring Stretford End.

Born: Oss, Holland, 1 September 1976
Signed: from PSV Eindhoven, 1 July 2001
Previous clubs: Den Bosch, Heerenveen
Senior United debut: 12 August 2001 v Liverpool, Cardiff, FA Charity Shield
United record: League: 62 (4) games, 48 goals; FA Cup: 3 (2) games, 6 goals; League Cup: 4 games, 1 goal; Europe: 24 (1) games, 24 goals; Others: 1 games, 1 goal
Total: 94 (7) games, 80 goals
International: 21 caps for Holland

After United's home defeat to Bolton in early September Sam Allardyce claimed that Ruud van Nistelrooy had been "found out", adding that he believed the Dutchman would struggle to emulate his goalscoring feats of 2001/02. Subsequent events prove two things: the first is that Ruud doesn't listen to criticism; and the second is that the Trotters boss is a lousy clairvoyant. Van Nistelrooy didn't match his goal tally of last season: he bettered it, becoming the first United striker since Denis Law to notch over 40 goals in a season (he finished on 44). Incredibly, he did this while playing largely as a lone striker.

The Dutchman's best spell came at the 'business end' of the season: in the last 10 crucial fixtures against Fulham, Real Madrid (home and away), Liverpool, Newcastle, Arsenal, Blackburn, Spurs, Charlton and Everton he scored 15 goals and prompted this tribute from Sir Alex: "Ruud is fantastic and he's improving. Everything about him is developing. His overall game is getting better." Sam Allardyce was unavailable for comment.

Ryan Giggs

11 **Position:** Forward

Magic moment: No contest. Giggs' second goal away at Juventus – a mesmerising fandango from 50 yards out – helped steer United into the Champions League quarter-finals and signalled his return to form.

Born: Cardiff, 29 November 1973
Signed: Trainee, 9 July 1990
Senior United debut: 2 March 1991 v Everton, home, Division 1
United record: League: 341 (41) games, 79 goals; FA Cup: 39 (4) games, 9 goals; League Cup: 21 (5) games, 6 goals; Europe: 77 (5) games, 19 goals; Others: 10 (1) games, 0 goals
Total: 488 (56) games, 113 goals
International: 40 caps for Wales

A testing season for the world's most coveted left-winger. After starting the campaign in top form – scoring twice in United's opening three Premiership skirmishes – Giggs, by his own admission, went off the boil. So it is a tribute to both his ability and character that, despite mounting criticism and speculation about his future during this time, the Welshman hauled himself out of his personal slump to play a pivotal role in the final stages of United's championship-winning campaign.

Operating behind van Nistelrooy, Giggs' movement brought fresh impetus to United's attack, and helped inspire goal gluts against Liverpool (home) and Newcastle (away). Ryan also weighed in with a Man of the Match performance in the 2-2 draw with Arsenal at Highbury, creating the opening goal for Ruud and heading in the second himself. Giggs reached two milestones during the season: he bagged his 100th goal, in a 2-2 draw at Chelsea in August, and made his 500th appearance as United shared two goals with Fulham at Loftus Road in October.

Roy Carroll

Magic moment: In the final throes of the championship race, Carroll was picked to start at Spurs. With the score at 0–0 he made a vital save at Robbie Keane's feet, helping lay the foundations for a crucial 2–0 victory.

13 **Position:** Goalkeeper

Born: Enniskillen, Northern Ireland, 30 September 1977
Signed: from Wigan, 1 July 2001
Previous club: Hull City
Senior United debut: 26 September 2001 v Aston Villa, away, Premiership
United record: League: 14 (3) games, 0 goals; FA Cup: 2 games, 0 goals; League Cup: 3 games, 0 goals; Europe: 4 games, 0 goal; Others: 0 games, 0 goals
Total: 23 (3) games, 0 goals
International: 12 caps for Northern Ireland

Following injury to Fabien Barthez, Roy Carroll – enjoying his second term at Old Trafford since arriving from Wigan Athletic in 2001 – began the 2002/03 season as United's first-choice netminder. The Northern Irishman kept goal in the first five fixtures, steering the Reds through both legs of the Champions League qualifier against tongue-twisting Hungarian outfit, Zalaegerszeg, as well as league meetings with West Brom, Chelsea and Sunderland. Barthez was restored to the No.1 slot in September, leaving Carroll to bide his time on the substitutes' bench.

Then came the arrival of Ricardo, signed from Valladolid in late August, and it seemed that Roy had fallen to third in the pecking order. But as the season came to the boil, Carroll was dramatically called up to the first team for the last three games ahead of both Barthez and Ricardo, leading to speculation that he may get the job full time. Whatever happens he's vowed to stick around: "I'm still young, so hopefully in the next two or three years I'll be pushing for that No.1 shirt."

David May

Magic moment: May was made skipper for the Worthington Cup tie at Burnley and did the captain's armband proud with an assured performance that helped inspire the youngsters alongside him.

14 **Position:** Defender

Born: Oldham, 26 July 1970
Signed: from Blackburn Rovers, 1 July 1994
Other clubs: Huddersfield Town (loan)
Senior United debut: 20 August 1994 v Queens Park Rangers, home, Premiership
United record: League: 68 (17) games, 6 goals; FA Cup: 6 games, 0 goals; League Cup: 9 games, 1 goal; Europe: 13 (2) games, 1 goal; Others: 2 (1) games, 0 goals
Total: 98 (20) games, 8 goals

Despite his limited involvement with the first-team this season, David May can justifiably lay claim to being Sir Alex Ferguson's lucky charm: the Reds won every game in which May got his boots dirty in 2002/03. Admittedly, he only appeared in four matches, and two of those were as a substitute, but his efforts in coming on to help shore up United's defence in the closing stages of matches in Switzerland, against FC Basel in the Champions League, and closer to home during the Premiership scuffle at Anfield, helped to ensure the Reds picked up important victories.

The centre-half also played an influential role in United's Worthington Cup run. May was a starter in the third round victory at home to Leicester City and in the fourth round, alongside Wes Brown at the heart of defence, he produced a typically no-nonsense display that enabled a young and inexperienced line-up that included Danny Pugh and John O'Shea (both operating in midfield), to get forward, express themselves and, ultimately, inspire a 2-0 victory.

Luke Chadwick

Magic moment: To be honest, more magic moments for Reading than United this season, but Chadwick still enjoyed a rare chance to impress at Turf Moor in the Worthington Cup win over Burnley.

15 **Position:** Midfield

Born: Cambridge, 18 November 1980
Signed: Trainee, 30 June 1997
Other clubs: Royal Antwerp (loan), Reading (loan)
Senior United debut: 13 October 1999 v Aston Villa, away, Worthington Cup
United record: League: 11 (14) games, 2 goals; FA Cup: 1 (2) game, 0 goals; League Cup: 5 games, 0 goals; Europe: 1 (5) game, 0 goals; Others: 0 games, 0 goals
Total: 18 (21) games, 2 goals

Operating in more or less the same position as David Beckham has always restricted Luke Chadwick's first team opportunities at United, and this season it was tougher than ever for him. The right-winger started just one game for the Reds – away to Burnley in the Worthington Cup – and made four substitute appearances, three of them in Europe.

In fact, the only time he tasted Premiership action was as a second-half substitute for Nicky Butt in the defeat to Leeds United. In October, Chadwick told *United Review*. "I just want to play regular football and at the moment it doesn't look like I'll get that here so I might have to look elsewhere." He did just that, and in February hooked up with Alan Pardew at Reading to help the Berkshire side's push for the Premiership.

With Chadwick signed up for the latter third of the First Division campaign, Reading ended up in fourth place and made it to the play-offs, only to lose to Wolves (and fellow Old Trafford old boys Paul Ince and Denis Irwin) in the semi-finals.

Roy Keane

Magic moment: Lifting the Premiership trophy at Goodison Park. Like many of his well-decorated team-mates, Keane enjoyed this one just as much as the first and it showed – that beaming smile said it all...

16 **Position:** Midfield

Born: Cork, Ireland, 10 August 1971
Signed: from Nottingham Forest, 19 July 1993
Previous clubs: Cobh Ramblers
Senior United debut: 7 August 1993 v Arsenal, Wembley, FA Charity Shield
United record: League: 252 (10) games, 29 goals; FA Cup: 36 (1) games, 1 goal; League Cup: 11 (2) games, 0 goals; Europe: 70 (1) games, 14 goals; Others: 10 games, 2 goals
Total: 379 (14) games, 46 goals
International: 58 caps for Ireland

Even by his own volcanic standards, Roy Keane endured an explosive start to the season. It began with a series of blows that would have knocked anyone for six: the exit from the Irish World Cup squad rolled into the publication of his controversial autobiography, followed quickly by a sending off at Sunderland and bust-up with Jason McAteer.

An operation to Roy's troubled hip followed, and it was December 26 before he returned to first team action. By this time Arsenal were leading the way, and critics were pointing the finger at United's talismanic captain.

If you could switch off your cliché radar for a second, it was a season of two halves. United's unbeaten streak in the league coincided with an almost unbroken run of games for Keano (save the month of March), and by the run-in he was, well, running it. During the final three games of the season, we were treated to the Roy Keane of old – hungrier than ever and most importantly, enjoying his football again. We've got a feeling Triggs the dog will enjoy his country walks a lot more this summer.

Michael Stewart

17 **Position:** Midfield

Born: Edinburgh, 26 February 1981
Signed: Trainee, 30 June 1997
Other clubs: Royal Antwerp (loan)
Senior United debut: 31 October 2000 v
Watford, away, Worthington Cup
United record: League: 5 (2) games, 0 goals;
FA Cup: 0 (1) games, 0 goals; League Cup:
2 (2) games, 0 goals; Europe: 0 (2) games,
0 goals; Others: 0 games, 0 goals
Total: 7 (7) games, 0 goals
International: 3 caps for Scotland

Magic moment: Stewart started against Burnley in the Worthington Cup and never let the side down as United's near–neighbours put up a fight for the Sky Sports audience.

United's Edinburgh-born midfield prospect would probably have hoped for more first-team chances this season. Last year he broke into the Scotland international first team (and took part in their ill-fated summer tour of south-east Asia), but has found opportunities at United harder to come by. His Old Trafford season mirrored Luke Chadwick's, with one start at Burnley and a few more substitute appearances being the sum of his first team run-outs, but unlike Chadwick, Stewart decided to stick it out in Manchester rather than go out on loan.

Stewart has discussed the prospect of spending next season out on loan but at time of going to press, nothing had been confirmed. Highly rated within the club, the midfielder is under no illusions as to how difficult it is to break into United's midfield. "There's a lot of fantastic players in front of me so I've got to concentrate and work hard to keep progressing. If I manage to be half the player Roy Keane is for Manchester United then I'll be happy." Scotland's international bosses will be pleased too.

Paul Scholes

18 **Position:** Midfield

Born: Salford, 16 November 1974
Signed: Trainee, 8 July 1991
Senior United debut: 21 September 1994
v Port Vale, away, League Cup
United record: League: 206 (54) games,
68 goals; FA Cup: 12 (8) games, 5 goals;
League Cup: 10 (4) games, 8 goals; Europe:
62 (11) games, 20 goals; Others: 8 games,
0 goals
Total: 298 (77) games, 101 goals
International: 54 caps for England

Magic moment: Well, three of them... it has to be the incredible hat-trick against Newcastle at St James Park. In this sort of form no-one could have dealt with Scholes, not even one of United's closest challengers.

A season to remember. This year Scholes could shout about a personal best goal tally, a place in the Premiership team of the season, his 100th goal for the Reds and, most importantly, yet another league winner's medal. Shouting about these achievements is one thing he won't do though – the only place he does his talking is on the pitch (generally about 16 yards from the opposition goal).

When 2002 became 2003, Scholes was devastating. He scored seven goals in the first six games of the year and ended the run against West Ham (who still had six knocked past them). His 20-goal haul was the first time an attacking midfielder in a United shirt had broken that barrier since Sir Bobby Charlton, and it was a major contribution to United's eighth Premiership title. Transfer speculation constantly follows United but while Paul Scholes is one man who could walk into any team on the planet, he admitted this year there would only be one team he would join if the unthinkable happened and he left Old Trafford – Oldham, of course.

Ricardo

Magic moment: Dramatically saving a David Dunn penalty against Blackburn moments after coming on as a sub. With the score at 2–1 the save was crucial, and the Reds went on to win 3–1.

Born: Madrid, Spain, 31 December 1971
Signed: from Valladolid, 30 August 2002
Senior United debut: 18 September 2002 v Maccabi Haifa, home, Champions League
United record: League: 0 (1) games, 0 goals; FA Cup: 0 games, 0 goals; League Cup: 0 games, 0 goals; Europe: 3 (1) games, 0 goals; Others: 0 games, 0 goals
Total: 3 (2) games, 0 goals
International: 1 cap for Spain

Ricardo Lopez Felipe, to give him his full name, was a summer deadline day signing and gave Sir Alex yet more goalkeeping options. He had made his debut for Spain the week before arriving at Old Trafford and was highly thought of in his native *La Liga*, but had Fabien Barthez and Roy Carroll to contend with. Ricardo was up for the challenge from day one, and said on his arrival, "When I heard Sir Alex wanted to see me I was delighted. I want to do well for the manager, the team and all the fans."

His first opportunity came away to Maccabi Haifa in the Champions League, when he gave away a penalty during a 3–0 defeat. The next chance came at home to Bayer Leverkusen when he gave away another spot kick, which Leverkusen's Simak blasted over the bar. His third start of the season was away to Deportivo La Coruña (with United already qualified for the next round, just like the Maccabi match). No penalties, but a 2–0 defeat all the same. His luck changed on his first league outing, as a sub for Barthez, which provided him with his first United magic moment...

Ole Gunnar Solskjaer

Magic moment: The final goal against Liverpool at Old Trafford, which condemned the Merseysiders to their worst defeat by United in 50 years. All the more galling considering Ole used to follow Liverpool as a kid...

Born: Kristiansund, Norway, 26 February 1973
Signed: from Molde, 29 July 1996
Previous clubs: Clausenengen FK
Senior United debut: 25 August 1996 v Blackburn, home, Premiership
United record: League: 135 (65) games, 84 goals; FA Cup: 9 (10) games, 6 goals; League Cup: 7 (3) games, 6 goals; Europe: 33 (40) games, 18 goals; Others: 5 (3) games, 0 goals
Total: 189 (121) games, 114 goals
International: 55 caps for Norway

One of Old Trafford's most-loved players celebrated his 300th appearance for United this season, and never has his influence been as important. In a campaign marred by a series of injuries to a number of key players, Solskjaer's versatility has been a godsend to Sir Alex. And for someone who has has been burdened with an unwanted "supersub" tag, it may be a surprise to hear that with 37 games, Ole made more Premiership appearances than any other United player this season (and only eight of them from the bench). Operating in a wider role than usual for much of the campaign, Solskjaer still managed to provide invaluable support for Ruud van Nistelrooy whenever needed and weighed in with 15 goals.

Ole's form in the wide right role was so impressive he was even given the nod ahead of David Beckham for the visit of Real Madrid. The selection provoked controversy but as Sir Alex said at the time, "I don't regard Solskjaer as a substitute any more – he deserved his place and has been in fantastic form in that position". And who are we to argue?

Diego Forlan

21 Position: Forward

Magic moment: A few clues: it happened somewhere down the East Lancs Road, it was the cue for major waterworks, and it inspired one of the Stretford End's most memorable chants in years. Altogether now...

Born: Montevideo, Uruguay, 19 May 1979
Signed: from Independiente, 22 January 2002
Senior United debut: 29 January 2002 v Bolton Wanderers, away, Premiership
United record: League: 13 (25) games, 6 goals; FA Cup: 0 (2) game, 0 goals; League Cup: 3 (2) games, 2 goals; Europe: 6 (12) games, 1 goal; Others: 0 games, 0 goals
Total: 22 (41) games, 9 goals
International: 5 caps for Uruguay

It took Diego Forlan some 24 Premiership appearances before he broke his Premiership duck, but when it came (a late equaliser against Aston Villa in October), it was crucial. In fact, most of his goals turned out to be pretty important. He scored an even later winner against Southampton in the next league match (and then couldn't get his top back on after a particularly frenzied celebration, but that's another story) and punished Jerzy Dudek by scoring a dramatic double at Anfield – guaranteeing folk hero status for life. His two late winners against Chelsea (one in the Premiership, one in the Worthington Cup) live on in the memory too.

Forlan found first team places hard to come by in 2003 but he can look back on his first full season at United with real satisfaction. Diego was on the golf course with his father when he discovered Arsenal had lost to Leeds and United were confirmed champions, so if your putting was disrupted by the ecstatic celebrations of a young Uruguayan back on 2nd May 2003, we can only apologise on his behalf.

John O'Shea

22 Position: Defender

Magic moment: Nutmegging the mighty Luis Figo when Real Madrid came to town. The magic thing about it being that no United fan was in the least bit surprised. Anything you can do, O'Shea can do better...

Born: Waterford, Ireland, 30 April 1981
Signed: Trainee, 3 August 1998
Previous clubs: Bournemouth (loan), Royal Antwerp (loan)
Senior United debut: 13 October 1999 v Aston Villa, away, Worthington Cup
United record: League: 30 (11) games, 0 goals; FA Cup: 1 game, 0 goals; League Cup: 7 games, 0 goals; Europe: 12 (7) games, 0 goals; Others: 0 games, 0 goals
Total: 50 (18) games, 0 goals
International: 4 caps for Ireland

Let's hear it for the boy. Last season John O'Shea made 13 first team appearances, eight as a substitute. This time his total broke 50, and 42 of those were in the starting 11 – remember the name, indeed. O'Shea's first full season exceeded all his (and the manager's) expectations. When *United Review* interviewed him in October 2002, his ambition was to play 20 Premiership games and gain some experience in Europe. He ended up taking part in over 30 league games and 16 Champions League matches, including the double-headers with Juventus and Real Madrid.

O'Shea was nominated for the PFA Young Player Of The Year award and broke into the Ireland side, after being unlucky to miss out on the 2002 World Cup. Keen to make one position his own, he has impressed whererever he's played – and there's been a few. He even stood out in central midfield when he played there against Burnley, but it doesn't look like he'll be challenging Ruud at the top of the scoring charts. O'Shea came close to breaking his duck at Newcastle, but you can't have everything.

Wes Brown

24 **Position:** Defender

Magic moment: Most of Brown's work takes place in United's box rather than the opposition's, but the timing of his first goal for the Reds couldn't have been better, just four minutes into the home game against Juve.

Born: Manchester, 13 October 1979
Signed: Trainee, 8 July 1996
Senior United debut: 4 May 1998 v Leeds United, home, Premiership
United record: League: 73 (9) games, 0 goals; FA Cup: 4 (1) games, 0 goals; League Cup: 6 (1) games, 0 goals; Europe: 23 (5) games, 1 goal; Others: 0 games, 0 goals
Total: 107 (16) games, 1 goal
International: 7 caps for England

Just five minutes into the opening game of the season (away to Zalaegerszeg), Wes Brown suffered a broken ankle which kept him out of United's next 21 matches. That the young defender returned stronger than ever and enjoyed arguably his best ever season in a United shirt says everything about his strength of character and an ability to deal with whatever fate throws at him. The cruciate injury suffered on the last day of the season at Everton was yet another cruel setback, but Brown will work harder than ever to reclaim his fitness, and his place in the team.

Brown was expected to form a new central defensive partnership with good friend Rio Ferdinand, but ironically he was at his strongest in December when partnering Mikael Silvestre, after Rio had his own spell on the sidelines. Arsenal's visit to Old Trafford on league business was a particular triumph for United's Anglo-Gallic combo, with the threat of Thierry Henry and Sylvain Wiltord completely snuffed out. Brown's versatility meant he filled in at right-back in the absence of Gary Neville.

Quinton Fortune

25 **Position:** Midfield

Magic moment: We'd hazard a guess that Fortune's most satisfying moment of the season was signing a brand new contract just days after United had lifted the Premiership trophy once again.

Born: Cape Town, RSA, 21 May 1977
Signed: from Club Atletico de Madrid, 1 August 1999
Previous clubs: Tottenham Hotspur, RCD Mallorca
Senior United debut: 30 August 1999 v Newcastle, home, Premiership
United record: League: 23 (13) games, 5 goals; FA Cup: 0 games, 0 goals; League Cup: 3 games, 0 goals; Europe: 7 (9) games, 0 goal; Others: 1 (2) games, 2 goals
Total: 34 (24) games, 7 goals
International: 43 caps for South Africa

The talented South African midfielder was restricted to 16 first team appearances for United this season, half of them as substitute, but Sir Alex knows this is one man he can rely on no matter the situation. In an impressive spell before Christmas, Fortune worked tirelessly in the wins over Bayer Leverkusen, Newcastle United and FC Basel, then played an important supporting role in the memorable 2-1 victory over Liverpool. He was substituted with 10 minutes to go at Anfield and tests showed he had suffered a broken leg, which kept him out for three months.

In an interview last year, Roy Keane revealed Fortune is one of the most committed Reds in training sessions at Carrington. This attitude and workrate has impressed the manager enough to reward the lad from Cape Town with a new three-year contract, saying: "He's been improving every year since he joined us and has shown great character to come back from his various injury problems. We look forward to him making a great contribution to the team in the next three years".

Danny Pugh

26 **Position:** Midfield

Magic moment: Starting against Deportivo was impressive but being part of the team that beat a Juventus side containing Davids, Trezeguet, Thuram and Nedved in only your fourth senior game? One for the scrapbook.

Born: Manchester, 19 October 1982
Signed: Trainee, 5 July 1999
Senior United debut: 18 September 2002 v Maccabi Haifa, home, Champions League
United record: League: 0 (1) games, 0 goals; FA Cup: 0 games, 0 goals; League Cup: 1 game, 0 goals; Europe: 1 (2) game, 0 goals; Others: 0 games, 0 goals
Total: 2 (3) games, 0 goals

Danny Pugh marked his third year at Manchester United's very own fame academy with five chances to prove himself on the big stage – and the stage doesn't get any bigger than the *Stadio delle Alpi* on a Champions League evening. The lad from Cheadle Hulme started on the bench against Juventus but when John O'Shea limped off injured with half an hour to go, the biggest night of his life suddenly got a whole lot bigger. Not a bad result either, all things considered.

The heady heights of Turin aside, Pugh also made his Premiership debut this season as a late sub against Spurs at Old Trafford, and featured in two other Champions League matches against Maccabi Haifa (home) and Deportivo La Coruña (away). He started against Burnley in the Worthington Cup and had three gilt-edged chances to open his scoring account for the Reds. Those misses proved difficult to live down in the merciless United dressing room, as Pugh later admitted: "I got a load of stick afterwards, but I thoroughly enjoyed the match".

Mikael Silvestre

27 **Position:** Defender

Moment: Like Wes Brown he's paid to defend and defend he does, but equally, there's no doubt Silvestre savoured his match-winning goal against Leeds United as much as Wes enjoyed his goal against Juve.

Born: Chambray-les-Tours, France, 9 August 1977
Signed: from Internazionale, 2 September 1999
Other clubs: Stade Rennais FC
Senior United debut: 11 September 1999 v Liverpool, away, Premiership
United record: League: 120 (10) games, 2 goals; FA Cup: 6 games, 0 goals; League Cup: 5 games, 0 goals; Europe: 38 (6) games, 1 goal; Others: 5 games, 0 goals
Total: 174 (16) games, 3 goals
International: 16 caps for France

After a rocky time at the back in the 2001/02 season, Manchester United steadied the ship and ended the latest campaign with the meanest defensive record in the Premiership. Mikael Silvestre's form was a major contributing factor. He made more league starts (32) than any other United player this season, and was equally impressive at left back or central defence – where he enjoyed his favourite match of the season against Arsenal at Old Trafford in the league.

"We should be inspired by that game and try to produce that type of display all the time," he said later. Evidently, his team-mates listened as they marched to an eighth Premiership title.

Silvestre was an ever-present for the French national side this season, adding nine caps to his growing total. No doubt he'll be looking forward to future international get-togethers, where he can talk his fellow countrymen Patrick Vieira, Robert Pires and Sylvain Wiltord through his latest championship-winning adventure...

Darren Fletcher

31 **Position:** Midfield

Magic moment: The ovation given to Fletcher when he was substituted after 71 minutes of his Old Trafford debut against FC Basel (to be replaced by one D Beckham) will be a moment he'll remember for a long time.

Born: Edinburgh, 1 February 1984
Signed: Trainee, 3 July 2000
Senior United debut: 12 March 2003 v FC Basel, home, UEFA Champions League
United record: League: 0 games, 0 goals; FA Cup: 0 games, 0 goals; League Cup: 0 games, 0 goals; Europe: 2 games, 0 goals; Others: 0 games, 0 goals
Total: 2 games, 0 goals

In recent times, United's promising reserve players have generally enjoyed their first taste of the big time in the League Cup. It's testament to the Reds' safe passage through the early phases of this year's Champions League that Darren Fletcher's two first-team appearances came in the European fixtures against FC Basel and Deportivo La Coruña.

Fletcher's United debut would have happened a lot sooner if the manager had got his way. Sir Alex planned to give him his first taste of first team football when he was just 16, but Premiership rules prevented it as he was still employed on schoolboy forms. A couple of injuries delayed his debut even further, but he fought his way back to fitness and the Reds are set to reap the benefits. United's experienced pros have known of Fletcher's potential for some time and Gary Neville, for one, is looking forward to playing alongside him a lot more: "He reminds me of a young David Beckham. Slightly different as a player, but still fantastic to have around. He looks like he can handle the big stage." High praise indeed.

Lee Roche

34 **Position:** Defender

Magic moment: Alan Shearer and Craig Bellamy don't often pop up in the Reserve League (North) so Roche will have enjoyed pitting his defensive wits against them for 20 minutes at OT... and coming out on top.

Born: Bolton, 28 October 1980
Signed: Trainee, 30 June 1997
Senior United debut: 5 November 2001 v Arsenal, away, Worthington Cup
United record: League: 0 (1) games, 0 goals; FA Cup: 0 games, 0 goals; League Cup: 1 game, 0 goals; Europe: 1 game, 0 goals; Others: 0 games, 0 goals
Total: 2 (1) games, 0 goals

Bolton-born defender Lee Roche has been a virtual ever-present in Ricky Sbragia's Reserve side this season, but found himself upgraded for a couple of first team games against two of the biggest teams around. In November, the young right back replaced a tiring Laurent Blanc in the stunning home win over Newcastle United. The blood would have been pumping as he stood on the touchline ready to make his Premiership debut, but given the Reds were 5-1 up at the time and coasting, the manager's advice was no doubt, "Just go out and enjoy it, son".

His other senior game this season came alongside a handful of his Reserves and Academy mates in the Champions League Phase 2 match against Deportivo La Coruña at the *Estadio Riazor*, when the young United player left Spain defeated but far from disgraced. There's no doubt Roche has been unfortunate that the man holding down his position in the first team has been Gary Neville, and he went on loan to Wrexham a couple of season ago to gain a prolonged taste of senior football.

Danny Webber

37 **Position:** Forward

Born: Manchester, 28 December 1981
Signed: Trainee, 6 July 1998
Senior United debut: 28 November 2000
v Sunderland, away, Worthington Cup
United record: League: 0 games, 0 goals;
FA Cup: 0 games, 0 goals; League Cup: 1 (1)
game, 0 goals; Europe: 0 (1) games, 0 goals;
Others: 0 games, 0 goals
Total: 1 (2) game, 0 goals

Moment: United may have lost 2–0 over in La Coruña, but the experience gained in facing up to some of *La Liga*'s toughest defenders will not have been lost on Webber, or his team-mates.

Like a lot of his Reserve colleagues this season, Danny Webber's taste of the big time came after his more experienced team-mates had already ensured United would be taking part in the next round of the Champions League. The Mancunian striker was a second-half replacement for Ryan Giggs away to Deportivo La Coruña in Phase 2 (Giggs being one of the few old heads on show), and he ran his socks off in an attempt to get United back in the match.

It wasn't Webber's only first team appearance this season however. He spent a second loan spell with Watford between August and October 2002 and impressed the Hornets with his strong running and eye for goal.

Watford hoped to retain his services for longer with manager Ray Lewington saying, "He's been absolutely magnificent since he's been here," but a dislocated shoulder forced the the England Under-20 international to return to Old Trafford – only to then suffer a broken leg in a Manchester Senior Cup tie at the tail-end of the season.

Mark Lynch

38 **Position:** Defender

Born: Manchester, 2 September 1981
Signed: Trainee, 6 July 1998
Senior United debut: 18 March 2003
v Deportivo La Coruña, away, Champions League
United record: League: 0 games, 0 goals;
FA Cup: 0 games, 0 goals; League Cup:
0 games, 0 goals; Europe: 1 game, 0 goals;
Others: 0 games, 0 goals
Total: 1 game, 0 goals

Magic moment: Giving away an own goal on your first team debut can't exactly be classed as a magic moment, but lining up alongside players such as Laurent Blanc, Ryan Giggs and Nicky Butt certainly can.

Anyone who watched Mark Lynch's first team debut for United will confirm he was one of the most impressive young players on display, but unfortunately the record books will point out he scored an own goal in the same match which put Deportivo La Coruña 2-0 up. The Manchester-born defender could do little to stop the goal, coming as it did after the gifted Valerón had fired in a practically undefendable cross. There's no doubt Lynch will have wanted the Spanish soil to open up when that own goal hit the net, but Sir Alex will have learned a lot more about the character of the player by the way he recovered and stuck to his task for the rest of the match. As the manager pointed out in his programme notes the following week, "Our youngsters were up against a team challenging for the Spanish championship and in those circumstances we came out of it rather well."

Lynch is another young hopeful to have spent some time honing his football away from United. He played 20 games in the Scottish Premier League with St Johnstone in 2001, mostly out-of-position in midfield.

Daniel Nardiello

40 Position: Forward

Magic moment: Nardiello was the only starting player making his home debut in the League Cup match against Leicester, and lining up alongside Beckham, Solskjaer and Ferdinand was a moment to savour.

Born: Coventry, 22 October 1982
Signed: Trainee, 5 July 1999
Senior United debut: 5 November 2001 v Arsenal, away, Worthington Cup
United record: League: 0 games, 0 goals; FA Cup: 0 games, 0 goals; League Cup: 1 (1) game, 0 goals; Europe: 0 (1) games, 0 goals; Others: 0 games, 0 goals
Total: 1 (2) game, 0 goals

Son of Coventry City and Wales' Donato Nardiello, Daniel featured in the League Cup tie against Leicester City, during which he was unfortunate not to open his first-team scoring account before giving way to Kieran Richardson, and the Maccabi Haifa away tie in the Champions League. A strong-running striker, Nardiello has been a prolific goalscorer for the under-19s and Reserves and scored 16 goals in 23 games for Ricky Sbragia's second string during this campaign.

Kieran Richardson

42 Position: Midfield

Magic moment: What more can you ask for than a goal on your home debut? Richardson rounded off an impressive late show against Leicester in the League Cup with a diving header in front of the Stretford End.

Born: Greenwich, 21 October 1984
Signed: Trainee, 2 July 2001
Senior United debut: 23 October 2002 v Olympiakos, away, Champions League
United record: League: 0 (2) games, 0 goals; FA Cup: 1 game, 0 goals; League Cup: 0 (1) games, 1 goal; Europe: 2 (3) games, 0 goals; Others: 0 games, 0 goals
Total: 3 (6) games, 1 goal

South Londoner Richardson made his senior home debut in the Worthington Cup against Leicester this season as a second half substitute for fellow Academy kid Daniel Nardiello, after taking part in the UNICEF friendly against Boca Juniors. He also scored in the pre-season match at Chesterfield. Snapped up from West Ham, Richardson has enjoyed several first-team outings in all competitions, and was a goalscorer in United's FA Youth Cup Final win over Middlesbrough.

Mads Timm

43 Position: Midfield

Magic moment: With qualification to Phase 2 of the Champions League in the bag, Sir Alex blooded some of his youngsters against Maccabi Haifa. With just over 10 minutes to go, Timm made his United debut, replacing Diego Forlan.

Born: Odense, Denmark, 31 October 1984
Signed: from OB Odense, 1 August 2002
Senior United debut: 29 October 2002 v Maccabi Haifa, away, Champions League
United record: League: 0 games, 0 goals; FA Cup: 0 games, 0 goals; League Cup: 0 games, 0 goals; Europe: 0 (1) games, 0 goals; Others: 0 games, 0 goals
Total: 0 (1) games, 0 goals

Mads Timm caught the eye starring for the Reserves and was rewarded with a place on the bench for the Maccabi Haifa away match in Phase 1 of the Champions League, in the neutral territory of Cyprus. Timm appeared as a second half substitute and while the lads lost the match 3-0, the experience gained could prove invaluable in the long run. The young Danish playmaker was another vital part of Brian McClair's successful FA Youth Cup winning team.

Arsenal 1 Sheffield United 0 FA Cup semi-final **Sunday 13 April 2003**
Sheffield United players embark on a lap of honour around Old Trafford after narrowly losing a hard-fought FA Cup semi-final against holders Arsenal

Manchester United Public training day **Thursday 8 August 2002**
The first team squad put the finishing touches to pre-season training in front of the fans

Bradford Bulls 18 St Helens 19 Super League Grand Final **19 October 2002**
Rugby league's showpiece occasion goes down to the wire once again

Old Trafford's goal king

Ruud van Nistelrooy was named Barclaycard Player of the Year for season 2002/03, and picked up the Golden Boot award for finishing the Premiership's top scorer. Barclaycard donated £1,000 for every league goal Ruud scored to charities of his choice.

United's No.10 also set a new club record by scoring in 10 consecutive games, and his impeccable finishing in the Champions League made him the highest-ever scorer in one season, with 12 goals.

"To win both the Barclaycard Golden Boot award and the Player of the Year rounds off a great season for me," said Ruud.

"There are so many great strikers in the Premiership with the likes of Thierry Henry, James Beattie and Alan Shearer, so it is a real honour to come top of the scorers' league.

"The goals I've scored also mean I can donate the £25,000 to two causes in Holland, the SOS Children's Village and a Creutzfeldt-Jakob Disease charity."

RUUD'S GOLDEN GOALS IN 2002/03

Date	Against	h/a	Game	Goals
Aug 27	Zalaegerszeg	h	CL qualifier	2
Sept 3	Middlesbrough	h	Prem	1 (pen)
Sept 18	Maccabi Haifa	h	CL phase 1	1
Sept 21	Tottenham	h	Prem	1 (pen)
Sept 24	Bayer Leverkusen	a	CL phase 1	2
Sept 28	Charlton	a	Prem	1
Oct 7	Everton	h	Prem	1
Nov 13	Bayer Leverkusen	h	CL phase 1	1
Nov 17	West Ham	a	Prem	1
Nov 23	Newcastle	h	Prem	3
Nov 26	Basel	h	CL phase 1	2
Dec 11	Deportivo	h	CL phase 2	2
Jan 4	Portsmouth	h	FAC3	2 (pens)
Jan 11	West Brom	a	Prem	1
Jan 22	Blackburn	a	WC semi	1 (pen)
Jan 26	West Ham	h	FAC4	2
Feb 1	Southampton	a	Prem	1
Feb 4	Birmingham City	a	Prem	1
Feb 9	Manchester City	h	Prem	1
Feb 19	Juventus	h	CL phase 2	1
Feb 25	Juventus	a	CL phase 2	1
Mar 22	Fulham	h	Prem	3 (1 pen)
Apr 5	Liverpool	h	Prem	2 (pens)
Apr 8	Real Madrid	a	CL QF 1	1
Apr 12	Newcastle	a	Prem	1 (pen)
Apr 16	Arsenal	a	Prem	1
Apr 19	Blackburn	h	Prem	1
Apr 23	Real Madrid	h	CL QF 2	1
Apr 27	Tottenham	a	Prem	1
May 3	Charlton	h	Prem	3
May 11	Everton	a	Prem	1 (pen)
Summary				
Premiership:			25 (7 penalties)	
Champions League:			14	
FA Cup:			4 (2 penalties)	
Worthington Cup:			1 (penalty)	
Total:			**44** (10 penalties)	

CELEBRATIONS

The Nevilles hail United's opening goal against West Ham at home in the league

Pure genius: Paul Scholes after completing his Newcastle treble

Rio on top of the pile after Seba opens the scoring against Olympiakos

Diego whips off his top after firing in a late winner against Southampton

Ruud is mobbed during the last home game against Charlton Athletic

ACTION

Roy Keane wins a header against Liverpool, Old Trafford, 5 April 2003

Rio Ferdinand shows his composure at home to Sunderland, 1 Jan 2003

Midfield tiger Nicky Butt evades Ian Harte at Elland Road, 14 Sept 2002

David Beckham puts John Arne Riise under pressure at Old Trafford, April 2003

Seba Veron up against Michel
Salgado as Real Madrid visit
Old Trafford, 22 April 2003

ON THE BENCH

Sir Alex has a word during
the second half against
Tottenham, 27 April 2003

Carlos Queiroz gets his
point across at the Valley,
September 28, 2002

Conducting the United orchestra at Anfield, 1 December 2002

The bench applauds David Beckham's opener against Charlton, 3 May 2003

GOALS

David Beckham scores his unforgettable free-kick against Real Madrid

Ole Gunnar Solskjaer makes it 4–0 against Liverpool, 5 April 2003

Ryan Giggs nets his second goal against Juventus, 25 February 2003

Ruud on the way to his amazing
second goal against Fulham,
Old Trafford, 22 March 2003

FA YOUTH CU

The lads celebrate a record ninth FA Youth Cup win

If the World Cup's spiritual home is Brazil and the European Cup's traditional keepers are Real Madrid, then United could be said to have a claim on the FA Youth Cup – junior football's most coveted trophy.

The Reds' love affair with this marvellous competition began in the mid-1950s when Matt Busby and Jimmy Murphy masterminded success in the contest's first five years. Ever since those wonderful days of Duncan Edwards, Bobby Charlton, Eddie Colman, Wilf McGuinness et al, there has been an inextricable link between United and the FA Youth Cup, and on a nostalgic and emotional night at Old Trafford, the club's latest bunch of young hopefuls completed a two-legged win over Middlesbrough to claim the trophy for a record ninth time.

Goals from Kieran Richardson and Ben Collett had given the Reds a two-goal cushion from the first leg at the Riverside, but nobody was foolhardy enough to think that the return was a mere formality. Middlesbrough, like United, didn't reach the final on favourable draws and lots of luck alone, and they more than proved their capabilities by holding United to a 1-1 draw at Old Trafford.

In front of 14,849 fans – including most of the first team – Eddie Johnson gave United the lead in the 15th minute with a sizzler that Boro keeper Ross Turnbull, exceptional on the night, had little chance of seeing, let alone stopping. But the visitors equalised 12 minutes from time when Gary Liddle was given the freedom of the United area, and took full advantage to power a header past Luke Steele from Andrew Davies' right-wing cross.

It was a case of too little, too late for Boro, though, who realistically lost their chance of collecting the

P

Quinton, Roy, David and Gary cheer on the new breed

United's Eddie Johnson wins the ball

Skipper David Jones lifts the Cup

rophy when Collett scored United's second goal during njury time in a tightly-contested first leg.

In the Old Trafford return, United dominated and nly Turnbull's heroics kept the goal count down. After he game, Under-19 manager Brian McClair was elighted with the addition to the trophy cabinet but efused to take any praise for himself.

"I've done very, very little," he said. "There's a lot of eople who deserve pats on the back – scouts, coaches ho have had the players from a young age and parents ho've had to make sacrifices to give them a chance to ecome professionals. And these lads have worked very ard and sacrificed a lot. They really wanted it – that's nown right through." Overall, it was another fine ccasion and a wonderful moment when skipper David nes held the gleaming trophy aloft. The FA Youth Cup, ke the Premiership trophy, is back where it belongs!

Wednesday 4 December 2002 – Third Round
v NEWCASTLE UNITED 3–1 (WON, AWAY, AT KINGSTON PARK, KENTON)
Scorers: Eagles, Richardson, Taylor (o.g.)
Team: Steele, Sims, Lawrence, Howard, McShane, Jones, Eagles, Calliste, Johnson, Richardson, Collett
Substitutes: Picken, Lee T, Eckersley, Ebanks-Blake (Calliste), Flanagan (Johnson)

Tuesday 21 January 2003 – Fourth Round
v SHEFFIELD WEDNESDAY 2–0 (WON, HOME, AT MOSS LANE, ALTRINCHAM)
Scorers: Collett, Richardson
Team: Steele, Sims, Lawrence, Howard, McShane, Jones, Eagles, Timm, Johnson, Richardson, Collett
Substitutes: Picken, Heaton, Byrne, Poole, Calliste (Timm)

Wednesday 5 February 2003 – Fifth Round
v SHEFFIELD UNITED 1–1* (DRAWN, HOME, AT MOSS LANE, ALTRINCHAM)
Scorer: Johnson
Team: Steele, Sims, Lawrence, Howard, McShane, Jones, Eagles, Timm, Johnson, Richardson, Poole
Substitutes: Nevins, Lee T., Byrne, Bardsley, Calliste (Poole)
*After extra time. Won 4–3 on penalties.
Penalty-scorers: Jones, Calliste, Eagles, Richardson

Thursday 6 March 2003 – Sixth Round
v TRANMERE ROVERS 3–1 (WON, HOME, AT MOSS LANE, ALTRINCHAM)
Scorers: Eagles, Timm, Ebanks-Blake
Team: Steele, Sims, Lawrence, Bardsley, McShane, Jones, Eagles, Timm, Calliste, Richardson, Collett
Substitutes: Howard, Heaton, Ebanks-Blake (Calliste), Byrne, Picken

Saturday 29 March 2003 – Semi Final, 1st Leg
v CHARLTON ATHLETIC 1–1 (DRAWN, AWAY)
Scorer: Richardson
Team: Steele, Sims, Lawrence, Bardsley, McShane, Jones, Eagles, Calliste, Johnson, Richardson, Collett
Substitutes: Poole, Heaton, Howard, Byrne, Ebanks-Blake (Calliste)

Wednesday 9 April 2003 – Semi Final, 2nd Leg
v CHARLTON ATHLETIC 2–0 (WON, HOME)
Scorers: Johnson, Richardson
Team: Steele, Sims, Lawrence, Bardsley, McShane, Jones, Eagles, Timm, Johnson, Richardson, Collett
Substitutes: Howard, Heaton, Byrne, Calliste, Ebanks-Blake (Timm)

Tuesday 15 April 2003 – Final, 1st Leg
v MIDDLESBROUGH 2–0 (WON, AWAY)
Scorers: Richardson, Collett
Team: Steele, Sims, Lawrence, Bardsley, McShane, Jones, Eagles, Timm, Johnson, Richardson, Collett
Substitutes: Howard, Heaton, Poole, Calliste, Ebanks-Blake (Timm)

Friday 25th April 2003 – Final, 2nd Leg
v MIDDLESBROUGH 1–1 (DRAWN, HOME)
Scorer: Johnson
Team: Steele, Sims, Lawrence, Bardsley, McShane, Jones, Eagles, Ebanks-Blake, Johnson, Richardson, Collett
Substitutes: Howard (McShane), Heaton, Poole (Richardson), Calliste (Ebanks-Blake), Picken

Filho's young Reds make a strong start but have to settle for second place as City steal the show

Chris Eagles in action against Everton

United's under-17s finished the season in a highly creditable runners-up spot in their group. An achievement even more meritorious when taking into account that neighbours Manchester City ran away with the honours after leading the chase from the earliest days. The Blues enjoyed a marvellous campaign – it would be churlish in the extreme not to acknowledge that – and were in command of the section throughout to claim their prize with a 15-point margin over Francisco Filho's charges.

United in turn showed their superiority over the remainder of the teams, finishing 12 points clear of third-placed Sheffield United. One defeat in the first five games provided an optimistic start to the season for the club's newest recruits, and the first-day goal glut – leaving Reading on the wrong end of a 6-1 thumping at Carrington – set the ball rolling.

As it turned out, that was the most comprehensive success of the term, but results aren't the be all and end all at this level. There's nothing wrong with a winning habit – football is after all a competitive sport – but the development of young players is always uppermost in the minds of the coaches and backroom staff. Whether these young hopefuls make a successful career in the game remains to be seen, but one thing is for sure, they could scarcely be in a better place to pursue their chosen profession.

Saturday 24 August 2002
v READING (Home) Won: 6-1
Scorers: Nevins 2, Picken (pen), Eagles, Jones, Marsh
Team: T Lee, Picken, Eckersley, Nevins, Howard, Hogg, Port, Eagles, Ebanks-Blake, Jones, Marsh
Subs: Simpson (Hogg), Heaton, Flanagan (Ebanks-Blake)

Friday 31 August 2002
v CHARLTON ATHLETIC (Away) Won: 4-1
Scorers: Picken, Ebanks-Blake, Eagles, Calliste
Team: Heaton, Simpson, Eckersley, Nevins, Howard, Picken, Eagles, Jones, Ebanks-Blake, Hogg, Marsh
Subs: Campbell (Hogg), T Lee, Flanagan (Ebanks-Blake), Calliste (Marsh), K Lee

Saturday 14 September 2002
v SHEFFIELD UNITED (Home) Lost: 1-3
Scorer: Marsh
Team: T Lee, Simpson, Eckersley, Nevins, Howard, Picken, Calliste, Hogg, Ebanks-Blake, Eagles, Port
Subs: Jones, Heaton, Flanagan (Ebanks-Blake), Marsh (Port), McShane (Nevins).

Wednesday 18 September 2002
v LIVERPOOL (Away) Won: 2-1
Scorers: Eagles, Jones
Team: Heaton; Nevins, Eckersley, McShane, Howard, Picken, Eagles, Jones, Ebanks-Blake, Hogg, Calliste
Subs: Flanagan (Calliste), T Lee, Port, Marsh (Hogg), Simpson (Nevins)

Saturday 21 September 2002
v NOTTINGHAM FOREST (Home) Won: 2-1
Scorers: Ebanks-Blake, Marsh
Team: T Lee, Simpson, Eckersley, McShane, Howard, Picken, Eagles, Jones, Ebanks-Blake, Hogg, Calliste
Subs: Flanagan, Heaton (T Lee), Port (Hogg), Marsh (Calliste), Nevins

Saturday 28 September 2002
v EVERTON (Home) Won: 1-0
Scorer: Ebanks-Blake
Team: Heaton, Simpson, Eckersley, Nevins, Howard, Picken, Eagles, Jones, Ebanks-Blake, Flanagan, Port
Subs: Marsh (Flanagan), Calliste (Port), Hogg (Jones)

Saturday 12 October 2002
v MANCHESTER CITY (Home) Lost: 1-2
Scorer: Hogg
Team: Heaton, Nevins, Howard, McShane, Picken, Eagles, Jones, Ebanks-Blake, Hogg, Calliste
Subs: Flanagan (Calliste), Port (Nevins), Marsh (Eagles), Rose

Saturday 19 October 2002
v EVERTON (Away) Won: 2-1
Scorers: Port, Eagles
Team: Heaton, Simpson, Hogg, Nevins, Howard,
Picken, Eagles, Jones, Ebanks-Blake, Calliste, Port
Subs: Flanagan (Calliste), Marsh (Blake),
Rose (Jones)

Saturday 26 October 2002
v NOTTINGHAM FOREST (Away) Won: 3-1
Scorers: Eagles 2, Rose
Team: Heaton, Simpson, Eckersley, Howard, Nevins,
Picken, Eagles, Jones, Ebanks-Blake,
Port, Calliste
Subs: Flanagan (Calliste), Marsh (Ebanks-Blake),
Rose (Eckersley)

Saturday 2 November 2002
v BIRMINGHAM CITY (Away) Won: 3-1
Scorers: Ebanks-Blake 2, Calliste
Team: Heaton, Simpson, Picken, McShane, Howard,
Nevins, Calliste, Jones, Ebanks-Blake,
Port, Flanagan
Subs: Marsh (Ebanks-Blake), T Lee, Campbell, Rose

Saturday 9 November 2003
v CREWE ALEXANDRA (Away) Won: 2-1
Scorers: Ebanks-Blake, Picken
Team: Heaton, Picken, Hogg, Howard, McShane,
Jones, Calliste, Nevins, Ebanks-Blake,
Flanagan, Port
Subs: Rose (Hogg), T Lee, Simpson (Port),
Marsh (Flanagan)

Saturday 16 November 2002
v WOLVERHAMPTON WANDERERS (Home) Drawn: 0-0
Team: Lee, Simpson, Eckersley, Howard, Lea,
Picken, Rose, Jones, Ebanks-Blake, Flanagan, Port
Subs: Marsh (Flanagan), Heaton, M Fox (Rose),
Booth (Jones)

Saturday 23 November 2002
v SHEFFIELD UNITED (Away) Lost: 2-5
Scorers: Calliste (pen), Blake
Team: T Lee, Picken, Eckersley, Lea, Howard,
K Lee, Calliste, Jones, Ebanks-Blake, Flanagan, Port
Subs: Fox (Flanagan), Heaton (T Lee), Marsh,
Campbell (Port)

Saturday 7 December 2002
v LIVERPOOL (Home) Won: 2-0
Scorers: Calliste, Ebanks-Blake
Team: Heaton, Simpson, Eckersley, Lea, Howard,
Picken, Flanagan, Jones, Ebanks-Blake, Calliste, Port
Subs: K Lee (Booth), Wallwork (Calliste), Booth (Port)

Saturday 14 December 2002
v MANCHESTER CITY (Away) Lost: 0-4
Team: T Lee, Simpson, Eckersley, Howard, McShane,
Picken, Nevins, Jones, Flanagan,
Eagles, Calliste
Subs: Port (Calliste), Heaton, Fox (Flanagan), Hogg

Saturday 18 January 2003
v CREWE ALEXANDRA (Home) Won: 2-1
Scorer: Ebanks-Blake 2
Team: Heaton, Simpson, Booth, Lea, Hogg,
Jones, Campbell, Fox, Ebanks-Blake,
Flanagan, Port
Subs: Rose (Fox), T Lee, Mullen (Port)

Saturday 25 January 2003
v WOLVERHAMPTON WANDERERS (Away) Won 2-1
Scorers: Ebanks-Blake, Flanagan
Team: Heaton, Picken, Hogg, Lea, Howard,
Nevins, Flanagan, Booth, Ebanks-Blake,
Rose, Calliste
Subs: Mullen (Calliste), T Lee, Marsh (Rose),
Fox (Booth)

Wednesday 19 February 2003
v BIRMINGHAM CITY (Away) Won: 3-1
Scorers: Ebanks-Blake, Calliste 2
Team: T Lee, Simpson, Eckersley, Howard, Hogg, Picken,
Flanagan, Jones, Ebanks-Blake, Calliste, Port
Subs: Marsh (Jones), Crockett, Booth, Campbell (Port)

Saturday 22 February 2003
v NEWCASTLE UNITED (Home) Lost: 2-3
Scorer: Ebanks-Blake
Team: Heaton, Simpson, Eckersley, Hogg, Howard,
Picken, Flanagan, Jones, Ebanks-Blake, Nevins, Marsh
Subs: Fox, Daniels, Campbell (Howard), K Lee

Saturday 1 March 2003
v BLACKBURN ROVERS (Away) Drawn: 1-1
Scorer: McShane
Team: Heaton, Simpson, Eckersley, Howard, McShane,
Picken, Eagles, Nevins, Ebanks-Blake,
Calliste, Flanagan
Subs: Marsh (Flanagan), Crockett, Fox (Marsh), Hogg

Saturday 8 March 2003
v WATFORD (Home) Won: 2-0
Scorer: Ebanks-Blake 2
Team: Heaton, Simpson, Eckersley, Howard, McShane,
Picken, Eagles, Nevins, Ebanks-Blake,
Calliste, Flanagan
Subs: Port (Calliste), Crockett, Hogg (McShane),
Marsh (Eagles)

Tuesday 18 March 2003
v SUNDERLAND (Away) Won: 1-0
Scorer: Ebanks-Blake
Team: Sanna, Simpson, Lea, Nevins, McShane,
Hogg, Flanagan, Marsh, Ebanks-Blake, Calliste, Port
Subs: Rose (Port), Crockett, Campbell (Flanagan),
Mullen (Simpson)

Saturday 22 March 2003
v CRYSTAL PALACE (Home) Lost: 0-1
Team: Heaton, Picken, Eckersley, Howard, McShane,
Hogg, Flanagan, Nevins, Ebanks-Blake, Calliste, Port
Subs: Marsh (Port), Crockett, Campbell (Flanagan),
Rose (Hogg)

Saturday 5 April 2003
v IPSWICH TOWN (Away) Lost: 1-2
Scorer: Hogg
Team: Heaton, Lea, Hogg, Nevins, McShane,
Picken, Calliste, Marsh, Ebanks-Blake,
Eagles, Rose
Subs: Flanagan (Rose), Crockett, Campbell (Marsh),
Mullen, K Lee

Saturday 26 April 2003
v DERBY COUNTY (Home) Won: 2-1
Scorers: Howard (pen), Eckersley
Team: Heaton, Simpson, Eckersley, Hogg, Howard,
Picken, Flanagan, Nevins, Calliste,
Campbell, Port
Subs: Rose (Port), Daniels, Marsh (Campbell),
K Lee, Mullen (Flanagan)

FA PREMIER ACADEMY LEAGUE UNDER-17							
Group A	P	W	D	L	F	A	Pts
Manchester City	22	20	2	0	66	11	62
Manchester United	22	15	2	5	44	29	47
Sheffield United	22	10	5	7	34	24	35
Wolves	22	10	5	7	21	19	35
Everton	22	8	5	9	31	27	29
Liverpool	22	8	4	10	22	35	28
Crewe Alexandra	22	5	7	10	35	42	22
Nottingham Forest	22	7	1	14	27	44	22
Birmingham City	22	5	3	14	28	47	18

FA PREMIER ACADEMY LEAGUE UNDER-17		
	APPS	GOALS
Mitchell BOOTH	2(2)	-
Fraizer CAMPBELL	2(7)	-
Ramon CALLISTE	19(2)	6
Chris EAGLES	13	6
Sylvan EBANKS-BLAKE	23	17
Adam ECKERSLEY	18	1
Callum FLANAGAN	16(8)	1
Mark FOX	1(5)	-
Tom HEATON	17(2)	-
Steven HOGG	16(2)	2
Mark HOWARD	22	1
Richard JONES	17	2
Michael LEA	7	-
Tommy LEE	7	-
Kieran LEE	1(1)	-
Paul McSHANE	11(1)	1
Phil MARSH	5(16)	3
Jamie MULLEN	0(4)	-
Adrian NEVINS	19	2
Phil PICKEN	23	3
Graham PORT	15(4)	1
Danny ROSE	3(7)	1
Christopher SANNA	1	-
Danny SIMPSON	17(3)	-
Kyle WALLWORK	0(1)	-

Cup triumph for McClair's youngsters but a severe case of the Blues denied United top spot in the league

Brian McClair's first season in charge of the senior Academy players went agonisingly close to being marked with a league and cup Double. The youngsters marched to glory in the FA Youth Cup but in the end had to be content with a third-place finish in the league after being one of the main contenders for the title for most of the season.

McClair's under-19s endured a stuttering start to the campaign – four defeats in the opening five fixtures – before settling down to put in a serious challenge for group honours. They turned the corner in late September and suffered only a further four defeats throughout the campaign. Easily the worse defeat of the season was the 7-3 drubbing by Newcastle United at Carrington during that early dismal sequence, but the books were balanced in January when United rattled half a dozen plus one past luckless Birmingham City.

United's interest in the title remained right up until their final fixture against Manchester City at Platt Lane. Victory would have given the Reds an outside chance of finishing on top, but the Blues won the game 2-1 and went on to win the group. Lee Sims was the under-19s' most regular performer, appearing in 25 of the season's league fixtures, while Colin Heath led the way in the scoring charts with 25 goals.

Colin Heath leads a Red charge against City

Saturday 24 August 2002
v READING (Home) Won: 2–0
Scorer: Heath 2
Team: Steele, Sims, Collett, Fox, Cogger, Bardsley, Mooniaruck, Taylor, Heath, Johnson, Timm
Subs: Humphreys, Heaton, Jones, Poole (Timm), Byrne

Friday 31 August 2002
v CHARLTON ATHLETIC (Away) Lost: 2–3
Scorer: Heath 2
Team: Steele, Sims, Collett, Fox, Cogger, Jones, Mooniaruck, Humphreys, Heath, Byrne, Richardson
Subs: Taylor, T Lee, Bardsley, Poole (Byrne), Johnson

Saturday 7 September 2002
v LEEDS UNITED (Away) Lost: 1–2
Scorer: Poole
Team: Steele, Sims, Collett, Fox, Cogger, Bardsley, Timm, Taylor, Poole, Johnson, Richardson
Subs: Heath (Timm), Jowsey, Mooniaruck, Jones (Taylor), Humphreys

Saturday 14 September 2002
v NEWCASTLE UNITED (Home) Lost: 3–7
Scorers: Timm, Heath, Johnson
Team: Jowsey, Sims, Collett, Bardsley, Cogger, Jones, Byrne, Fletcher, Heath, Humphreys, Timm
Subs: Taylor (Cogger), Steele, Mooniaruck (Byrne), Johnson (Humphreys), Poole

Saturday 21 September 2002
v SUNDERLAND (Away) Lost: 2–3
Scorers: Bardsley, Fox
Team: Steele, Sims, Collett, Fox, Cogger, Bardsley, Mooniaruck, Taylor, Heath, Johnson, Timm
Subs: Humphreys, Richardson, Byrne, Jones

Saturday 28 September 2002
v BLACKBURN ROVERS (Home) Won: 4–0
Scorers: Timm 3, Heath
Team: Steele, Sims, Lawrence, Bardsley, Taylor, Jones, Byrne, Humphreys, Heath, Johnson, Timm
Subs: Fox, Cogger, Mooniaruck (Byrne), Poole (Johnson), Collett (Lawrence)

Saturday 5 October 2002
v STOKE CITY (Away) Won: 4–1
Scorers: Heath 2, Taylor, Poole
Team: Steele, Sims, Bardsley, Fox, Cogger, Taylor, Mooniaruck, Poole, Heath, Richardson, Jones
Subs: Byrne, Heaton, Flanagan

Saturday 12 October 2002
v MANCHESTER CITY (Home) Lost: 0–2
Team: Steele, Sims, Bardsley, Fox, Cogger, Taylor, Mooniaruck, Poole, Heath, Richardson, Timm
Subs: Johnson (Heath), Jones, Collett (Timm), Byrne

Saturday 19 October 2002
v EVERTON (Away) Won: 2–1
Scorers: Johnson, Sims

Team: Steele, Sims, Collett, Fox, Bardsley, Jones, Mooniaruck, Poole, Johnson, Taylor, Timm
Subs: Heath (Mooniaruck), Cogger

Saturday 26 October 2002
v NOTTINGHAM FOREST (Home) Drawn: 2-2
Scorers: Heath, Johnson
Team: Jowsey, Sims, Collett, Fox, Cogger, Bardsley, Poole, Taylor, Heath, Johnson, Timm
Subs: Mooniaruck, Steele, Jones

Saturday 2 November 2002
v BIRMINGHAM CITY (Away) Lost: 1-2
Scorer: Heath (pen)
Team: Jowsey, Sims, Eckersley, Fox, Cogger, Bardsley, Mooniaruck, Taylor, Poole, Eagles, Jones
Subs: Heath (Mooniaruck), Humphreys, Collett

Saturday 9 November 2002
v CREWE ALEXANDRA (Away) Won: 3-2
Scorer: Heath 3
Team: Steele, Sims, Eckersley, Fox, Taylor, Bardsley, Mooniaruck, Jones, Heath, Eagles, Collett.
Subs: Cogger, Humphreys, Poole, Johnson (Eagles), Lawrence (Collett)

Saturday 16 November 2002
v WOLVERHAMPTON WANDERERS (Home) Won: 2-0
Scorer: Eagles 2
Team: Steele, Sims, Lawrence, Bardsley, McShane, Timm, Eagles, Jones, Johnson, Poole, Collett
Subs: Fox (Bardsley), Jowsey, Heath (Timm)

Saturday 23 November 2002
v SHEFFIELD UNITED (Away) Won: 2-0
Scorer: Heath 2
Team: Steele, Sims, Lawrence, Fox, McShane, Jones, Mooniaruck, Eagles, Heath, Johnson, Collett
Subs: Cogger (Lawrence), Jowsey, Taylor (Collett)

Saturday 7 December 2002
v LIVERPOOL (Home) Drawn: 0-0
Team: Jowsey, Sims, Lawrence, Fox, McShane, Taylor, Mooniaruck, Fletcher, Johnson, Richardson, Eagles
Subs: Cogger, Steele, Collett, M Fox

Saturday 14 December 2002
v NOTTINGHAM FOREST (Away) Drawn: 0-0
Team: Jowsey, Sims, Lawrence, Fox, Cogger, Taylor, Mooniaruck, Fletcher, Heath, Johnson, Humphreys
Subs: Collett (Humphreys), Steele, Byrne Mooniaruck)

Saturday 11 January 2003
v BIRMINGHAM CITY (Home) Won: 7-2
Scorers: Eagles 2, Timm 2, Howard, Byrne, Picken
Team: Steele, Sims, Lawrence, McShane, Howard, Jones, Eagles, Byrne, Calliste, Timm, Collett
Subs: Eckersley, T Lee, Picken (Jones), Ebanks-Blake (Timm), Flanagan (Byrne)

Saturday 18 January 2003
v CREWE ALEXANDRA (Home) Won: 3-0
Scorers: Fox, Humphreys, Poole
Team: Jowsey, Picken, Eckersley, Fox, Cogger, Nevins, Byrne, Fletcher, Poole, Humphreys, Mooniaruck
Subs: Sims, Steele, Howard, Collett

Saturday 25 January 2003
v WOLVERHAMPTON WANDERERS (Away) Won: 3-1
Scorers: Fox 2, Timm
Team: Steele, Sims, Collett, Fox, McShane, Bardsley, Byrne, Jones, Heath, Eagles, Timm
Subs: Humphreys, Jowsey, Lawrence, Johnson (Heath), Poole (Bardsley)

Saturday 8 February 2003
v DERBY COUNTY (Away) Lost: 2-3
Scorers: Collett, Eagles
Team: Steele, Sims, Lawrence, Bardsley, Howard, Jones, Byrne, Nevins, Johnson, Eagles, Collett
Subs: Poole (Howard), Heaton, Picken (Lawrence), Calliste (Johnson)

Saturday 15 February 2003
v MIDDLESBROUGH (Home) Won: 3-2
Scorers: Jones, Heath 2
Team: Jowsey, Sims, Lawrence, Bardsley, McShane, Jones, Eagles, Collett, Heath, Timm, Poole
Subs: Picken (Eagles), Steele, Howard, Byrne (Timm)

Saturday 22 February 2003
v SHEFFIELD WEDNESDAY (Away) Won: 3-2
Scorers: Heath, Calliste, Humphreys
Team: Steele, Sims, Lawrence, Bardsley, McShane, Jones, Byrne, Humphreys, Heath, Calliste, Collett
Subs: Cogger, Jowsey (Steele), Fox, Timm

Saturday 1 March 2003
v BARNSLEY (Home) Won: 3-2
Scorers: Heath, Timm, Mooniaruck
Team: Jowsey, Fox, Lawrence, Bardsley, Cogger, Jones, Mooniaruck, Humphreys, Heath, Timm, Byrne
Subs: Collett (Cogger), Steele

Tuesday 18 March 2003
v SHEFFIELD UNITED (Home) Won: 3-0
Scorers: Poole, Howard, Heath
Team: Steele, Sims, Picken, Bardsley, Howard, Jones, Byrne, Timm, Poole, Eagles, Collett
Subs: Humphreys (Eagles), Heaton, Lawrence (Sims), Heath (Timm)

Saturday 15 March 2003
v LIVERPOOL (Away) Lost: 0-1
Team: Steele, Sims, Picken, Bardsley, McShane; Jones, Eagles, Timm, Heath, Richardson, Collett
Subs: Calliste (Heath), Nevins, Howard (McShane), Flanagan

Saturday 22 March 2003
v STOKE CITY (Home) Won: 4-0
Scorers: Heath 3, Humphreys

Team: Steel, Sims, Lawrence, Fox, Cogger, Bardsley, Byrne, Humphreys, Heath, Poole, Collett
Subs: Timm, Johnson (collett), Eagles

Friday 11 April 2003
v MANCHESTER CITY (Away) Lost: 1-2
Scorer: Ebanks-Blake
Team: Jowsey, Picken, Eckersley, Fox, Howard, Mooniaruck, Calliste, Poole, Heath, Ebanks-Blake, Nevins
Subs: Hogg, Heaton, Port, Flanagan (Poole)

Saturday 5 April 2003
v EVERTON (Home) Won: 3-2
Scorers: Heath 2, Humphreys
Team: Steele, Sims, Fox, Cogger, Bardsley, Byrne, Humphreys, Heath, Johnson, Poole
Subs: Richardson, Jones, Collett (Johnson)

FA PREMIER ACADEMY LEAGUE UNDER-19							
Group A	P	W	D	L	F	A	Pts
Manchester City	28	18	5	5	50	27	59
Nottm Forest	28	15	9	4	37	25	54
Manchester United	28	16	3	9	65	42	51
Everton	28	14	3	11	52	32	45
Liverpool	28	12	7	9	45	40	43
B'ham City	28	10	9	9	31	35	39
Crewe Alexandra	28	11	4	13	37	49	37
Wolves	28	8	9	11	38	35	33
Sheffield United	28	7	4	17	37	57	25
Stoke City	28	3	8	17	25	62	17

APPEARANCES AND GOALS		
	APPS	GOALS
Phillip BARDSLEY	21	1
Danny BYRNE	12(2)	1
Ramon CALLISTE	3(2)	1
John COGGER	14(1)	-
Ben COLLETT	18(5)	1
Chris EAGLES	11	1
Sylvan EBANKS-BLAKE	1(1)	1
Adam ECKERSLEY	4	-
Callum FLANAGAN	0(2)	-
Darren FLETCHER	4	-
David FOX	19(1)	4
Colin HEATH	19(5)	25
Mark HOWARD	4(1)	2
Chris HUMPHREYS	9(1)	4
David JONES	17(1)	1
Eddie JOHNSON	12(5)	3
James JOWSEY	9(1)	-
Lee LAWRENCE	12(2)	-
Paul McSHANE	8	-
Kalam MOONIARUCK	14(2)	1
Adrian NEVINS	3	-
Phil PICKEN	4(3)	1
David POOLE	13(5)	4
Kieran RICHARDSON	6	-
Lee SIMS	25	1
Luke STEELE	19	-
Kris TAYLOR	12(2)	1
Mads TIMM	15	8

RESERVES

The team enjoyed a solid run-in to their league campaign, but had to settle for a mid-table finish

In terms of results, the Reserves' season could hardly be described as a roaring success. They eventually finished in mid-table, but for most of the time hovered just below the halfway mark. United's second 11 started the season with Mike Phelan job-sharing with his first team coaching duties, but just before Christmas, Ricky Sbragia arrived to provide full-time stewardship.

The side struggled to find any real consistency after Sbragia's arrival, and continually changing personnel didn't help matters. Away wins at Sheffield Wednesday, West Brom and Bradford City helped compensate for the largely poor home form. United, who started the campaign as reigning champions, rarely looked capable of retaining their crown, but there was room for optimism during the run-in, with only one defeat in the last seven games.

And there was a dramatic ending to the campaign when United entertained Middlesbrough at Moss Lane. Steve McClaren's team needed to win to claim the title ahead of north-east rivals Sunderland, but they could only manage a draw so the trophy ended up going to Wearside.

There was little cheer in the Manchester Senior Cup, where United finished third in the group stage – therefore failing to reach the final. Oldham Athletic and Manchester City contested the destination of the wonderful old trophy whilst Bury were wooden-spoonists.

Wednesday 21 August 2002
v WEST BROMWICH ALBION (Home, at Old Trafford)
Won: 1–0 **Scorer**: Nardiello
Team: Steele, Roche, Hilton, Tate, May, Pugh, Chadwick, Fletcher, M Williams, Nardiello, Djordjic
Subs: Muirhead, Heaton, Rankin (Fletcher), Lynch (Hilton), Bardsley (Pugh)

Wednesday 4 September 2002
v EVERTON (Away, at Halton Stadium, Widnes)
Lost: 0–1
Team: Ricardo, G Neville, Pugh, Roche, May, Rankin, Chadwick, Lynch, Forlan, Nardiello, Richardson
Subs: Tate, B Williams, Eagles (Richardson), Muirhead (Rankin), Jones

Thursday 19 September 2002
v LIVERPOOL (Away, at Deva Stadium, Chester)
Drawn: 1–1 **Scorer**: Nardiello (pen)
Team: Carroll, G Neville, Tierney, Tate, May, Fletcher, Chadwick, Stewart, Forlan, Nardiello, Pugh
Subs: M Williams (Forlan), B Williams, Lynch (Pugh), Richardson (G Neville), Roche

Thursday 26 September 2002
v BRADFORD CITY (Home, at Moss Lane, Altrincham)
Won: 2–0 **Scorers**: Stewart, Humphreys
Team: Ricardo, Lynch, Tierney, Roche, May, Taylor, Chadwick, Stewart, Nardiello, M Williams, Pugh
Subs: Mooniaruck (Roche), B Williams, Collett (May), Humphreys (Taylor)

Luke Chadwick made 12 starts for the Reserves

Tuesday 8 October 2002
v BLACKBURN ROVERS (Away, at Christie Park, Morecambe)
Won: 5-0 Scorers: Forlan 4, Richardson
Team: Ricardo, Roche, Tierney, Tate, May, P Neville, Chadwick, Richardson, Forlan, Muirhead, Fortune
Subs: Nardiello (May), B Williams (Ricardo), Lynch, Rankin (Tierney), Pugh

Thursday 17 October 2002
v BIRMINGHAM CITY (Home, at Moss Lane, Altrincham)
Won: 3-0 Scorers: Forlan, Nardiello 2 (1 pen)
Team: Ricardo, Lynch, Rankin, Tate, May, Pugh, Chadwick, Richardson, Forlan, Nardiello, Fortune
Subs: Roche, B Williams, Fox (Fortune), Timm (Chadwick), Johnson (Forlan)

Tuesday 22 October 2002
v MANCHESTER CITY (Away, at Ewen Fields, Hyde)
Lost: 0-5
Team: B Williams, Lynch, Tierney, Cogger, Tate, Taylor, Mooniaruck, Rankin, Nardiello, Heath, Pugh
Subs: Eckersley (Tierney), Jowsey, Nevins, Port

Thursday 31 October 2002
v SUNDERLAND (Home, at Moss Lane, Altrincham)
Lost: 1-3 Scorer: Nardiello (pen)
Team: Carroll, Roche, Tierney, Tate, May, Lynch, Chadwick, Rankin, Heath, Nardiello, Pugh
Subs: Richardson (Rankin), B Williams, Taylor, Fox, Bardsley

Thursday 21 November 2002
v ASTON VILLA (Home, at Moss Lane, Altrincham)
Won: 6-2 Scorers: Nardiello 2 (1 pen), Wood, Chadwick, Davis, Pugh
Team: Carroll, Lynch, Rankin, Roche, Taylor, Wood, Chadwick, Richardson, Nardiello, Davis, Pugh
Subs: Heath (Nardiello), B Williams, Sims (Chadwick), Fox (Richardson), Johnson

Thursday 19 December 2002
v NEWCASTLE UNITED (Home, at Old Trafford)
Lost: 2-3 Scorer: Nardiello 2
Team: Ricardo, Rankin, Pugh, Lynch, Roche, Keane, Chadwick, Stewart, Nardiello, Davis, Richardson
Subs: Fletcher, Jowsey, M Williams (Davis), Muirhead, Taylor

Tuesday 14 January 2003
v SHEFFIELD WEDNESDAY (Away)
Won: 2-0 Scorers: Butt, Nardiello
Team: Carroll, Lynch, Rankin, Pugh, Roche, Stewart, Chadwick, Butt, Nardiello, Davis, Richardson
Subs: Fletcher (Stewart), Lee, Wood (Butt), M Williams, Muirhead

Thursday 23 January 2003
v EVERTON (Home, at Moss Lane, Altrincham)
Lost: 1-4 Scorer: Wood
Team: Ricardo, Lynch, Pugh, Roche, Muirhead, Stewart, Chadwick, Butt, Nardiello, Davis, Wood
Subs: Fox, Jowsey (Ricardo), Lawrence (Stewart), Heath (Muirhead), M Williams

Monday 3 February 2003
v WEST BROMWICH ALBION (Away)
Won: 3-1 Scorers: M Williams, Davis, Nardiello
Team: Jowsey, Lynch, Rankin, Roche, Pugh, Fox, Davis, Humphreys, Nardiello, M Williams, Chadwick
Subs: Muirhead, Heaton, Heath (M Williams), Collett, Fletcher (Humphreys)

Monday 10 February 2003
v LIVERPOOL (Home, at Moss Lane, Altrincham)
Lost: 0-2
Team: Jowsey, Lynch, Rankin, Roche, Pugh, Fletcher, Davis, Fox, Nardiello, Heath, Richardson
Subs: Cogger, Steele, Muirhead, Hilton, Jones (Fletcher)

Thursday 27 February 2003
v BLACKBURN ROVERS (Home, at Moss Lane, Altrincham)
Lost: 1-3 Scorer: Fletcher
Team: Ricardo, Lynch, Hilton, Roche, Pugh, Fletcher, Davis, Wood, Richardson, Webber, Fortune
Subs: Fox (Fletcher), Jowsey, M Williams, Nardiello (Davis), Humphreys

Thursday 6 March 2003
v BIRMINGHAM CITY (Away)
Lost: 0-1
Team: Carroll, Lynch, Hilton, Roche, Pugh, Fletcher, Davis, Stewart, Webber, Nardiello, Wood
Subs: Heath, Jowsey, Fox (Wood), M Williams (Webber)

Thursday 13 March 2003
v MANCHESTER CITY (Home, at Moss Lane, Altrincham)
Won: 1-0 Scorer: Webber
Team: Ricardo, Lynch, Wood, Roche, Pugh, Humphreys, Davis, Stewart, Nardiello, Webber, Fox
Subs: M Williams, Steele, Heath (Humphreys), Jones, Bardsley

Monday 24 March 2003
v SUNDERLAND (Away, at Archibalds Stadium, Durham)
Lost: 0-1
Team: Carroll, Lynch, Pugh, Roche, Fox, Wood, Davis, Fletcher, Nardiello, M Williams, Fortune
Subs: Heath (M Williams), Steele, Picken, Humphreys (Fortune), Ebanks-Blake

Thursday 27 March 2003
v BRADFORD CITY (Away)
Won: 3-1 Scorer: Nardiello 3 (1 pen)
Team: Ricardo, Lynch, Pugh, Roche, P Neville, Wood, Davis, Fletcher, Nardiello, Heath, Fortune
Subs: Hilton (Wood), Steele, Picken, Fox (Fortune)

Monday 31 March 2003
v BOLTON WANDERERS (Away, at Gigg Lane, Bury)
Drawn: 1-1 Scorer: Nardiello (pen)
Team: Carroll, Lynch, Pugh, Roche, P Neville, Fletcher, Davis, Wood, Nardiello, Heath, Fortune
Subs: Fox, Steele, Hilton, M Williams, Humphreys

Thursday 3 April 2003
v BOLTON WANDERERS (Home, at Moss Lane, Altrincham)

Lost: 1-2 Scorer: Wood
Team: Ricardo, Lynch, Pugh, M Williams, Fox, Fletcher, Davis, Humphreys, Nardiello, Heath, Wood
Subs: Hilton (M Williams), B Williams, Jones, Sims, Cogger

Wednesday 9 April 2003
v ASTON VILLA (Away)
Drawn: 2-2 Scorers: Heath, Nardiello
Team: Carroll, Lynch, Pugh, Wood, May, Fox, Davis, Heath, Nardiello, M Williams, Fortune
Subs: Cogger (Fortune), B Williams, Roche, Mooniaruck

FA PREMIER RESERVE LEAGUE NORTH		
	APPS	**GOALS**
Phillip BARDSLEY	3(1)	–
Nicky BUTT	2	1
Danny BYRNE	1(1)	–
Roy CARROLL	9	–
Luke CHADWICK	12	1
John COGGER	1(1)	–
Ben COLLETT	1(1)	–
Jimmy DAVIS	18	3
Bojan DJORDJIC	1	–
Christopher EAGLES	2(3)	–
Sylvan EBANKS-BLAKE	3(2)	–
Adam ECKERSLEY	0(2)	–
Darren FLETCHER	12(2)	1
Quinton FORTUNE	7	–
Diego FORLAN	4	5
David FOX	9(6)	1
Colin HEATH	10(5)	3
Kirk HILTON	8(2)	–
Mark HOWARD	1(1)	–
Chris HUMPHREYS	3(2)	1
Eddie JOHNSON	0(1)	–
David JONES	0(1)	–
James JOWSEY	4(2)	–
Roy KEANE	1	–
Lee LAWRENCE	1(1)	–
Mark LYNCH	25(2)	–
David MAY	8	–
Kalam MOONIARUCK	5(2)	–
Ben MUIRHEAD	2(1)	–
Daniel NARDIELLO	21(2)	16
Gary NEVILLE	2	–
Phil NEVILLE	3	–
David POOLE	0(1)	–
Danny PUGH	25	1
John RANKIN	9(2)	–
RICARDO	10	–
Kieran RICHARDSON	11(3)	1
Lee ROCHE	20	–
Lee SIMS	2(1)	–
Luke STEELE	2	–
Michael STEWART	8	1
Alan TATE	6	–
Kris TAYLOR	3	–
Paul TIERNEY	5	–
Mads TIMM	0(1)	–
Danny WEBBER	3	1
Ben WILLIAMS	3(1)	–
Matthew WILLIAMS	12(3)	6
Neil WOOD	10(1)	3

Wednesday 21 August 2002
v WEST BROMWICH ALBION (Home, at Old Trafford)
Won: 1–0 Scorer: Nardiello
Team: Steele, Roche, Hilton, Tate, May, Pugh, Chadwick,
Fletcher, M Williams, Nardiello, Djordjic
Subs: Muirhead, Heaton, Rankin (Fletcher),
Lynch (Hilton), Bardsley (Pugh)

Wednesday 4 September 2002
v EVERTON (Away, at Halton Stadium, Widnes)
Lost: 0–1
Team: Ricardo, G Neville, Pugh, Roche, May,
Rankin, Chadwick, Lynch, Forlan,
Nardiello, Richardson
Subs: Tate, B Williams, Eagles (Richardson), Muirhead
(Rankin), Jones

Thursday 19 September 2002
v LIVERPOOL (Away, at Deva Stadium, Chester)
Drawn: 1–1 Scorer: Nardiello (pen)
Team: Carroll, G Neville, Tierney, Tate, May,
Fletcher, Chadwick, Stewart, Forlan,
Nardiello, Pugh
Subs: M Williams (Forlan), B Williams, Lynch (Pugh),
Richardson (G Neville), Roche

Thursday 26 September 2002
v BRADFORD CITY (Home, at Moss Lane, Altrincham)
Won: 2–0 Scorers: Stewart, Humphreys
Team: Ricardo, Lynch, Tierney, Roche, May,
Taylor, Chadwick, Stewart, Nardiello,
M Williams, Pugh
Subs: Mooniaruck (Roche), B Williams, Collett (May),
Humphreys (Taylor)

Tuesday 8 October 2002
v BLACKBURN ROVERS (Away, at Christie Park, Morecambe)
Won: 5–0 Scorers: Forlan 4, Richardson
Team: Ricardo, Roche, Tierney, Tate, May, P Neville,
Chadwick, Richardson, Forlan, Muirhead, Fortune
Subs: Nardiello (May), B Williams (Ricardo), Lynch,
Rankin (Tierney), Pugh

Thursday 17 October 2002
v BIRMINGHAM CITY (Home, at Moss Lane, Altrincham)
Won: 3–0 Scorers: Forlan, Nardiello 2 (1 pen)

Thursday 4 October 2002
v MANCHESTER CITY (Home, at Moss Lane, Altrincham)
Won: 1–0 Scorer: Muirhead
Team: Carroll; Roche, Rankin, Tate, May; Fletcher,
Chadwick, Stewart, Muirhead; Nardiello, Fortune
Subs: Lynch, B Williams, Heath (Nardiello),
Pugh (Fortune), Tierney

Monday 27 January 2003
v MANCHESTER CITY (Away, at Ewan Fields, Hyde)
Lost: 0–3
Team: Carroll; Lynch, Pugh, Roche, May; Wood,
Chadwick, Stewart, Nardiello; Davis, Richardson
Subs: Muirhead, Jowsey, M Williams, Fox
(Chadwick), Heath

Thursday 13 February 2003
v OLDHAM ATHLETIC (Away)
Lost: 1–2 Scorer: Fletcher
Team: Steele; Rankin, Hilton, Roche, Pugh;
Fox, Davis, Fletcher, Nardiello; M Williams, Richardson
Subs: Muirhead (Nardiello), T Lee, Webber
(M Williams), Wood (Richardson)

Thursday 20 March 2003
v OLDHAM ATHLETIC (Home, at Moss Lane, Altrincham)
Drawn: 2–2* Scorer: Webber 2 (1 pen)
Team: Carroll; Lynch, Pugh, Roche, May;
Stewart, Davis, Wood, M Williams;
Webber, Richardson
Subs: Nardiello (M Williams), Steele,
Humphreys (Stewart), Heath (Webber), Cogger
***Lost 7–6 on penalties**
Penalty–scorers: May, Nardiello, Davis, Richardson,
Pugh, Wood

Monday 14 April 2003
v BURY (Home, at Moss Lane, Altrincham)
Drawn: 2–2* Scorers: Nardiello, Heath
Team: B Williams; Lynch, Pugh, Roche, May;
Fletcher, Nardiello, Fox, Heath; Davis, Hilton
Subs: M Williams (May), Jowsey, Picken, Nevins
***Won 2–0 on penalties**
Penalty–scorers: Nardiello, Fox

v BURY (Away)
Match cancelled

Daniel Nardiello was top scorer in the Reserves

BARCLAYCARD PREMIERSHIP RESERVES (NORTH)							
	P	W	D	L	F	A	Pts
Sunderland	28	17	4	7	51	26	55
Middlesbrough	28	16	7	5	47	26	55
Manchester City	28	17	3	8	55	27	54
Aston Villa	28	16	4	8	59	44	52
Liverpool	28	13	5	10	48	34	44
Everton	28	12	7	9	44	36	43
Leeds United	28	10	13	7	45	37	41
Manchester United	28	12	5	11	45	37	41
Bolton Wanderers	28	11	5	12	45	48	38
Birmingham City	28	11	4	13	33	39	37
West Brom	28	8	11	9	27	31	35
Newcastle United	28	8	9	11	44	43	33
Blackburn Rovers	28	10	3	15	34	51	33
Sheffield W'day	28	3	5	20	21	55	14
Bradford City	28	3	3	22	20	84	12

ROLL CALL

ACADEMYSCHOLARS2003/04

	Position	Birthdate	Birthplace	Date signed
THIRD YEAR				
Phillip Bardsley	Defender	28 June 1985	Salford	2 July 2001
Danny Byrne	Midfield	30 November 1984	Frimley	2 July 2001
Ben Collett	Midfield	11 September 1984	Bury	2 July 2001
Eddie Johnson	Forward	20 September 1984	Chester	2 July 2001
David Jones	Midfield	4 November 1984	Southport	2 July 2001
Lee Lawrence	Defender	1 December 1984	Boston	2 July 2001
David Poole	Forward	12 November 1984	Manchester	2 July 2001
Kieran Richardson	Midfield	21 October 1984	Greenwich	2 July 2001
Lee Sims	Defender	6 September 1984	Manchester	2 July 2001
Luke Steele	Goalkeeper	24 September 1984	Peterborough	13 May 2002
Mads Timm	Forward	31 October 1984	Odense, Denmark	2 July 2001
SECOND YEAR				
Sylvan Blake	Forward	29 March 1986	Cambridge	8 July 2002
Ramon Calliste	Forward	16 December 1985	Cardiff	8 July 2002
Christopher Eagles	Midfield	19 November 1985	Hemel Hempstead	8 July 2002
Adam Eckersley	Defender	7 September 1985	Salford	8 July 2002
Callum Flanagan	Forward	19 September 1985	Manchester	8 July 2002
Tom Heaton	Goalkeeper	15 April 1986	Chester	8 July 2002
Steven Hogg	Forward	1 October 1985	Bury	16 September 2002
Mark Howard	Defender	29 January 1986	Salford	8 July 2002
Tommy Lee	Goalkeeper	3 January 1986	Keighley	8 July 2002
Paul McShane	Defender	6 January 1986	Wicklow	8 July 2002
Adrian Nevins	Midfield	31 January 1986	Manchester	8 July 2002
Phil Picken	Defender	12 November 1985	Manchester	8 July 2002
Graeme Port	Midfield	13 April 1986	York	8 July 2002
FIRST YEAR				
Richard Jones	Midfield	26 September 1986	Manchester	7 July 2003
Philip Marsh	Forward	15 November 1986	St Helens	7 July 2003
Daniel Simpson	Defender	4 January 1987	Salford	7 July 2003

MANCHESTER UNITEDDEPARTURES

John Cogger	Contract cancelled by mutual agreement	9 May 2003
Nick Culkin	Free transfer	7 July 2002
Chris Humphreys	Contract cancelled by mutual agreement	8 April 2003
Ben Muirhead	Contract cancelled by mutual agreement	28 February 2003
John Rankin	Contract cancelled by mutual agreement	26 March 2003
Kris Taylor	Contract cancelled by mutual agreement	5 February 2003
Dwight Yorke	To Blackburn Rovers	27 July 2002
Laurent Blanc	Free transfer	30 June 2003
Kirk Hilton	Free transfer	30 June 2003
David May	Free transfer	30 June 2003
Kalam Mooniaruck	Free transfer	30 June 2003
Lee Roche	Free transfer	30 June 2003

YOUNG PRO

Jimmy Davis

Position: Forward

Born: Bromsgrove, 6 February 1982
Signed trainee: 6 July 1999
Signed professional: 31 August 1999
Senior United debut: 5 November 2001
v Arsenal, away, League Cup

Bojan Djordjic

Position: Midfield

Born: Belgrade, Yugoslavia, 6 February 1982
Signed professional: Brommapojkarna IF,
Sheffield Wednesday (loan)
Senior United debut: 19 May 2001
v Tottenham Hotspur, away, Premiership

David Fox

Position: Midfield

Born: Stoke-on-Trent, 13 December 1983
Signed trainee: 3 July 1999
Signed professional: 31 December 2000

Colin Heath

Position: Forward

Born: Chesterfield, 31 December 1983
Signed trainee: 3 July 2000
Signed professional: 31 December 2000

Kirk Hilton

Position: Defender

Born: Flixton, 2 April 1981
Signed trainee: 30 June 1997
Signed professional: 1 July 1999
See departures, p211

James Jowsey

Position: Goalkeeper

Born: Scarborough, 24 November 1983
Signed trainee: 3 July 2000
Signed professional: 24 November 2000

FESSIONALS

Kalam Mooniaruck

Position: Forward

Born: Yeovil, 22 November 1983
Signed trainee: 3 July 2000
Signed professional: 22 November 2000
See departures, p211

Alan Tate

Position: Forward

Born: Chesterfield, 31 December 1983
Signed trainee: 3 July 2000
Signed professional: 31 December 2000

Paul Tierney

Position: Midfield

Born: Salford, 15 September 1982
Signed trainee: 5 July 1999
Signed professional: 12 July 2000

Ben Williams

Position: Goalkeeper

Born: Manchester, 27 August 1982
Signed trainee: 27 August 1999
Signed professional: 1 July 2001

Matthew Williams

Position: Forward

Born: St Asaph, 5 November 1982
Signed trainee: 5 July 1999
Signed professional: 26 January 2000

Neil Wood

Position: Forward

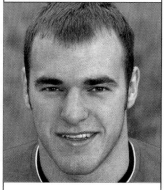

Born: Manchester, 4 January 1983
Signed trainee: 5 July 1999
Signed professional: 4 January 2000

MEMBERSHIP

General information

During the football season, the Ticketing & Membership Services office hours are as follows:

Monday to Friday: 9.00am – 5.00pm
Home Match Days: 9.00am – kick-off

Members' personal accident insurance

Under our special personal accident insurance policy with Lloyds Underwriters, all members are insured whilst in attendance and travelling to and from the stadium (until safe return to current place of residence), for all competitive games played by the Manchester United 1st team, both home and away, anywhere in the world.

The following accidental death and bodily injury benefits apply:
Death £10,000 (limited to £1,000 for persons under 16 years of age).
Total and irrecoverable loss of sight of both eyes £10,000.
Total an irrecoverable loss of sight in one eye £5,000.
Loss of two limbs £10,000.
Loss of one limb £5,000.
Total and irrecoverable loss of sight in one eye and loss of one limb £10,000.
Permanent Total Disablement (other than total loss of sight of one or both eyes or loss of limb) £10,000.

The above is subject to the policy conditions and exclusions. Further details are available from the Membership Secretary to whom enquiries should be addressed.

& TRAVEL

Branches of the supporters' club

A full list of all our official branches of the supporters club can be found on pages 218 to 226.

Away travel

Domestic games:

All club members, which include Private Box holders, Executive Suite & Club Class members and season ticket and League Match Ticket Book holders, are automatically enrolled in our Away Travel Club and, as such, are entitled to book coach travel from Old Trafford to all Premiership venues. Full details can be found on this page.

How to make a booking:

You can book a place on a coach, subject to availability, upon personal application at the Ticketing & Membership Services office, in which case you must quote your MUFC membership number. Alternatively, you can make a postal application by submitting the relevant payment, a stamped addressed envelope and a covering letter quoting your MUFC membership number. Telephone reservations are also acceptable during normal office hours on 0870 442 1994 if making payment by credit/debit card. Cancellations must be made in advance of the day of the game.

It should be noted that this season all coaches will be of an Executive standard, ie. toilet facilities, video entertainment and refreshment availability.

Car park attendants will be on duty should you wish to park your car on one of our car parks before travelling to an away game. This service is offered at no extra charge but we wish to point out that the club will not be held responsible for any damage or theft from your vehicle.

Members are advised to check match ticket availability before booking a place on a coach. Details can be obtained by telephoning our Ticket & Match Information line on 0870 757 1968.

European travel

Ticketing & Membership Services is also responsible for organising members travel and distribution of match tickets for our European away games. Full details will be made known when available, via all usual channels.

MEMBERS' TRAVEL

	Return Fare	*Departure Time	**Estimated return time to Old Trafford
Arsenal	£22.00	8.30am	9.30pm
Aston Villa	£15.00	11.30am	7.30pm
Birmingham City	£15.00	11.30am	7.30pm
Blackburn Rovers	£12.00	1.00pm	6.15pm
Bolton Wanderers	£12.00	1.00pm	6.15pm
Charlton Athletic	£22.00	8.00am	10.00pm
Chelsea	£22.00	8.30am	9.30pm
Everton	£12.00	1.00pm	6.15pm
Fulham	£22.00	8.30am	9.30pm
Leeds United	£12.00	1.00pm	6.15pm
Leicester City	£15.00	11.30am	7.30pm
Liverpool	£12.00	1.00pm	6.15pm
Manchester City	£12.00	1.00pm	6.00pm
Middlesbrough	£18.00	11.00am	8.00pm
Newcastle United	£18.00	10.30am	8.30pm
Portsmouth	£22.00	8.30am	10.00pm
Sheffield United	£12.00	12.30pm	7.15pm (subject to Play-offs)
Southampton	£22.00	8.30am	10.00pm
Tottenham Hotspur	£22.00	8.30am	9.30pm
Wolverhampton Wanderers	£15.00	11.30am	7.30 pm(subject to Play-offs)
Millennium Stadium, Cardiff	£25.00	7.00am	11.00pm

* All times based on games with a 3.00 pm kick-off

* Departure times are subject to change and it is vital to check the actual time when making your booking

** Return times shown are only estimated and are subject to traffic congestion

---

If you have any query or require further information regarding membership, domestic away travel, European away games, personal insurance or branches of the supporters' club, please write to this address: Manchester United Football Club, Ticketing & Membership Services, Department M, Old Trafford, Manchester M16 0RA. Or, if you prefer, you can telephone the office on 0870 442 1994 or send a fax on 0161 868 8837. R.N.I.D. Textphone 0161 868 8668

SUPPORTERS

1958 THE FLOWERS OF MANCHESTER

UK Branches

ABERDEEN
Branch Secretary: **Michael Stewart**, 26 Dubford Crescent, Bridge of Don, Aberdeen, AB23 8FT;
Tel: 01224 822826 (after 7pm); **Mobile: 07740 980967; Email: stewart_m@btinternet.com**
Departure points (excluding early kick-offs): Guild Street, Aberdeen 6.00am; Forfar Bypass
6.45am; The Kingsway, Dundee 7.00am; Stirling Services 8.15am (coach for home games
only). New members welcome – contact branch secretary for further information.

ABERGELE AND COAST
Branch Secretary: **Eddie Williams**, 14 Maes-y-Dre, Abergele, Clwyd, North Wales, LL22 7HW.
Tel: 01745 823694
Departure points: Aber; Llanfairfechen; Penmaen Mawr; Conwy; Llandudno Junction;
Colwyn Bay; Abergele; Rhyl; Rhuddlan; Dyserth; Prestatyn; Mostyn; Holywell; Flint; Deeside.

ABERYSTWYTH AND DISTRICT
Branch Secretary: **Alan Evans**, 6 Tregerddan, Bow Street, Dyfed, SY24 5AW.
Tel: 01970 828117 after 6pm. Chairman: **A Howe, Tel: 01970 615757**
Departure points: Please contact branch secretary.

ASHBOURNE
Branch Secretary: **Diane O'Connell**, 1 Milldale Court, Ashbourne, Derbyshire, DE6 1SN.
Tel: 01335 346105
Departure points: The Maypole, Bridge Street, Derby, 3½ hours before kick-off; McDonalds,

Markeaton Roundabout, Derby, 3½ hours before kick-off; Hanover Hotel, Ashbourne, 3 hours
before kick-off; Ashbourne bus station, 3 hours before kick-off. Contact branch secretary for
details of travel to away fixtures.

BARNSLEY
Branch Secretary: **Mick Mitchell**, 12 Saxon Crescent, Worsbrough, Barnsley, S70 5PY.
Tel: 01226 283 983
Departure points: 12.30pm (5.30pm) Locke Park Working Men's Club, Park Road, Barnsley
via A628. Or 2½ hours before any other kick-off times.

BARROW AND FURNESS
Branch Secretary: **Robert Bayliff**, 183 Chapel Street, Dalton-in-Furness, Cumbria, LA15 8SL.
Mobile: 07788 762936
Departure points: Barrow, Ramsden Square 9.30am (4pm); Dalton 9.45am (4.15pm);
Ulverston 10am (4.30pm) and A590 route to M6. Times in brackets denote evening fixtures.

BEDFORDSHIRE
Branch Secretary: **Craig Dilley**, 33 Tennyson Avenue, Biggleswade, Bedfordshire SG18 8QD.
Mobile: 07977 501133 (up to 9pm only)
Departure points: Bedford bus station, 'Coachways', Junction 14, M1

BERWICK–UPON–TWEED
Branch Secretary: **Margaret Walker**, 17 Lords Mount, Berwick-Upon-Tweed, Northumberland,
TD15 1LY. Chairman: **Raymond Dixon**, 92 Shielfield Terrace, Berwick-upon-Tweed.

CLUBS

Tel: **01289 308671**. SAE for all enquiries please.
Departure points: Berwick, Belford, Alnwick, Stannington, Washington; Scotch Corner, Leeming Bar and anywhere on the main A1 - by arrangement.

BIRMINGHAM
Branch Secretary: **Paul Evans**, 179 Longbridge Lane, Longbridge, Birmingham B31 4LA.
Tel: **0121 604 1385** (6.30pm–9pm). Coaches operate to all home games. For times and additional information, please telephone or send a stamped addressed envelope.
Departure points: Longbridge; Birmingham City Centre; Tennis Courts Public House (A34); Scott Arms and Junction 7 (M6).

BLACK COUNTRY
The branch operate to all home games. Coach details are as follows:
Departure points: Talk of the Town, Darlaston 11am (4pm); Woden Public House, Wednesbury; 11.10am (4.10pm) Friendly Lodge Hotel, J10 M6, 11.15am (4.20pm); The Chase Gate Public House, off J11 M6, 11.25am (4.30pm). Times in brackets denote evening fixtures. For further information contact branch secretary **Ade Steventon, Tel: 0121 531 0826** (6.30pm –9pm). Mobile: **07796 307487**

BLACKPOOL, PRESTON AND FYLDE
Chairman: **Martin Day, Tel: 07971 963264; Email: martin.day@endeavour.co.uk**
Coach travel: **Jean Halliday 01772 635887;** Membership Secretary: **Sharon Randall, Tel: 07879 683744;** Social Secretary: **Tony Nicholson, Tel: 07760 226893**
Departure points: Bispham, Blackpool, St Annes, Lytham, Freckleton, Preston. Away travel to Blackburn, Bolton, City, Leeds, Liverpool, Everton and other north west clubs in Cup competitions. Out-of-town Reds welcome to travel with branch.

BRADFORD AND LEEDS
Branch Secretary: **Sally Hampshire**, PO Box 87, Cleckheaton, West Yorkshire, BD19 6YN.
Tel: **07973 904554; Email: ian.Hampshire@btinternet.com; www.bradfordreds.co.uk**

BRIDGNORTH AND DISTRICT
Branch Secretary: **Ann Saxby**, 30 Pitchford Road, Albrighton, Near Wolverhampton, WV7 3LS
Tel: **01902 373260**
Departure points: Ludlow, Bridgnorth, Albrighton, Wolverhampton.

BRIDGWATER AND SOUTH WEST:
Branch Secretary: **Ray White**, 4 Spencer Close, Bridgwater, Somerset, TA6 5SP.
Tel: **01278 452186**, Mobile: **07973 816190; Email: raywhite@bridgwater-reds.co.uk,**
website: **www.bridgwater-reds.co.uk**
Departure points: Taunton, Bridgwater, Weston-Super-Mare, Clevedon, Aztec West (Bristol).

BRIGHTON
Branch Secretary: **Colin Singers**, 34 Meadowview Road, Sompting, Lancing, West Sussex.
Tel: **01903 761679,** Mobile: **07931 540723**
Departure points: 6.30am Worthing Central, 6.40am Shoreham (George Pub); 7am Brighton Railway Station; 7.45am Gatwick Airport.

BRISTOL, BATH & DISTRICT
Chairman: **Ashley Powell;** Branch Secretary: **Eve Berry**, 9 Whitestone Road, Frome, Somerset BA11 2DN. Tel/Fax: **01373 467309** (h) Mobile: **07973 816190;** Treasurer: **Margaret Pettinger;** Administrator: **Les Purnell;** Committee Members: Karen Pettinger, Sue Hedges

BURTON-ON-TRENT
Branch Secretary: **Mrs Pat Wright**, 45 Foston Avenue, Burton-on-Trent, Staffordshire, DE13 0PL. Tel: **01283 532534**
Departure points: Moira (garage), Swadlincote, Burton (B&Q Lichfield Street), Stoke area.

CARLISLE AND DISTRICT
Branch Secretary: **Arnold Heard**, 28 Kentmere Grove, Morton Park, Carlisle, Cumbria, CA2 6JD.
Tel/Fax: **01228 538262,** Mobile: **07860 782769**
Departure points: For departure times and details please contact branch secretary.

CENTRAL POWYS
Branch Secretary: **Bryn Thomas**, 10 Well Lane, Bungalows, Llanidloes, Powys, SY18 6BA.
Tel: **01686 412391**(h) **01686 413 200**(w)
Departure points: Crossgates 10.30am; Rhayader 10.45am; Llanidloes 11.05am; Newtown 11.25am.

CHEPSTOW AND DISTRICT
Branch Secretary: **Anthony Parsons**, 56 Treowen Road, Newbridge, Newport, Gwent, NP11 3DN. Tel: **01495 246253**

Departure points: Newbridge, Pontypool, Cwmbran Bus Station; Newport; Coldra Langstone; Magor; Caldicot; Chepstow. For further details contact branch secretary.

CHESTER AND NORTH WALES
Branch Chairman: **Eddie Mansell**, 45 Overlea Drive, Hawarden, Deeside, Flintshire, CH5 3HR.
Tel: **01244 520332;** Branch Secretary: **Kate Reynolds**, 139 Park Avenue, Bryn-Y-Baal, Mold, Flintshire CH7 6TR, Tel: **01352 753962;** Ticket/Travel Secretary: **Des Wright**, 2 Church Lane, Backford, Chester CH2 4BE, Tel: **01244 851603;** Membership Secretary: **Irene Keidel**, 3 Springfield Drive, Buckley, Flintshire CH7 2PH, Tel: **01244 550943.**
Departure points: Oswestry; Ellesmere; Wrexham; Chester; Rhyl; Greenfield; Flint; Queensferry (ASDA Store); Whitby (Woodlands); Ellesmere Port (Bus Station); Frodsham.

CLEVELAND
Chairman: **Paul McClaren**, Mobile: **07867 563757**. Branch Secretary: **Brian Tose**, 5 Cowbar Cottages, Staithes, Saltburn by Sea, Cleveland TS13 5DA; Mobile: **07811 612949.**
Departure points: Please contact branch secretary for details.

COLWYN BAY AND DISTRICT
Branch Secretary: **Clive Allen**, 62 Church Road, Rhos-on-Sea, Colwyn Bay, North Wales, LL28 4YS, Tel: **01492 546400;** Branch Chairman: **Bill Griffith**, Whitefield, 60 Church Road, Rhos-on-Sea, Colwyn Bay, North Wales, LL28 4YS, Tel: **01492 540240.**
Departure points: Bus stop, Mostyn Broadway (opposite Asda stores) 11.00am (4pm); Bus stop opposite Llandudno Junction Railway Station 11.15am (4.15pm); Guy's Newsagents, Conway Road, Colwyn Bay 11.30am (4.30pm); bus stop opposite Marine Hotel, Old Colwyn 11.35am (4.35pm); Top Shop, Abergele Road, Old Colwyn 11.40am (4.40pm); bus stop, Fair View Inn, Llandudlas 11.45am (4.45pm); Slaters Showrooms bus stop, Abergele 11.50am (4.50pm); Talardy Hotel, St. Asaph 12 noon (5pm); Plough Hotel, Aston Hill, Queensferry 12.45pm (5.45pm). Times in brackets denote evening fixtures.

CORBY & KETTERING
Branch Secretary: **Andy Hobbs**, 32 Lower Pastures, Great Oakley, Corby, Northants
Tel: **01536 744 838,** Mobile: **07855 507338.** Branch Meetings: 1st Sunday of the month 7.15pm alternating from the Wayfarers, London Road, Kettering and the following month at the Corby Rugby Club, Rockingham Road, Corby.
Departure points: Co-op Extra Store, Alexander Rd, Corby 8.30am (1.30pm); Co-op Extra Superstore, Northfield Ave, Kettering 8.40am (1.40pm). Times in brackets for evening fixtures.

CRAWLEY
Branch Secretary: **Robert Tweddle**, 206 Gossops Drive, Crawley, West Sussex RH11 8LJ
Mobile: **07986 115832**

CREWE AND NANTWICH
Branch Secretary: **Andy Ridgway**, 38 Murrayfield Drive, Willaston, Nantwich, Cheshire.
CW5 6QF Tel: **01270 568418**
Departure points: Nantwich Barony 12.30pm (5.00pm); Earl of Crewe 12.40pm (5.10pm); Cross Keys 12.50pm (5.20pm). Away travel subject to demand. Times in brackets denote evening fixtures.

DONCASTER AND DISTRICT
Branch Secretary: **Albert Thompson**, 89 Anchorage Lane, Sprotboro, Doncaster, South Yorkshire, DN5 8EB Tel: **01302 782964;** Branch Treasurer: **Sue Moyles**, 217 Warningtongue Lane, Cantley. Tel: **01302 349203** Mobile: **01302 349203** Mobile: **07740 699824; Email: sfmoyles@hotmail.com** Branch Chairman: **Paul Kelly**, 58 Oak Grove, Conisbrough DN12 2HN. Tel: **01709 324058** Membership Secretary: **Mrs L Sudbury**, 8 Parkway, Armthorpe, Doncaster Tel: **01302 834323**
Departure points: Broadway Hotel, Dunscroft 10.30am (4.30pm); Edenthorpe 10.40am (4.40pm); Waterdale (opposite main library) 10.45am (4.45pm); The Highwayman, Woodlands 11am (5pm). Times in brackets denote 8pm kick-off. Meetings held first Monday of every month (unless there is a home match) in the Co-op Social Club (at the back of B&Q) at 7.30pm.

DORSET
Branch Secretary: **Mark Pattison**, 89 Parkstone Rd, Poole, Dorset, BH15 2NZ. Tel: **01202 744348**
Departure points: Poole Train Station 6.15am (10.30am); Banksome (Courts) 6.20am (10.35am); Bournemouth 6.30am (10.45am); Christchurch (Bargates) 6.45am (11.00am); Ringwood 7.00am (11.15am); Rownham Services 7.15am (11.30am); Chieveley Services 8.30am (12.30pm). Times in brackets denote evening fixtures.

DUKINFIELD AND HYDE
Branch Secretary: **Marilyn Chadderton**, 12 Brownville Grove, Dukinfield, Cheshire, SK16 5AS
Tel: **0161 338 4892**
Departure points: details of meetings and travel available from the above or from **S Jones** Tel: **0161 343 5260**

EAST ANGLIA
Branch Secretary: **Mark Donovan**, 55 The Street, Holywell Row, Mildenhall, Bury St Edmunds, Suffolk, IP28 8LT. **Tel: 01638 717075** (9am–6pm). Details of your local representative can also be obtained by telephoning this number. Executive travel available to all home fixtures via the following services: Service No.1: Clacton; Colchester; Braintree; Great Dunmow; Bishop Stortford. Service No.2: Felixstowe; Nacton; Ipswich; Stowmarket; Bury St. Edmonds. Service No.3: Thetford; Mildenhall; Newmarket; Cambridge; Huntingdon. Service No.4: Lowestoft; Great Yarmouth; Norwich; East Dereham; Kings Lynn. Coaches also operate to all away games for which departure details are dependent on demand and ticket availability.

EAST MANCHESTER
Branch Secretary: **Tony McAllister**, 10 Walmer Street, Abbey Hey, Gorton, Manchester M18 8QP. **Tel: 0161 230 7098; Mobile: 07786 222596; Email: anthony.mcallister1@ntlworld.com** Branch meetings held on the last Thursday of each month (8pm) at Gorton Labour Club, Ashkirk Street, Gorton, Manchester.

EAST YORKSHIRE
Branch Secretary: **Ian Baxter**, 18 Soberhill Drive, Holme Moor, York YO43 4BH **Mobile: 07768 821844**; Hull Administrator: **Fred Helas, Mobile: 07774 775 078.**
Departure points: Hull Coach: Hull Marina 10.30am (3.30pm); Howden Coach: Bay Horse, Market Weighton: 10.30am (3.30pm); Redbrick Café, Howden; 11am (4pm). Times in brackets denote evening fixtures.

ECCLES
Branch Secretary: **Gareth Morris**, 11 Brentwood Drive, Monton, Eccles, Manchester, M30 9LP. **Tel: 0161 281 9435**
Departure point: (away games only) Rock House Hotel, Peel Green Road, Peel Green, Eccles. For departure times please contact branch secretary.

FEATHERSTONE & DISTRICT
Branch Secretary: **Paul Kingsbury**, 11 Hardwick Rd, Featherstone, W Yorks WF7 5JA. **Tel: 01977 793910; Mobile: 07789 040536. Email: paul@kingsbury.freeserve.co.uk** Website: mysite.freeserve.com/fevreds. Treasurer: **Andrew Dyson**, 46 Northfield Drive, Pontefract, W Yorks WF8 2DL. **Tel: 01977 709561; Mobile: 07956 464953. Email: andy.dyson@totalise.co.uk**
Departure points: Pontefract Sorting Office 10.30am (3.30pm); Corner Pocket, Featherstone 10.40am (3.40pm); Green Lane, Featherstone 10.45am (3.45pm); Castleford Bus Station 10.55am (3.55pm); times in brackets denote evening fixtures. Meetings held every fortnight (Mondays) at the Girnhill Lane WMC, Girnhill Lane, Featherstone.

FLEETWOOD
For details contact Branch Secretary **Stuart Gill, Tel: 01253 865450** or **Brian Houten, Tel: 01253 875876. Email: fleetwoodreds@eudoramail.com**

GLAMORGAN AND GWENT
Branch Secretary: **Neil Chambers**, 201 Malpas Road, Newport, South Wales NP20 5PP. Branch Chairman: **Cameron Erskine, Tel: 02920 623705** (10am–1pm Monday–Friday. Answerphone at other times). **Mobile: 07885 615546, Email: c.erskine@ntlworld.co.uk**
Departure points: Skewen; Port Talbot; Bridgend; Cardiff; Newport.

GLASGOW
Branch Secretary: **David Sharkey**, 45 Lavender Drive, Greenhills, East Kilbride G75 9JH **Tel: 01355 902592** (7–11pm). Coach runs to all home games.
Departure points: 8am (1pm) Queen Street Station, Glasgow; 8.15am (1.15pm) The Angel, Uddingston; Any M74 service stations. Times in brackets denote evening fixtures.

GLOUCESTER AND CHELTENHAM
Branch Secretary: **Paul Brown**, 59 Katherine Close, Churchdown, Gloucester, GL3 1PB **Tel: 01452 859553; Mobile: 07801 802593; Email: muscglos@aol.com;**
Departure points: Bennetts Yard, Eastern Ave, Glos. 8.45am (1,45pm); Station Rd, Gloucester 9am (2pm); Cheltenham Railway Station (outside Midland Hotel), 9.10am (2.10pm); Cheltenham Gas Works Corner 9.15am (2.15pm). Times in brackets for evening fixtures.

GRIMSBY AND DISTRICT
Branch Secretary: **Bob England**, 5 George Butler Close, Laceby, Grimsby, DN37 7WA. **Tel: 01472 752130, Email: redbob68@hotmail.com;** Travel: **Craig Collins** (Branch Chairman) **Tel: 01472 314273;** Membership Secretary: **Sarah Bell, Tel: 01472 314273.**

GUERNSEY
Branch Secretary: **Eddie Martel**, Timanfaya, Summerfield Road, Vale, Guernsey, Channel Isles GY3 5UH. **Tel: 01481 246285; Mobile: 07781 128 089.**

GWYNEDD
Branch Secretary: **Gwyn Hughes**, Sibrwd y Don, Tan y Cefn, Llanwnda, Caernarfon, Gwynedd, LL54 7YB. **Tel: 01286 830073, Tel: 07050 380804, Email: Gwyn.Hughes@manutd.com**
Departure points: Pwllheli; Llanwnda; Caernarfon; Bangor. For departure times please contact branch secretary.

HAMPSHIRE
Branch Secretary: **Pete Boyd**, 22 Weavers Crofts, Melksham Wilts SN12 8BP.

Tel/Fax: 01225 700354; Email: pete@muschants.com; Website: www.muschants.com Membership Secretary/Treasurer: **Roy Debenham**, 11 Lindley Gardens, Alresford, Hampshire, SO24 9PU; **Tel/Fax: 01962 734420;** Chairman: **Paul Marsh**, Oaktree Cottage, Commonhill Road, Braishfield, Hants SO51 0QF; **Tel: 07732 473570.**
Departure points: (1) King George V Playing Fields, Northem Rd, Cosham 7.30am (12 noon); (2) Sainsburys, Hedge End 7.50am (12.20pm); (3) Bullington Cross Inn, Junction of A34 & A303 8.20am (12.50pm) (4) Tot Hill Services (A34), just south of Newbury 8.40am (1.10pm).

HARROGATE AND DISTRICT
Branch Secretary: **Michael Heaton**, Railway Cottage, Grange Rd, Dacre Banks, Harrogate, N Yorks HG3 4EF; **Tel & Fax: 01423 780679; Mobile: 07790 798328; website: www.heatonsheroes.co.uk**
Departure points include: Nidderdale, Rippon, Northallerton, Leyburn, Harrogate, Skipton and Earby areas. Coaches also operate to all away games, incl. European ties. For further information, contact branch secretary. Send sae for membership details. Meetings held every 3rd Thursday of each month at the Hopper Lane Public House on the A59 leaving Harrogate.

HASTINGS
Branch Secretary: **Tim Martin**, 94 Gillsmans Hill, St Leonards-on-Sea, East Sussex TN38 0SL (no personal callers please); **Tel: 01424 442073** (6pm–8pm); **Mobile: 07973 656716** (daytime); **Email: martin@silvan.fsnet.co.uk** For match bookings phone Tim at the above. For membership details and other enquiries, contact **Chris Fry; Tel: 01424 437595, Mobile: 07973 309382;** or **Steve Whitelaw; Tel: 07881 610345; Rod Beckingham, Tel: 01424 443477** (6pm–8pm)
Departure points: Eastbourne, Tesco Roundabout 5.40am; Bexhill, Viking Chip Shop 6.00am; Silverhill Traffic lights 6.15am; Hurst Green, George Pub 6.40am; Pembury, Camden Arms Pub 7.00am. All above times for 3 or 4pm kick-off. For details of travel to away games please contact branch secretary.

HEREFORD
Branch Secretary: **Norman Elliss**, 40 Chichester Close, Abbeyfields, Belmont, Hereford, HR2 7YU **Tel: 01432 359923, Fax: 01432 342880.**
Departure points: 8.30am (2pm) Leominster; 9am (2.30pm) Bulmers Car Park, Hereford; 9.30am (3pm) Ledbury; 9.45am (3.15pm) Malvern Link BP Garage; 10am (3.30pm) Oak Apple Pub, Worcester; Times in brackets denote midweek fixtures.

HERTFORDSHIRE
Organised travel to home & away games. Pick-up points at Hertford, Welwyn, Stevenage, Hitchin and Luton. For travel arrangements, contact **Mick Prior, Tel: 01438 361900;** For membership, contact **Mick Slack, Tel: 01462 622451.** Correspondence to: **Steve Bocking**, 64 Westmill Road, Hitchin, Herts. SG5 2SD **Tel: 01462 622076.**

HEYWOOD
Branch Secretary: **Denis Hall**, 2 Hartford Ave, Summit, Heywood, Lancs OL10 4H; **Tel: 01706 364475.** Chairman: **Lee Swettenham**, 30 Wilton Grove, Heywood, Lancs. OL10 1AZ; **Tel: 01706 368953.**
Departure points: Bay Horse, Torrington St, Hopwood/ Heywood 1pm (6pm midweek).

HIGHLANDS & ISLANDS
Branch Secretary: **Ronnie McKay**, Creag Ard House, 5 Longrigg Road, Strontian, Argyll PH36 4HY. **Tel/Fax: 01967 402012; Mobile: 07818 243284; Email: Ronniemckay@btinternet.com**

HIGH PEAK
Chairman: **Dave Rhodes**, 21 Park Rd, Whaley Bridge, High Peak SK23 7DJ. **Tel: 01663 732484;** Branch Secretary: **Keith Udale**, 101 Station Rd, Marple, Stockport SK6 6PA **Tel: 0161 427 1805; Mobile: 07810 567953; Email: k.udale@rds.co.uk; Fax: 0208 543 7330**
Departure points: Memorial Club, Chapel; Jodrell Arms, Whaley Bridge; Bus Station, New Mills; Navigation, Marple. The Branch holds meetings last Thursday in the month at the White Horse, Whaley Bridge.

HYNDBURN & PENDLE
Branch Secretary: **Alan Haslam**, 97 Crabtree Avenue, Edgeside, Waterfoot, Rossendale, BB4 9TB. **Tel: 01706 831736**
Departure points: Barnoldswick 11.15am (4.45pm); Nelson 11.30am (5pm); Burnley 11.45am (5.15pm); Accrington 12.15pm (5.45pm); Haslingden 12.20pm (5.50pm); Rawtenstall 12.30pm (6pm). Times in brackets denote evening fixtures.

INVICTA REDS (KENT)
Branch Secretary: **Vic Hatherly, Tel: 01634 865613; Mobile: 0773 668 6962** Tickets and Travel: **Shaun or Louise Rogers, Tel: 01622 721344** (not after 9pm), **Mobile: 0781 388 0616** (not after 9pm). Correspondence to: **Invicta Reds** (Kent), 19 Tarragon Road, Maidstone, Kent, ME16 0UR. **Email: invictareds@manutd.com** website: **www.invictareds.org.uk**
Departure points: Pop-In Newsagents, Ramsgate; Mill Lane, Herne Bay; Magistrates Court, Canterbury; M2 Medway Services; M2, Junction 3, Chatham; Little Chef Services, A2 by Cobham; Dartford Tunnel; M25, Junction 28; M25, A10; Junction 26, Waltham Abbey.

ISLE OF MAN
Branch Secretary: **Gill Keown**, 5 King Williams Way, Castletown, Isle of Man, IM9 1DH **Tel: 01624 823143 E-mail: reddevil@manx.net**

JERSEY
Branch Secretary: **Mark Jones**, 5 Rosemount Cottages, James Road, St.Saviour, Jersey, Channel Islands **Tel:** 01534 734786(h); 01534 885885(w). Should any members be in Jersey during the football season, the branch shows television games in private club. Free food provided – everybody welcome, including children. Contact branch secretary for details.

KEIGHLEY
Branch Secretary: **Kevin Granger**, 3 Spring Terrace, Long Lee, Keighley, West Yorkshire, BD21 4SZ. **Tel:** 01535 661862, **Mobile:** 01709 555653, **Fax:** 01535 600564 **Email:** k.d.granger@talk21.com
Departure points: Coach leaves from Keighley Technical College in Cavendish Street then travels to Colne and joins M65 & M66 to Manchester. Contact branch secretary for more details.

KNUTSFORD
Branch Secretary: **John Butler**, 4 Hollingford Place, Knutsford WA16 9DP. **Tel:** 01565 651360; **Fax:** 01565 634792; **Email:** johnmbutler@onetel.net.uk Treasurer: **John Aston**; Chairman: **Angus Campbell**. Please contact the secretary for details of meetings.

LANCASTER AND DISTRICT
Branch Secretary: **Andy Baker**, 78 Highland Brow, Galgate, Nr Lancaster LA2 0NB. **Tel:** 01524 751035 (6pm–7pm weekdays); **Mobile:** 07808 395488; **Email:** a.baker@lancasta.ac.uk
Departure points: Carnforth Ex-Servicemens 11.45am (4.45pm); Morecambe Shrimp Roundabout 12pm (5pm); Lancaster Dalton Square 12.20pm (5.20pm), then A6 route to Broughton Roundabout for M6 – M61. Times in brackets denote evening fixtures.

LEAMINGTON SPA
Branch Secretary: **Norma Worton**, 23 Cornhill Grove, Kenilworth, Warwickshire, CV8 2QP. **Tel:** 01926 859476, **Email:** norma.worton@virgin.net
Departure points: Newbold Terrace, Leamington Spa; Leyes Lane, Kenilworth; London Road, Coventry

LINCOLN
Branch Secretary: **Steve Stone**, 154 Scorer St, Lincoln LN5 7SX. **Tel:** 01522 885671
Departure points: Unity Square at 10am on Saturdays (3pm kick-off). Midweek matches, depart at 3pm from Unity Square.

LONDON
Branch Secretary: **Ralph Mortimer**, 55 Boyne Avenue, Hendon, London, NW4 2JL
Departure points: Semley Place, Victoria 8pm (12.30pm); Staples Corner 8.30am (1.15pm); Junction 11 M1, 9am (1.45pm). Times in brackets refer to midweek games. A coach will run to all away games subject to sufficient numbers/tickets. **Email:** mortijr@aol–com or **Tel:** 0208 203 1213 after 6pm.

LONDON ASSOCIATION
Branch Secretary: **Najib Armanazi**, **Tel:** 07941 124591; **Email:** najcantona@hotmail.com Membership Secretary: **Alison Watt**, **Tel:** 01322 558333 (7pm – 9pm only) **Email:** alisonwatt@redlodge.freeserve.co.uk

LONDON FAN CLUB
Branch Secretary: **Paul Molloy**, 65 Corbylands Road, Sidcup, Kent, DA15 8JQ. **Tel/Fax:** 020 8302 5826. Travel Secretary: **Mike Dobbin**, **Email:** info@mulfc65.freeserve.co.uk
Departure points: Euston Station by service train – meeting point at top of escalator from Tube). Cheap group travel to most home and away games.

MACCLESFIELD
Branch Secretary: **Ian Evans**, 25 Pickwick Road, Poynton, Cheshire SK12 1LD. Chairman: **Mark Foster**, **Tel:** 01625 434362; Treasurer: **Rick Holland**, 97 Pierce St, Macclesfield. SK11 6EX **Tel:** 01625 427762; Membership Secretary: **Neil McCleland**, **Tel:** 01625 613183
Departure points: Home games, meet Macclesfield Rail Station 11.45am (4.45pm midweek fixtures). For away games, please contact branch secretary.

MANCHESTER UNITED DISABLED SUPPORTERS' ASSOCIATION – (MUDSA)
Branch Secretary: **Phil Downs**, MUDSA., PO Box 141, South DO, M20 5BA
Tel: 0161 434 1989, **Fax:** 0161 445 5221, **Email:** disability@manutd.co.uk

MANSFIELD
Branch Secretary: **Peggy Conheeney**, 48 West Bank Ave, Mansfield, Nottinghamshire, NG19 7BP. **Tel/Fax:** 01623 625140, **Mobile:** 0776 1107104, **Email:** peg.con.musc@faxvia.net
Departure points: Kirkby Garage 10am (4pm); Northern Bridge, Sutton 10.10am (4.10pm); Mansfield Shoe Co. 10.20am (4.20pm); Peg's Home 10.30am (4.30pm); Young Vanish, Glapwell 10.40am (4.40pm); Hipper Street School, Chesterfield 10.55am (4.55pm); Times in brackets denote evening fixtures. Away games are dependent on ticket availability.

MID-CHESHIRE
Branch Secretary: **Leo Lastowecki**, 5 Townfield Court, Barnton, Northwich, Cheshire, CW8 4UT. **Tel:** 01606 784790

MIDDLETON & DISTRICT
Branch Secretary: **Kevin Booth**, 8 Wicken Bank, Hopwood, OL10 2LW **Tel:** 01706 624196 **Mobile:** 07762 741438 Chairman: **Mike Conroy**, 12 Lulworth Rd, Middleton, M24.

Tel: 0161 653 5696
Departure points: Home games: coaches depart Crown Inn, Middleton, 1 hour prior to kick-off. Away games: contact secretary

MILLOM AND DISTRICT
Branch Secretary/Chairman: **Clive Carter**, 47 Settle St, Millom, Cumbria, LA18 5AR. **Tel:** 01229 773565 Treasurer: **Malcom French**, 4 Willowside Park, Haverigg, Cumbria, LA18 4PT. **Tel:** 01229 774850. Assistant Treasurer: **Paul Knott**, 80 Market Street, Millom, Cumbria. **Tel:** 01229 772826.

NEWTON-LE-WILLOWS
Branch Chairman: **Mark Coleman**, 14 Avocet Close, Newton-le-Willows **Tel:** 01925 222390; Branch Secretary: **Mrs Joan Collins**, Birley Street, Newton-le-Willows **Tel:** 01925 228959; Ticket Secretary: **Anthony Hatch**, Newton-le-Willows **Tel:** 01925 276298; **Website:** http/nlwmust.ukong.com. Meetings once a month in the Legh Arms Public House, Newton-le-Willows. Call any of the above for date of meeting – all telephone enquiries before 9pm. Coach travel for selected home games to be booked and paid in advance. Most games available at Legh Arms. Junior and family membership welcome.

NORTH DEVON
Branch Secretary: **Dave Rogan**, Leys Cottage, Hilltop, Fremington, Nr Barnstaple, EX31 3BL. **Tel/Fax:** 01271 328280, **Mobile:** 07967 682167
Departure points: Please contact Branch Secretary.

NORTH EAST
Branch Secretary: **John Burgess**, 10 Streatlam Close, Stainton, Barnard Castle, Co Durham, DL12 8RQ. **Tel:** 01833 695200
Departure points: Newcastle Central Station, 8.30am (1pm); A19/A690 Roundabout 8.50am (1.20pm); Peterlee A19–B1320 Slip Road, Southbound 9am (1.30pm); Hartlepool Baths 9.15am (1.45pm); Hartlepool Owton Lodge 9.20am (1.50pm); Hartlepool Sappers Corner 9.25am (1.55pm); Billingham, The Swan Pub 9.30am (2pm); Darlington Feethams on dual carriageway 10am (2.30pm); Scotch Corner 10.10am (2.40pm); Leeming Bar Services A1 10.20am (2.50pm).

NORTH MANCHESTER
Branch meetings at Leggatts Wine Bar, Oldham Road, Failsworth. Coaches to all home and away games. Secretary: **Graham May**, **Mobile:** 07931 505488. All home coach details: **Garry Chapman**, **Tel:** 07748 970225. All away coach details: **Dixie**, **Tel:** 07968 121872. All other enquiries contact **Graham**, **Tel:** 07931 505488

NORTH POWYS
For all enquiries please contact Branch Secretary, **Glyn T Davies**, 7 Tan-y-Mur, Montgomery, Powys, SY15 6PR. **Tel:** 01686 668841 (24hr answerphone).
Departure points: Saturdays, early KO 8.30am; evening games 4pm; Saturday 3pm KO 10.30am. Departure points Castle Caereinion Clock Park, Newtown, calling in at Abermule (Waterloo Hotel), Welshpool (Spar car park) Four Crosses and Mile End service station. If secretary is unavailable please contact the following officials and reps: Chairman **B Benyon**, Oswestry 01691 670611; Treasurer: **B Foulkes**, Newton 01938 810 979 or Branch Managers: Knighton – **R Davies** 01547 528318; Newton – **P Owen** 01686 610545; Branch meetings held every six weeks on a rota basis. For Welshpool area please contact secretary or treasurer.

NORTH STAFFORDSHIRE
Branch Secretary: **Peter Hall**, Cheddleton Heath House, Cheddleton Heath Rd, Leek ST13 7DX. **Tel:** 01538 360364
Departure points: 12.30pm (5.15pm) Leek bus station. Times in brackets for evening fixtures.

NORTH YORKSHIRE
Branch Secretary: **Andy Kirk**, 80 Trafalgar Road, Scarborough, YO12 7QR **Tel/Fax:** 01723 372876; **Mobile:** 07766 338164; **E-mail:** andykirk25@yahoo.co.uk
Departure points: Executive coaches to all home games from Whitby, Scarborough, Malton and York – booking in advance is required. Please phone secretary for further details.

NOTTINGHAM
Branch Secretary: **Wayne Roe**, Vine Cottages, 15 Platt Street, Pinxton, Notts NG16 6NX **Tel:** 07870 604269 (home travel): **Email:** wainy@aol.com
Martyn Meek, **Tel:** 01773 768424 (away travel)
Departure points: 10am (3pm) Nottingham; 10.30am (3.30pm) Ilkeston; 10.45am (3.45pm) Eastwood; 11am (4pm) Junction 28, M1. Times in brackets denote evening fixtures.

OLDHAM
Branch Secretary: **Dave Cone**, 67 Nelson Way, Washbrook, Chadderton, Lancashire, OL9 8NL. **Tel:** 0161 345 1793; **Mobile:** 07760 203258. Chairman: **Martyn Lucas**, 1 Wickentree Holt, Norden, Rochdale OL12 7PQ; **Tel:** 01706 355728. Meetings held on Sunday afternoons at 1pm at Horton Arms, 1 Ward Street, off Middleton Road, Chadderton, Oldham (unless a match day).
Departure points: (Coach to all home matches; midweek – leaves at 6pm; weekend 3pm ko. leaves at 1pm; w/end 4pm ko. – leaves at 1.30pm; away travel – subject to receiving match tickets.

OXFORD, BANBURY AND DISTRICT
Branch Secretary: **Mick Thorne**, The Paddock, 111 Eynsham Road, Botley, Oxford OX2 9BY. **Tel/Fax:** 01865 864924 **Email:** mickthorne@tinyworld.co.uk
Departure points: McLeans Coach Yard, Witney 6.30am for 12–1pm ko., 8am for 3–4pm ko.,

continued overleaf

1.30pm for evening ko; Botley Road Park-n-Ride, Oxford 7am for 12–1pm ko, 8.30am for 3–4pm ko., 2pm for evening ko; Plough Inn, Bicester 7.15am for 12–1pm ko, 8.45am for 3–4pm ko., 2.15pm for evening ko; Bus Station, Banbury 7.30am for 12–1pm ko, 9am for 3–4pm ko., 2.30pm for evening ko. Coach fares for all home games adults £13, Junior & OAPs £9.00. All coach seats must be booked in advance. Coaches are non-smoking & no alcohol is allowed on the coaches. Away match coaches subject to demand. European away trips subject to match tickets, itineraries available after the draw. Please send sae or email for full details.

PETERBOROUGH AND DISTRICT
Branch Secretary: **Andrew Dobney**, 3 Northgate, West Pinchbeck, Spalding, Lincs, PE11 3TB.
Tel: 01775 640743; Email: andrew@dobney.fsnet.co.uk
Departure points: Spalding bus station 8.30am (1.15pm); Peterborough, Key Theatre 9.15am (2pm); Grantham, Foston Services 10am (2.45pm). Times in brackets for evening fixtures.

PLYMOUTH
Branch Secretary: **Dave Price**, 34 Princess Avenue, Plymstock, Plymouth PL9 9EP
Tel: 01752 482049 Regular coach service to home games.
Departure points (Saturday/Sunday games): Tamar Bridge 6.30am (4am); Bretonside 6.45am (4.15am); Plympton 7am (4.30am); Ivybridge 7.10am (4.40am); Buckfastleigh 7.25am (4.55am); Exeter Services 7.50am (5.20am). Times in brackets are for 12.30pm kick-offs. (Midweek games): Tamar Bridge 10.30am and then other pick-up points at time intervals shown above.

PONTYPRIDD
Branch Secretary: **Lawrence Badman, Tel: 01443 406894; Mobile: 07966 588457; Email: lawrence@pmusc.fsnet.co.uk** 11 Laura Street, Treforest, Pontypridd, Mid Glamorgan, South Wales, CF37 1NW. Phone calls between 5pm & 7pm only. Answer phone at other times.
Departure points: Treorchy, Porth, Pontypridd, Caerphilly and Newport.
Away Travel Secretary: **Gareth Williams, Tel: 01443 674505; Mobile: 07879 036206**
Branch Chairman: **Steve Pember, Tel: 01291 431720; Mobile: 07989 441683**

REDDITCH
Branch Secretary: **Mark Richardson**, 90 Alcester Road, Hollywood, Worcestershire, B47 5NS.
Tel/Fax: 0121 246 0237 Departure points: Redditch & Bromsgrove.

ROSSENDALE
Branch Secretary: **Ian Boswell**, 44 Cutler Lane, Stacksteads, Bacup, Lancs OL13 0HW
Tel: 01706 874764; Mobile: 07802 502356. Meetings: The Royal Hotel, Waterfoot – see local press or email ROYALREDS@theroyal-hotel.co.uk. Coach travel arrangements – contact **Paul Stannard, (T) 01706 214493; (F) 01706 215371 or Paul@theroyal-hotel.co.uk**

RUGBY AND NUNEATON
Branch Secretary: **Greg Pugh**, 67 Fisher Avenue, Rugby, Warwickshire CV22 5HW;
Tel: 01788 567900. Chairman: **Mick Moore**, 143 Marston Lane, Attleborough, Nuneaton, Warwickshire; **Tel: 01203 343 868.**
Departure points: St Thomas Cross Pub, Rugby; McDonalds, Junction 2, M6, Coventry; Council House, Coton Road, Nuneaton. Departure times vary according to kick-off.

RUNCORN AND WIDNES
Branch Secretary: **Elizabeth Scott**, 39 Park Road, Runcorn, Cheshire, WA7 4SS.

SCUNTHORPE
Branch Secretary: **Pat Davies, Tel: 01724 851359.** Chairman: **Guy Davies,
Tel: 01724 851359** Transport Manager: **Tony Fish, Tel: 01724 341029**

SHEFFIELD & ROTHERHAM
Branch Secretary: **Roger Everitt**, 27 South Street, Kimberworth, Rotherham, South Yorkshire, S61 1ER. **Tel: 01709 563613.** Coach Travel available to all home games.
Departure points: Midweek games: Conisboro Star Inn 4pm; Rotherham Nellie Denes 4.15pm; Meadowhall Coach Park 4.30pm. Weekend games: Conisboro Star Inn; Rotherham Nellie Denes; Sheffield Midland Station; Departure times depend on Sky TV kick-offs – phone secretary for confirmation of departure times at weekend games.

SHOEBURYNESS, SOUTH END AND DISTRICT
Branch Secretary: **Bob Lambert**, 23 Royal Oak Drive, Wickford, Essex, SS11 8NT.
Tel: 01268 560168. Chairman: **Gary Black, Tel: 01702 219072**
Departure points: 7am Cambridge Hotel, Shoeburyness; 7.15am Bell Public House, A127; 7.20am Rayleigh Weir; 7.30am McDonalds, A127; 7.40am Fortune of War Public House, A127; 8.00am Brentwood High St; 8.05am Little Chef, Brentwood By-pass. Additional pick-ups by arrangement. Coach seats should be booked in advance. Ring for details of midweek fixtures.

SHREWSBURY
Branch Secretary: **Martyn Hunt**, 50 Whitehart, Reabrook, Shrewsbury, SY3 7TE.
Tel: 01743 350397; Chirk Secretary: **Mike Davies, Tel: 01691 778678**
Departure points: Reabrook Island; Abbey Church; Monkmoor Inn; Heathgates Island; Harlescott Inn; Hand Hotel, Chirk. 3 & 4pm kick-off – Depart Reabrook 10.30am; 7.30 & 8pm kick-off – Depart Reabrook 3pm.

SOUTH ELMSALL & DISTRICT
Branch Secretary: **Bill Fieldsend**, 72 Cambridge St, Moorthorpe, South Elmsall, Pontefract,

W Yorkshire, WF9 2AR **Tel: 01977 648358, Mobile: 07818 245954;** Treasurer: **Mark Bossons, Tel: 01977 650316.** Meetings held Tuesdays at the South Kirkby British Legion.
Departure points: Cudworth Library 11.30am (4.30pm); Hemsworth Market 11.45am (4.45pm); Mill Lane 11.50am (4.50pm); Pretoria WMC 12 noon (5pm). Times in brackets denote evening fixtures.

SOUTHPORT
Branch Secretary: **B Budworth**, 51 Dawlish Drive, Marshside, Southport PR9 9RB **Tel: 01704 211361.** Chairman: **J Mason**, 57 Claremont Road, Birkdale, Southport **Tel: 01704 565466;** Treasurer: **J A Johnson, Email: joseph.johnson1@btinternet.com;** Membership Secretary: **Mrs C Rothwell**, 37 Eamont Ave, Marshside, Southport **Tel: 01704 213920;** Transport Secretary: **Mr N Rimmer**, 41 Everton Road, Birkdale, Southport PR8 4BT.

STALYBRIDGE
Branch Secretary: **Walt Petrenko, Mobile: 07980 698964;** Chairman: **S Hepburn, Tel: 0161 344 2328.** Treasurer: **R A Wild, Tel: 0161 338 7277.** Membership Secretary: **A Baxter, Tel: 07885 809777;** Away travel: **Nigel Barrett, Mobile: 07802 799482;** Home travel: **B Williamson, Tel: 0161 338 6832.**
Departure point: Home coach leaves from the Pineapple, Stalybridge, 1½ hours before kick-off. Landlord: **M Mitchell, Tel: 0161 338 2542.** Away coaches are arranged when applicable.

STOKE-ON-TRENT
Branch Secretary: **Geoff Boughey**, 63 Shrewsbury Drive, Newcastle, Staffordshire, ST5 7RQ.
**Tel/Fax: 01782 561680 (home); Mobile: 07768 561680;
E-mail: geoff.boughey@btinternet.com**
Departure points: 12noon (5pm) Hanley bus station; 12.10pm (5.10pm) School Street, Newcastle; 12.15pm (5.15pm) Little Chef A34; 12.30pm (5.30pm) The Millstone Pub, Butt Lane. Times in brackets denote evening fixtures. Branch meetings every Monday night. Contact branch secretary for details.

STOURBRIDGE & KIDDERMINSTER
Branch Secretary: **Robert Banks**, 7 Croftwood Road, Wollescote, Stourbridge, West Midlands DY9 7EU. **Tel: 01384 826636.**
Departure points: Contact branch secretary for departure points and times.

SURREY
Branch Membership Secretary: **Mrs Maureen Asker**, 80 Cheam Road, Ewell, Surrey, KT17 1QF. **Tel: 0208 393 4763.** Home League Games Co-ordinator: **John Ramsden**, 22 Pound Lane, Godalming, Surrey **Tel: 01483 420909;** Cup Games Co-ordinator: **John Fuggle**, Flat 9, The Shrubbery, 22 Hook Road, Surbiton, Surrey; **Mobile: 07703 650869.**

SWANSEA
Branch Secretary: **Dave Squibb**, 156 Cecil Street, Manselton, Swansea, SA5 8QJ.
Tel: 01792 641981 Email: david.squibb@manutd.com
Departure points: Swansea (via Heads of Valleys Road); Neath; Hirwaun; Merthyr; Tredegar; Ebbw Vale; Brynmawr; Abergavenny; Monmouth.

SWINDON
Branch Secretary: **Martin Rendle**, 19 Cornfield Road, Devizes, Wiltshire, SN10 3BA.
Tel: 01380 728358 (between 8pm–10pm Monday to Friday).
Departure points: Kingsdown Inn; Stratton St Margaret; Swindon.

SWINTON
Branch Secretary: **John Berry**, 20 Castleway, Clifton, Swinton, M27 8HX **Mobile: 07887 676811**

TELFORD
Branch Secretary: **Sal Laher**, 4 Hollyoak Grove, Lakeside, Priorslee, Telford, TF2 9GE.
Tel: 01952 299224.
Departure points: Saturday (3pm kick-off) 10.30am Cuckoo Oak, Madeley; 10.40am Heath Hill, Dawley; 10.50am Bucks Head, Wellington; 11.00am Oakengates; 11.10am Bridge, Donnington; 11.20am Newport. Midweek (8pm kick-off) departure starts 4.30pm with 10 minutes later for each of the above locations. Contact branch secretary for further details.

TORBAY
Branch Secretary: **Vernon Savage**, 5 Courtland Road, Shiphay, Torquay, Devon TQ2 6JU.
Tel: 01803 616139 (answer machine); **Mobile: 07765 394238.**
Departure points: Upper Cockington Lane (Torquay); Newton Abbot railway station; The Avenue (Newton Abbot); Willcocks Garage (Kingsteignton) Countess Wear Roundabout (Exeter); Junction 25, M5 (Taunton); All departure times will be confirmed by branch secretary dependent on match kick-off time – additional departure points en-route can be arranged via Branch Secretary. The branch runs a coach to all w/end Premiership & Cup games at Old Trafford plus selected midweek European fixtures. The branch does not organise coach travel to away fixtures. The branch produces four editions of its newsletter every season, which culminates in the AGM at the Jolly Abbot, East Street, Newton Abbot. Full details from branch secretary. All branch members must be registered at Old Trafford.

UTTOXETER & DISTRICT
Branch Secretary: **Mrs T A Bloor**, 63 Carter Street, Uttoxeter, Staffordshire ST14 8EY.
Branch Chairman: **Mr R Phillips**, 77 Bentley Road, Uttoxeter, **Tel: 01889 567323.**
Departure points: Smithfield Hotel, Uttoxeter 11.30am Saturday, 4.30pm night games.

WALSALL
Branch Secretary: **Ian Robottom**, 157 Somerfield Road, Bloxwich, Walsall WS3 2EN. **Tel: 01922 861746.**
Departure points: 10.50am (4.15pm) Junction 9 (M6); 11.15am (4.50pm) Bell Pub, Bloxwich; 11.30am (5.15pm) Roman Way Hotel, A5 Cannock; 11.50am (5.35pm) Dovecote Pub, Stone Road, Stafford.

WARRINGTON
Branch Secretary: **Su Buckley**, 4 Vaudrey Drive, Woolston, Warrington, Cheshire, WA1 4HG. **Tel: 01925 816966.**
Departure points: Blackburn Arms 1pm (6pm); Churchills 1.10pm (6.10pm); Chewvies 1.15pm (6.15pm); Highway Man/ Kingsway 1.20pm (6.20pm); Rope 'n' Anchor 1.25pm (6.25pm). Times in brackets denote evening fixtures.

WELLINGBOROUGH
Branch Secretary: **Phil Walpole**, 7 Cowgill Close, Cherry Lodge, Northampton NN3 8PB. **Tel/ Fax: 01604 787612.**
Departure points: Shoe Factory, Irchester Road, Rushden 8.30am (1.30pm); Doc Martens Shoe Factory, Irchester 8.35am (1.35pm); The Cuckoo Public House, Woolaston 8.45am (1.45pm); Police Station, Wellingborough 8.55am (1.55pm) ; Duke of York Public House, Wellingborough 9am (2pm); Trumpet Public House, Northampton 9.10am (2.10pm); Abington Park Bus Stop, Northampton 9.15 am (2.15pm); Campbell Square, Northampton 9.20am (2.20pm); Mill Lane Lay-by (opposite Cock Hotel Public House), Kingsthorpe 9.25am (2.25pm); Top of Bants Lane (opposite Timken), Dugton 9.30am (2.30pm).

WEST CUMBRIA
Branch Secretary: **Robert Wilson**, 42 Wedgwood Road, Flimby, Maryport, Cumbria CA15 8QX. **Tel: 01900 819033, Mobile: 07786 542607, Email: rob_in_the_trafford@hotmail.com**
Departure points: Coach 1 departs: Egremont 9.45am (3.15pm): Cleator Moor 10am (3.30pm); Whitehaven 10.15am (3.45pm); Distington 10.20am (3.50pm); Cockermouth 10.35am (4.05pm). Coach 2 departs: Salterbeck 9.45am (1.45pm); Harrington Road 9.50am (1.50pm); Workington 10am (2.00pm); Station Inn 10.10am (2.10pm); Netherhall Cr 10.12am (2.12pm); Netherton 10.15am (2.15pm); Dearham 10.20am (2.20pm). Times in brackets denotes 8pm kick-off – contact branch secretary for other kick-off times.

WEST DEVON
Branch Secretary: **Mrs R M Bolt**, 16 Moorview, North Tawton, Devon, EX20 2HW. **Tel: 01837 82682** (all enquiries).
Departure points: North Tawton; Crediton; Exeter

WESTMORLAND
Branch Secretary: **Dennis Alderson**, 71 Calder Drive, Kendal, Cumbria, LA9 6LR. **Tel: 01539 728248; Mobile: 07973 965373.**
Departure points: Ambleside; Windermere; Staveley, Kendal and Forton Services. For departure times and further details, please contact branch secretary.

WORKSOP
Branch Secretary: **Mick Askew**, 20 Park St, Worksop, Nottinghamshire. **Tel: 01909 486194.**

YEOVIL
Branch Secretary: **Richard Chapman-Cox**, Hozen Cottage, 59 Water Street, Martock Somerset, TA12 6JP. **Mobile: 07930 505349; Email: richard.chapmancox@btinternet.com**
Departure points: Yeovil and Taunton. Transport available to non-branch members. Please contact branch secretary for departure times.

Irish Branches

ABBEYFEALE & DISTRICT
Branch Secretary: **Denis O'Sullivan, Tel: 068 32525** or **086 8157146;** Chairman: **Denis Daly, Tel: 068 31712** or **087 9880015;** Vice Chairman: **Gerard Foley, Tel: 068 32979** or **087 4125748;** Treasurer: **Paddy Finucane, Tel: 068 32036;** Youth officer: **Richard O'Mahony, Tel: 068 32305** or **087 2055031;** Public relations officer: **Tomas Mann, Tel: 068 31025** or **087 9130180.** Regular meetings held at Donal and Ann's Bar, Abbeyfeale – contact secretary for more details.

ANTRIM TOWN
Branch Secretary: **Brendan O'Neill**, 86 Ballycraigy Road, Glengormley, Co Antrim BT36 4SX; **Tel: 028 90 842929.** Chairman: **William Cameron**, 92 Donegore Drive, Parkhall, Antrim, N Ireland; **Tel: 02894 461634.** Club meetings held every other Thursday in the Top of the Town Bar, Antrim. All members must be registered with United's official membership scheme.

ARKLOW & SOUTH LEINSTER
Branch Secretary: **James Cullen**, 52 South Green, Arklow, Co Wicklow, Eire. **Tel: 087 2327859** or **0402 39816.** All trips arranged via local committee members.
Departure points: Waterford to Dublin – please contact the secretary for further details.

BALLYCASTLE
Branch Secretary: **Patricia McKendry**, 20 Carnduff Park, Ballycastle, Co. Antrim, Northern Ireland BT54 6LN; **Tel: 028 207 69269.** Chairman: **Derek McKendry.** Meetings: First Sunday every month, Scout Den, Ballycastle. New members welcome.

BALLYMONEY
Branch Secretary: **Malachy McAleese**, 8 Riverview Park, Ballymoney, Co Antrim, Northern Ireland BT53 7QS; **Tel: 028 276 67623.** Chairman: **Gerry McAleese**, 11 Greenville Avenue, Ballymoney, Co Antrim, Northern Ireland; **Tel: 028 276 65446.**
Departure points: Ballymoney United Social Club, Grove Road, Ballymena; Belfast Harbour or Belfast International Airport. Meetings: last Thursday of every month at Ballymoney United Social Club, 35 Castle Street, Ballymoney; **Tel: 028 276 66054** – new members welcome.
Website: www.musc-ballymoney.co.uk; Email: info@musc-ballymoney.co.uk

BANBRIDGE
Branch Secretary: **James Loney**, 83 McGreavy Park, Derrymacash, Lurgan, Northern Ireland BT66 6LR. **Tel: 028 38 345058; Mobile: 07901 833076.**
Email: james@mcgreavy4027freeserve.co.uk Chairman: **Kevin Nelson**, 10 Ballynamoney Park, Derrymacash, Lurgan, N Ireland. **Tel: 028 38 344232; Mobile: 07879 436358.**
Departure Points: Corner House, Derrymacash; Lurgan Town Centre; Newry Road, Banbridge

BANGOR
Branch Secretary: **Gary Wilsdon**, 4 Bexley Road, Bangor, Co Down BT19 7TS. **Tel: 028 91 458485; Email: gary.wilsdon@virgin.net**
Branch meetings: every other Monday 8pm at the Imperial Bar, Central Avenue, Bangor.

BELFAST REDS
Branch Secretary: **John Bond**, 53 Hillhead Crescent, Belfast, Northern Ireland, BT11 9FS. **Tel: 028 90 627861.**

BRAY
Branch Secretary: **Ravi Antour**, c/o Lower Dargle Road, Bray **Tel: 028 60477;**
Branch Chairman: **Noel Ryder**, 3 Avondale Court, Kerry Road, Bray, Col Wicklow; **Tel: 205 0578.**

BUNDORAN
Branch Secretary: **Rory O'Donnell**, Doonan Court, Donegal Town, Co. Donegal. **Tel: 073 23629; Mobile: 087 245 6994.**
Departure points: Rory's Autospares, Donegal Town and The Chasing Bull, Bundoran. All bookings to be made through branch secretary only. Bookings should be made early to avoid disappointment. New members always welcome.

CARLINGFORD LOUTH
Branch Secretary: **Harry Harold**, Mountain Park, Carlingford, Co Louth, Ireland. **Tel: 00 353 42 9373379.**

CARLOW
Branch Secretary: **Michael Lawlor**, Trafford House, 20 New Oak Estate, Carlow, Ireland. **Tel: 0503 43759, Mobile: 086 8950030** (Mon–Friday 7pm–9pm only).
Treasurer: **William Carroll, Mobile: 086 8593062** (Mon–Fri 9am–5pm only).

CARRICKFERGUS
Branch Secretary: **Gary Callaghan**, 3 Red Fort Park, Carrickfergus, Co Antrim, Northern Ireland BT38 9EW. **Tel: 028 93 355362; Fax: 028 93 369995; Email: aca@globalnet.co.uk**
The branch holds meetings fortnightly on a Monday evening at 8pm in the Quality Hotel, Carrickfergus. New members are welcome, especially family and juniors. The branch organises trips to Old Trafford for all home games and away matches including whenever possible.

CARRYDUFF
Branch Secretary: **John White**, Stretford End, 4 Baronscourt Glen, Carryduff, Co Down, Northern Ireland BT8 8RF. **Tel: 028 90 812377; E-mail: jw@carryduffmusc.com.** Chairman: **John Dempsey**, 16 Baronscourt Glen, Carryduff BT8 8RF, **Tel/Fax: 028 90 812823;**
Email: jd@carryduffmusc.com; Vice-Chairman: **Wilson Steele, Tel: 028 94 464987.**
Carryduff Junior Reds Branch Secretary: **Marc White;** Chairman: **Paul White;**
Branch website: www.carryduffmusc.com
Departure points: The branch organises coach trips to Old Trafford for every home game from The Royal Ascot, Carryduff and The Grand Opera House, Belfast. Branch meetings are held every week. No alcohol and no other club colours are permitted on the coach. New members, particularly juniors, are always welcome as the branch has a strong family and cross-community ethos. All members must be registered with Manchester United's official membership scheme.

CASTLEDAWSON
Branch Secretary: **Niall Wright**, 22 Park View, Castledawson, Co Londonderry, Northern Ireland. **Tel: 028 79 468779.**

CASTLEPOLLARD
Branch Secretary: **Anne Foley**, Coole, Mullingar, Co Westmeath, Ireland. **Tel/Fax: 00 353 44 61613; E-mail: muscpollard@hotmail.com**
Departure points: The Square, Castlepollard. Additional pick-up points by arrangement with branch secretary. Branch meetings on third Monday of every month. Notification of additional meetings by newsletter.

CASTLEWELLAN
Branch Secretary: **Seamus Owens**, 18 Mourne Gardens, Dublin Road, Castlewellan, Co Down, Northern Ireland, BT31 9BY. **Tel: 028 437 78137; Fax: 028 437 70762; Mobile: 07714 756 455.** Chairman: **Tony Corr, Tel: 028 437 22885** Treasurer: **Michael Burns Tel: 028 437 78665**

CITY OF DERRY
Branch Secretary: **David Kee**, 35 Curlew Way, Waterside, Londonderry BT47 6LQ.
Tel: 028 71 34 4059; Mobile: 07801 812829; E-mail: secretary@codmusc.org.uk
Meetings: first Tuesday of every month at the Gallery Bar, Dungiven Rd, Londonderry at 8.30pm.

CLARA
Branch Secretary: **Michael Kenny**, River Street, Clara, Co Offaly, Ireland.

CLONMEL
Branch Secretary: **Anthony O'Sullivan**, No. 41 Honeyview Estate, Clonmel, Co. Tipperary,
Ireland. **Tel: 052 26596** (home); **Mobile: 086 837 9836.** Chairperson: **Hughie O'Meara,**
Tel: 086 3120422. Regular meetings at Gleeson's Bar, Clonmel. For further information
contact the branch secretary. **Club branch mobile: 087 754 3028.**

COLERAINE
Branch Secretary: **Maud Doherty**, 12 Blackthorn Court, Coleraine, Co Derry, Northern Ireland.
Tel: 028 703 54773.

COMBER
Branch Secretary: **Derek Hume**, 14 Carnesure Hts., Comber, Co Down. **Tel: (028) 91 872608.**
Chairman: **Stephen Irvine. Email: Comberbranch@onetel.net.uk;** Branch meetings are held
on various Tuesdays. Details of these meetings are printed in *The Newtownards Chronicle*
newspaper and also available to view on our website: **www.propertysnaps.co.uk/CD**

COOKSTOWN
Branch Secretary: **Geoffrey Wilson**, 10 Cookstown Road, Moneymore, Co Londonderry,
Northern Ireland BT45 7QF. **Tel: 028 86748625; Mobile: 07855 760981** Meeting: first
Monday of every month at Royal Hotel, Cookstown, 9pm. New members welcome. However,
all members must be registered with Manchester United's official membership scheme.

CORK AREA
Branch Secretary: **Paul Kearney**, Beech Road, Passage West, Co Cork, Republic of Ireland.
Tel: 021 841190.

COUNTY CAVAN
Chairman: **Owen Farrelly, Tel: 046 42184;** Secretary: **Gerry Heery, Tel: 087 6181295.**
Assistant Secretary: **Jimmy Murray, Tel: 086 8289504; Email: co.cavanbranch@eircom.net;**
Website: **www.cocavanbranch.homestead.com;** Meetings: third Monday of each month in
Tyrrells, Main St, Mullagh, Co. Cavan.

COUNTY LONGFORD
Branch Secretary: **Seamus Gill**, 17 Springlawn, Longford, Republic of Ireland. **Tel: 043 47848;**
Fax: 043 41655. Chairman: **Harry Ryan**, 58 Teffia Park, Longford, Co. Longford; Treasurer:
Nicola King, 18 Harbour Row, Longford, Co Longford; President: **George Wenman.**

COUNTY MONAGHAN
Chairman: **Peter O'Reilly**; Branch Secretary: **Seamus Gallagher**; Assistant Secretary: **John
Hughes**; Treasurers: **Ann Devine & Jane Flynn**. Meetings fortnightly throughout the season at
Bellevue Tavern, Dublin Street, Monaghan; secretary phone nos. **Tel: 047 83265/81577** or
0868 307689, Email: seamusgallagh16@hotmail.com

COUNTY ROSCOMMON
Branch Secretary: **Noel Scally**, Cashel, Boyle, Co Roscommon, Ireland. **Tel: 079 64995;
Mobile: 087 2228466.** Chairman: **Seamus Sweeney**, Croghan, Boyle, Co Roscommon,
Tel: 079 68061; Mobile: 087 6484931. Treasurer: **Ray Livingstone**, Shankill, Elphin,
Co Roscommon, **Mobile: 087 6771230.** Meetings are held third Thursday of every month
at the Royal Hotel, Boyle, Co Roscommon.

COUNTY TIPPERARY
Branch Secretary: **Mrs Kathleen Hogan**, 45 Canon Hayes Park, Tipperary, Republic of Ireland.
Tel: 062 51042

COUNTY WATERFORD
Branch Secretary: **Kevin Moore**, 92 Childers Estate, Dungarvan, Co Waterford.
Tel: 086 3925677. Chairman: **Oliver Drummy**, 8 Cloneety Tce., Dungarvan, Co Waterford;
Vice–Chairman: **Tommy Keating**, Ringnasillogue, Childers Estate, Dungarvan, Co Waterford;
Treasurer: **Judy Connors**, Hillview Drive, Dungarvan, Co Waterford; Committee meetings held
at least once a month and general meetings whenever necessary. New members welcome.

CRAIGAVON
Branch Secretary: **Eamon Atkinson**, 8 Rowan Park, Tullygally Road, Craigavon, Co Armagh,
Northern Ireland BT65 5AY, **Tel: 028 38 343870.** Chairperson: **Cathy Flynn**, 2 Avondale
Manor, Craigavon, **Tel: 028 38 327788.** Treasurer: **Susan Atkinson**, 8 Rowan Park, Craigavon
BT65 5AY, **Tel: 028 38 343870.**
Departure Points: Lurgan; Craigavon; Portadown; Tandragee; Dundalk; Dublin Port. Meetings
held first Tuesday of each month at the Goodyear Sports & Social Club, Silverwood, Craigavon.

DONEGAL
Chairman: **Paul Dolan**; Branch Secretary: **Liam Friel, Tel: 087 6736967;** Treasurer: **Paddy
Delap, Tel: 074 22240;** Travel Organiser: **Tony Murray, Tel: 074 24111;** Public Relations

Officer: **Willie Diver 074 57156;** Vice Chairman: **Sean McLaghlin.** Club meetings held in Club
Room in the Dry Arch, Letterkenny. Notice of meetings put in local press and on Highland Radio.

DOWNPATRICK
Branch Secretary: **Terry Holland**, 137 Ballyhoman Road, Downpatrick, Co Down, Northern
Ireland. **Tel/Fax: 028 44 842550; Mobile: 07712 622242**

DUNDALK
Chairman: **Michael McCourt**; Secretary: **Arthur Carron**; Treasurer: **Mary Laverty**; Ticket &
Travel: **Dickie O'Hanrahan;** Committee Members: **Ollie Kelly, Gery Dullaghan.**

DUNGANNON
Branch Secretary: **Ian Hall**, Silveridge, 229 Killyman Rd, Dungannon, Co Tyrone, Northern Ireland
BT71 6RS. **Tel/Fax: 028 87 723085** (h); **Tel/Fax: 028 87 752255** (w); **Mobile: 07787 124765**
Meetings every two weeks (all year) at Cobbles Bar, Church St, Dungannon. For details on
membership, meetings, trips, etc. contact branch secretary or **Keith Houston** on **028 87 722735
(mobile 07813 208925)** or **Alan Carroll** on **028 87 727786 (mobile 07733 382937).**

EAST BELFAST
Branch Secretary: **Girvin Miskimmin**, 39 The Brambles, Lisburn Northern Ireland BT28 2XY.
Tel: 028 92 604527; Email: g.miskimmin@bt282xy.fsnet.co.uk. Meetings held at The
Ulster Maple Leaf Club on match nights and/ or fortnightly. All members must be registered with
Manchester United official membership scheme and must participate in Manchester United
Development Association's Super Pools Scheme.

ENNIS
Branch Secretary: **Seamus Hughes**, Old Trafford, Quin, Ennis, Co Clare, Republic of Ireland.
Tel: 065 68 20282; Mobile: 086 239 3975. Branch Chairman: **Eamon Murphy**, Knockboy,
Ballynacally, Co Clare, Ireland, **Tel: 065 68 28105.** Meetings held at Roslevan Arms,
Tulla Rd, Ennis.

FERMANAGH
Branch Secretary: **Gabriel Maguire**, 80 Glenwood Gardens, Enniskillen, BT74 5LT.
Tel: 028 66 325 950; Mobile: 07788 421739. Chairman: **Eric Brown**, 166 Main Street,
Lisnaskea. Treasurer: **Raymond McBrien**, Ardlougher Road, Irvinestown. Meetings held in
Charlie's Lounge, Enniskillen.

FIRST BALLYCLARE
Branch Secretary: **Alan Munce**, 7 Merion Park, Ballyclare, Co Antrim, Northern Ireland
BT39 9XD. **Tel: 028 93 324126.**

FIRST NORTH DOWN (BANGOR)
Branch Secretary: **Robert Quee**, Stretford End, 67 Springhill Road, Bangor West, Co Down,
Northern Ireland. **Tel: 028 91 453094.** Chairman: **Walter Geary**, 25 Beaumont Drive, Bangor BT19 6WH.
1st North Down supporters meet on alternative Monday evenings at 8pm at Ballykillaire Sports
Complex, Old Belfast Road, Bangor. New members always welcome. Branch operates a 'Family
Package Membership'. For further details please ring the secretary, **Tel: 028 91 453094;
Mobile: 07790 761828** or the Chairman, **Tel: 028 91 462732; Mobile: 07803 109429.**

FIRST PORTAFERRY
Branch Secretary: **Aiden Hughes**, Mermaid Bar, Kirkcubbin, Co Down, Northern Ireland.
Tel: 028 427 38215. Chair: **Tony Cleary;** Treasurer: **Hugh Conlon**. Branch meetings held on
first Tuesday of every month at 9.00pm at McNamara's, High Street, Portaferry.

FOYLE
Branch Secretary: **Martin Harkin**, 2 Harvest Meadows, Dunlade Road, Greysteel, Co Derry,
Northern Ireland BT47 3BG. Meeting point: Ulsterbus Club, Bishop Street, Derry City.
Departure points: Meet Ulsterbus at midnight, boat at 0250 on matchday. Hotel Comfort
Friendly, Hyde Road. Return boat 1430, arrive Ulsterbus Club 2030.

GALWAY
Branch Secretary: **Patsy Devlin**, 22 St James Crescent, Mervue, Galway, Ireland.
Mobile: 00 353 87 2530366. Monthly meetings at Cobblers Bar, Henry Street, Galway.
Membership open all year round. Trips by plane and ferry to all home games.

GLENOWEN
Branch Secretary: **Jim Turner**, 4 Dermot Hill Drive, Belfast, Northern Ireland BT12 7GG.
Tel: 02890 242682; Mobile: 07990 848 961 (day).
Email: **musc.glenowen@ntlworld.com** Meetings held every week on Wednesday evening
in Biddy Duffys Bar, Andersonstown Road, Belfast. Contact branch secretary for further details.

HILLTOWN
Branch Secretary: **Gery Durkin**, 14 Meadowlands Avenue, Warrenpoint, Co Down, Northern
Ireland BT34 3FY. **Mobile: 07742 198217.**

IVEAGH YOUTH
Branch Secretary: **Russell Allen**, 2 Iveagh Crescent, Belfast, Northern Ireland BT12 6AW.
Tel: 028 90 542651 (office); **028 90 329621** (home).
Assistant Branch Secretary: **Brendan McBride**, 3 Gransha Park, Belfast BT11 8AT.
Tel: 028 90 522400 (work); 028 90 203171 (home).

IRELAND (DUBLIN)
Branch Secretary: **Eddie Gibbons**, 19 Cherry Orchard Crescent, Ballyfermont, Dublin 10. **Tel: 01 626 9759; Fax: 01 6236388; Email: muscirlbranch@hotmail.com.** Membership Secretary: **Michael O'Toole**, 49 Briarwood Lawn, Mulmuddart, Dublin 15, **Tel: 01 821 5702.** The committee meets every Monday night in The INTO, Teachers Club, 36 Parnell Square, from 6.30–8.00pm for bookings/ membership etc, except when United play live on TV or Bank Holidays, when the branch meets on Tuesday night.

KILKENNY
Branch Secretary: **John Joe Ryan**, Priory Lodge, John's Quay, Kilkenny, **Tel: 056 65827** (day); **056 65136** (after 6pm); **Fax: 056 64043.** Assistant Secretary: **Mr Patrick Moran**, Ardra, Castlecomer, Co Kilkenny, **Tel: 056 41439.**

KILLALOE & ROSCREA
Branch Secretary: **Michael Flynn**, 611 Cross Roads, Killaloe, Co Clare, Ireland. **Tel: 061 376031.** Chairman: **Seamus Doran**, 7 Limerick Street, Roscrea, **Tel: 0505 23194.**

KILLARNEY
Branch Secretary: **Frank Roberts**, St Margaret's Road, Killarney, Co Kerry, Republic of Ireland. Chairman: **Bill Keefe**; Treasurer: **Denis Spillane**. Meetings held on the first Wednesday of every month at which future trips are organised.

KILLMALLOCK Branch Secretary: **Kieran Conba**, Emmet Street, Kilmallock, Co Limerick. **Tel: 087 204 4941; Email: Kieran.Conba@arise-europe.com**

LAGAN Branch Secretary: **John Mooreland**, 29 Ashgrove Road, Newtownabbey, Co Antrim, BT36 6LJ.

LAOIS Branch Secretary: **Denis Moran**, Newpark, Portlaoise, Co Laois, Ireland **Tel: 0502 22681** .

LARNE Branch Secretary: **Brian Haveron**, 69 Croft Manor, Ballygally, Larne, Co Antrim BT40 2RU. **Tel: 028 28 261197** (day); **028 28 583027** (night); **Mobile: 07785 388959.** Branch Chairman: **John Hylands**, 43 Olderfleet Road, Larne, Co Antrim BT40 1AS. **Tel: 028 28 277888.** Meetings: every Monday night 8.00pm at St. John's Social Club, Mill Brae, Larne. The branch has an allocation for every home fixture and is a family orientated branch. New members always welcome.

LIMAVADY
Branch Secretary: **Gerry Cooke**, 20 Whitehill Park, Limavady, Co. Derry BT49 0QE. **Tel: 028 77 768080** (after 6pm); **Mobile: 07903 236108.**

LIMERICK
Branch Secretary: **Dennis O'Sullivan**, 14 Rossa Avenue, Mulgrave Street, Limerick, Republic of Ireland. **Tel: 061 311502; Mobile: 086 8435828.**

LISBURN
Branch Secretary: **Mark Hutton**, 46 Lyndhurst Parade, Belfast BT13 3PB; **Tel: 02890 717242; Mobile: 07732 921257**
The branch meets each Tuesday night at 8.30pm at the Club Rooms on Sackville Street. To join you must be an official member of Manchester United. The branch travels to all home games and some away. Anyone interested in joining – families and kids welcome – should contact the branch secretary.

LISTOWEL Branch Secretary: **Aiden O'Connor**, 55 Pytha Fold Road, Withington, Manchester M20 4UR. **Tel: 0161 434 4713.** Assistant Secretary: **David O'Brien**, Bedford, Listowel, Co Kerry Ireland. **Tel: 068 22250.**

LURGAN Branch Secretary: **John Furphy**, 123 Drumbeg North, Craigavon, Co Armagh, N Ireland BT65 5AE. **Tel: 028 38 341842.**

MAYO
Branch Secretary: **Seamus Moran**, Belclare, Westport, Co Mayo, Ireland. **Tel: 00 353 982 7533** (h); **00 353 985 5202** (w); **Mobile: 00 353 872 417966; Fax: 00 353 982 8874.** Chairperson: **Liam Connell**, 70 Knockaphunta, Castlebar, Co Mayo, Ireland. Treasurer: **T J Gannon**, 4 The Paddock, Castlebar Road, Westport, Co Mayo, Ireland. PRO **Kieran Mongey**, Blackfort, Castlebar, Co Mayo, Ireland.

MEATH
Branch Secretary: **Colm McManus**, 46 Beechlawn, Kells, Co Meath, Republic of Ireland. **Tel: 046 49831.** Departure points: Jack's Railway Bar, Kells; Fairgreen, Naven.

MOURNE
Branch Secretary: **Michael Peacock**, 3 Meadowlands, Kilkeel, Co Down Northern Ireland BT34 4YD. **Tel: 028 417 63409.**

NEWRY
Branch Secretary: **Brendan McConville**, 14 Willow Grove, Newry, Co Down, Northern Ireland, BT34 1JH. **Tel: 028 3026 6996; Email: brendan.mcconville@manutd.com** Chairman: **Jeffrey Clements, Tel: 028 3026 7158.** Meetings: first Tuesday of each month at the Cue Club, Newry. **Tel: 028 3026 6066.**

NEWTOWNARDS
Branch Secretary: **Leo Cafolla, Tel: 07710 820300; Fax: 028 91 822200.** Chairperson: **Mrs Ruth Quann.** A family orientated club who meet once a fortnight at Nixx Sport's Bar, Newtownards. New members always welcome.

NORTH BELFAST
Branch Secretary: **Robert Savage**, 47 Mayfield Road, Newtownabbey, Northern Ireland, BT36 7WD. **Tel: 028 90 847237.** Meetings are no longer held at the Shamrock Social Club; please contact Branch Secretary if you require additional information.

OMAGH
Branch Secretary: **Brendan McLaughlin**, 4 Pinefield Court, Killyclougher, Omagh, Co Tyrone, Northern Ireland BT79 7YT. **Tel: 028 82 250025; Mobile: 077 10 366 486.**

PORTADOWN
Branch Secretary: **Harold Beck**, 23 Kernan Grove, Portadown, Co Armagh, BT63 5RX. **Tel: 028 3 833 6877; Mobile: 07703 360423; Email: harrybeck@mail.com;** Treasurer: **Harold Blevins**, 47 Creenagh Road, Loughgall, Co Armagh, BT61 8JL. **Tel: 028 38 891103; Mobile: 07753 640714.**
Departure points: Loughgall, Portadown, Lurgan, Lisburn, Moira, Banbridge. Meetings held 3rd Monday each month at Gary's Lounge, Bridge Street, Portadown.

PORTAVOGIE
Branch Secretary: **Robert McMaster**, 6 New Road, Portavogie, Co Down BT22 1EN. **Tel: 028 38 336877; Mobile: 07703 360423; Email: harrybeck@mail.com.** Treasurer: **Harold Blevins**, 47 Creenagh Road, Loughgall, Co Armagh BT61 8JL. **Tel: 028 38 891103; Mobile: 07753 640714.**
Departure points: Loughgall, Portadown, Lurgan, Lisburn, Moira, Banbridge. Meetings are held on the 3rd Monday of each month at Gary's Lounge, Bridge Street, Portadown.

PORTRUSH
Chairman: **Mr Lynn Mitchell**; Treasurer; **Hugo Clements**; Branch Secretary: **Jennifer McKane**, 231 Ballybogey Rd, Portrush, Co Antrim, Northern Ireland BT56 8NF. **Tel: 028 70 824605.**

PORTSTEWART
Branch Secretary: **Ryan McLaughlin, Mobile: 07736 248642 446; Tel: 028 777 50281** (home); **Email: ryan.mclaughlin2@btopenworld.com** Club meetings are held every second Wednesday of the month at Cromore Holt, Portstewart.

ROSTREVOR
Branch Chairman: **John Parr**, 16 Drumreagh Park, Rostrevor BT34 3DU. **Tel: 028 417 39797;** Branch Secretary: **Roger Morgan**, 23 Ardfield Crescent, Warrenpoint, Co Down, Northern Ireland. **Tel: 028 417 54783;** Treasurer: **John Franklin**, 14 Rosswood Park, Rostrevor, Co Down BT34 3DZ, **Tel: 028 417 38906;** Ass. Secretary: **M Rea**, 8 The Square, Rostrevor, Co. Down. **Tel: 028 417 39808;** Club President: **Paul Braham.**

SION MILLS
Branch Secretary: **Jim Hunter**, 122 Melmount, Sion Mills, Co Tyrone, Northern Ireland, BT82 9EU. **Tel: 028816 58226** (h); **02882 252491** (w).

SLIGO
Branch Chairman: **Eddie Gray**, 27 Cartron Heights, Sligo, Republic of Ireland. **Tel: 00 353 71 44387; Mobile: 086 607 5855.**

SOUTH BELFAST
Branch Secretary: **James Copeland**, 17 Oakhurst Avenue, Blacks Road, Belfast BT10 0PD. **Tel: 028 90 615184; Mobile: 07769 594875.** Chairman: **Danny Nolan;** Vice–Chairman: **Michael Murphy;** Treasurer: **James McLaughlin;** Fundraising Officer: **Simon Murray;** Fundraising Officer: **Pól Mead** Departure points: for all matches: Balmoral Hotel, Blacks Road.

STEWARTSTOWN
Branch Secretary: **Stephen Coyle**, 8 Coolnafranky Park, Cookstown, Co Tyrone, Northern Ireland BT80 8PN. **Tel: 028 86 765511.**

STRABANE
Branch Secretary: **Gerry Donnelly**, 27 Dublin Road, Strabane, Co Tyrone, Northern Ireland, BT82 9EA. **Tel: 02871 883376.**

TALLAGHT
Branch Secretary: **Jimmy Pluck**, 32 Kilcarrig Cresent, Fettercaim, Tallaght, Co Dublin 24, Republic of Ireland. **Tel/ Fax: 00 353 1 2442413** (h); **Mobile: 086 8030123** (anytime).

TIPPERARY TOWN
Branch Secretary: **John Ryan**, 35 O'Brien Street, Tipperary Town, Co Tipperary, Eire. **Tel: 00 353 86 883 1456** (24 hours); **Email: johncantona.ryan11@talk21.com**

TOWER ARDS
Branch Secretary: **Stephen Rowley, Tel: 028 91 810457** (h); **028 90 432014** (w). Meetings are held on the every second Sunday in the Tower Inn, Mill Street, Newtownards.

TRALEE
Branch Secretary: **Johnny Switzer**, Dromtacker, Tralee, Co Kerry, Ireland. **Tel: 066 7124787.**

WARRENPOINT
Branch Secretary: **Pat Treanor**, 31 Oakland Grove, Warrenpoint. **Tel: 028 417 73921; Mobile: 07775 968595.** Chairman: **John Bird**, 23 Greendale Crescent, Rostrevor, Co Down, **Tel: 028 417 3837.** Treasurer: **Leo Tohill**, 46 Carmen Park, Warrenpoint, Co Down, **Tel: 028 417 72453; Website: www.muwp.ukgateway.net** Club based at The Square Peg, Warrenpoint, Co Down, N Ireland. **Tel: 028 417 53429.** Meets last Friday of every month 8pm.

WEST BELFAST
Branch Secretary: **John McAllister**, 25 Broadway, Belfast BT12 6AS. **Tel: 028 90 329423. Email: hoyt@lineone.net** Branch Chairman: **George McCabe**, 21 Beechmount Street, Belfast, BT12 7NG. Treasurer: **Mr G Burns.** Committee: **Liam Curran, Michael Curran, Hugh Kerr, John McLarnon.** Meetings held fortnightly in The Red Devil Bar, Falls Road, on Tuesday evenings at 8pm. Families and new members always welcome.

Overseas Branches

BELGIUM
Chairman: **Peter Bauwens**, Grote Markt 78/2, 9060 Zelzate, Belgium. **Tel: 00 32 934 20403; Fax: 00 32 934 20406.** Branch Secretary: **Kristof Haes**, John Schenkelstraat 3, 9060 Zelzate, Belgium. **Tel: 00 32 934 56474.**

CANADA
Manchester United Supporters' Club, 12 St Clair Avenue East, PO Box 69057, Toronto, Ontario, M4T 3AI, Canada. Chairman: **Kevin Kerr. Email chairman@muscc.com Website: www.muscc.com; Fax: 00 1 416 480 0501** FAO: Maureen

CYPRUS
Branch Chairman: **Ronis Soteriades**, P.O. Box 51365, 3504 Limassol, Cyprus. **Tel: 00 357 25337690; Fax: 00 357 25388652.**

GERMAN FRIENDS
Branch President: **Marco Homfeck**, Silberstein 36, 95179 Geroldsgrün, Germany. **Tel: 09267 8111.**

GERMAN KREFELD REDS
Branch Secretary: **Andy Marsh**, Innsbrucker Str, 47807 Krefeld, Germany. **Tel/Fax 00 49 (0) 2151 392908; Mobile: 00 49 (0) 173 250 3390** Assistant Branch Secretary: **Stuart Dykes**, Grete Schmitz Str. 8, 47829 Kreffeld, Germany. **Tel: 00 49 (0) 2151 435 167; Fax: 00 49 2151 435 168; Mobile: 00 49 (0) 172 398 5152. Email: stuart.dykes@t-online.de**

GERMAN REDS
Branch Chairman: **Markus Nerlich**, Eissendorfer Str 28, D–21073 Hamburg, Germany. **Tel: 00 49 40 76 75 32 02; Fax: 00 49 40 30 01 41 11; Email: markusnerlich@aol.com**

GIBRALTAR
PO Box 22, Gibraltar; Branch Chairman: **C A Moberley, Tel: 00 350 74391; Email: divemob@gibnet.gi** or **cardmand@gibnynex.gi.** Branch/ Membership Secretary: **Brian Cardona Tel: 00 350 76653;** Treasurer: **D R Peralta;** Committee Members: Anthony Barnett, Christabelle Barnett, John Calderon, Damian Cruz, Billy Lima, Anthony Segovia.

HOLLAND
Branch Chairman: **Ron Snellen**, PO Box 33742, 2503 BA Den Haag, Holland. **Tel: 00 31 70 329 8602; Fax: 00 31 70 367 2247; Website: www.dutch-mancunians.nl Email: dennisvandervin@hetnet.nl**

HONG KONG
12B Shun Ho Tower, 24–30 Ice House Street, Central, Hong Kong. **Tel: 00 852 2869 1993; Fax: 00 852 2869 4312.** Branch Secretary/Treasurer: **Rick Adkinson;** Chairman: **Mark Saunders. Email: muschkb@pacific.net.hk**

ICELAND
Branch Secretary: **Bubbi Avesson**, Studningsmannaklubbur, Manchester United á Íslandi, PO Box 12170, 132 Reykjavik, Iceland.

KREFELD REDS
Branch Secretary: **Andrew Marsh**, Innsbrucker Str 7, 47807 Krefeld, Germany. **Tel: 00 49 (0) 2151 392908;** Email: **AndrewM63@aol.com** Chairperson: **Stuart Dykes**, Grete-Schmitz 8, Krefeld, Germany. **Tel: 00 49 (0) 2151 435167; Email: stuart.dykes@t-online.de; John McFadyen**, Wisseler Str 13, 47574 Gcoh, Germany. **Tel: 00 49 (0) 2823 928504; Mobile: 00 49 (0) 173 5203 933; Email: john.mcfadyen@manutd.com** or **djandboys@hotmail.com**

LUXEMBOURG
Branch Secretary: **Steve Kaiser. Tel: 00 352 4301 33073 (w); 00 352 340265 (h).**

MALTA
Quarries Square, Msida MSD 03, Malta (since 1959). **Tel: 00 356 21223531;**

Fax: 00 356 22131902; Email: **musc@maltanet.net; Website: www.manutd-malta.com.** Branch Secretary: **Joseph Tedesco;** Branch President: **Franco Mizzi.**

MAURITIUS
Branch Secretary: **Yacoob Atchia**, Flamingo Pool House, Remeno Street, Rose Hill, Mauritius, Indian Ocean. **Tel: 464 7382/ 454 7761/ 454 3570/ 464 7750; Fax: 454 7839; Email: abyss.manutd@intnet.mu** Chairman: **Swallay Banhoo Tel: 464 4450 (h);** Treasurer: **Naniel Baichoo, Tel: 454 3570 (w); 465 0387 (h).**

NEW SOUTH WALES
Chairperson: **Steve Griffiths;** Vice-Chairperson: Tony Redman. Branch Address: P.O. Box 693, Sutherland 1499, New South Wales, Australia. **Mobile: 00 61 2 0408 028766; Fax: 00 61 2 464 85931; Website: manutd–nsw.one.net.au;** Club website: **www.manutdnsw.com** Founders: Fred & Ann Pollitt. **Email: fredthered@muscuk.fsnet.co.uk**

NEW ZEALAND
Branch Chairman: **Brian Wood**, 55 Pine Street, Mount Eden, Auckland, New Zealand; Secretary: **Gillian Goodinson**, 20 Sandown Road, Rothesay Bay, Auckland, New Zealand. **Email: woody.utd@xtra.co.nz**

SCANDANAVIAN
Branch Secretary: **Per H Larsen**, PO Box 4003 Dreggen, N–5835 Bergan, Norway. **Tel: +47 5530 2770** (Mon - Fri 08.00–16.00); **Fax: +47 5596 2033 Email: muscsb@united.no**

SOUTH AFRICA
PO Box 2540, Capetown 8000, S Africa. **Tel: 00 27 82 231 64364** (customer care); **Fax: 00 27 21 438 8295; Email: m.united@mweb.co.za**

SOUTH EAST ASIA
Manager: **Jeremy Goon**, 6–B Orange Grove Road, Singapore 258332. **Tel: 00 65 737 0677; Fax: 00 65 733 5073; Email: members@manutd-sea.com.sg**

SOUTH AUSTRALIA
PO Box 276, Ingle Farm, South Australia 5098. **Fax: 08 82816731.** Branch Secretary: **Mick Griffiths, Tel: 08 82644499;** Branch Chairman: **Chris Golder, Tel: 08 82630602;** Vice-Chairman: **John Harrison, Tel: 08 82603413;** Treasurer: **Charlie Kelly, Tel: 08 82652248.** Meetings are held at the Para Hills Soccer Club, Bridge Road, Para Hills, SA. The Manchester United Supporters Amateur League Soccer team trains and plays at Para Hills Soccer Club.

SWISS DEVILS
Branch Secretary: **Marc Tanner**, Dorfstrasse 30d, 5430 Wettingen, Switzerland. **Tel: (00 41 56) 426 94 80; Website: www.swissdevils.ch; Email: info@swissdevils.ch**

TOKYO
Branch Secretary: **Hiroki Miyaji**, 2–24–10 Minami-Ayoma, Minato-ku, Tokyo, Japan. **Tel: +81 3 3470 3441.** English Information: **Stephen Ryan, Tel: +81 3 3380 8441. Email: best-oz@kk.iij4u.or.jp**

MUSC USA EAST
Headquarters, PO Box 4199, Huntington, N.Y. 11743, U.S.A. Founder General Secretary: **Peter Holland Tel: 00 1 631 547 5500** (day); **Fax: 00 1 631 547 6800; Tel: 00 1 631 261 7314** (evening); **Email: muscusa@muscusa.com;** Membership Secretary: **Trevor Griffiths Tel: 00 1 718 381 5300 Ext 23** (day); **00 1 516 759 8634** (evening); **Fax: 00 1 718 821 5229; Email: tgmufc@aol.com**

MUSC USA MIDWEST
Contact: **Paul MacFarlane**, 415 North 10th Street, 3rd Floor, St Louis, MO 63101; **Tel: 00 1 314 621 0220; Fax: 00 1 314 421 5954; Email: pmacfarlane@the 1101experiment.org**

MUSC USA SOUTH
Contact: **James Murray**, 670 North Orlando Avenue, Suite 101, Maitland, FL 32751; **Tel: 00 1 407 331 6881; Fax: 00 1 407 331 7712; Email: jameskmurray@earthlink.net**

MUSC USA WEST
Contact: **Siamak Emadi**, 13765 Alton Parkway Unit F, Irvine, CA 92618. **Tel: 00 1 949 859 6274** or **00 1 800 262 0291** or **00 1 800 410 2745 Ext. 127; Fax: 00 1 949 859 4380** or **00 1 949 859 6274; Email: siamakemadi@yahoo.com**

VICTORIA, AUSTRALIA
President: **Kieran Dunleavy; Tel/ Fax: (03) 9 850 8109.** Postal Address: Manchester United Supporters Club of Victoria, PO Box 1199, Camberwell, 3124 Victoria. Website: **www.vicmanutd.com; Email: muscovic@vicnet.net.au**

WESTERN AUSTRALIA
Branch Chairman: **Graham Wyche**, 19 Frobisher Ave, Sorrento 6020, Perth, Western Australia. **Tel/Fax: (08) 9 447 1144; Mobile: 0417 903 101; Email: freobook@omen.com.au**